# World History

*World History: An Introduction* provides readers with the knowledge and tools necessary to understand the global historical perspective and how it can be used to shed light on both our past and our present. A concise and original guide to the concepts, methods, debates and contents of world history, it combines a thematic approach with a clear and ambitious focus.

Each chapter traces connections with the past and the present to explore major questions in world history:

- How did humans evolve from an endangered species to the most successful of them all?
- How has nature shaped human history?
- How did agricultural societies push human history in a new direction?
- How has humankind organized itself in ever more complex administrative systems?
- How have we developed new religious and cultural patterns?
- How have the paths of 'The West' and 'The Rest' diverged over the last five centuries?
- How, at the same time, has the world become more interconnected and 'globalized'?
- How is this world characterized by growing gaps in wealth, poverty and inequality?

Sharp and accessible, Eric Vanhaute's introduction to this exciting field demonstrates that world history is more of a perspective than a single all-encompassing narrative: an instructive new way of seeing, thinking and doing. It is an essential resource for students of history in a global context.

**Eric Vanhaute** is Professor of Economic and Social History and World History at Ghent University in Belgium. He has been Visiting Research Fellow at the Fernand Braudel Center, Binghamton and at Utrecht University, Fellow-in-Residence at the Netherlands Institute for Advanced Study in the Humanities and Social Sciences, and Visiting Professor at the University of California at Berkeley, the Institute of Economic and Social History at the University of Vienna and the Institute for Social Economy and Culture at Peking University.

# World History
## An introduction

## Eric Vanhaute

Translated by Linda Weix

Routledge
Taylor & Francis Group

LONDON AND NEW YORK

First published 2013
by Routledge
2 Park Square, Milton Park, Abingdon, Oxon OX14 4RN

Simultaneously published in the USA and Canada
by Routledge
711 Third Avenue, New York, NY 10017

*Routledge is an imprint of the Taylor & Francis Group, an informa business*

*British Library Cataloguing in Publication Data* A catalogue record for this
book is available from the British Library

*Library of Congress Cataloging in Publication Data*
Vanhaute, E.
[Wereldgeschiedenis. English]
World history: an introduction / Eric Vanhaute.
p. cm.
1. World history. I. Title.
D20.V3613 2012
909—dc23
2012018551


ISBN: 978-0-415-53578-6 (hbk)
ISBN: 978-0-415-53579-3 (pbk)
ISBN: 978-0-203-08214-0 (ebk)


Typeset in Times New Roman
by Book Now Ltd, London

MIX
Paper from
responsible sources
FSC
www.fsc.org   FSC® C004839

Printed and bound in Great Britain by the MPG Books Group

# Contents

# Illustrations

## Figures

# Preface

The one duty we owe to history is to rewrite it.

(Oscar Wilde)

The past is a foreign country. We have never been there; we only know about it from others. It is to all those other people that I dedicate this book. Those who have accumulated, analyzed and passed the knowledge on for generations. Those who have repeatedly rewritten history with innovative in-depth investigations and skilful syntheses. It is their wisdom that I collect here; I stand on their shoulders. It is not possible to do justice to every insight that I have assembled here. The literature guide at the end of the book is my modest tribute to the historians and scientists that laid the foundations of the fascinating discipline that world history has become over the last few years. My thanks also go out to the many hundreds of students at Ghent University that have digested this knowledge over the years – sometimes enthusiastically, sometimes reluctantly. They contributed to the critical review of this book more than they will ever know. I particularly want to thank Jan-Frederik Abbeloos, Frank Caestecker, Alexander Jocqué and Peer Vries, as well as three referees and the members of my *Communities/Comparisons/Connections Research Group* in Ghent for their critical reading of the text. I also want to thank Linda Weix for translating the text, Alexander Jocqué for preparing the index and Peter Laroy of Academia Press and Michael Strang of Routledge for their enthusiastic support during the preparation of this revised and translated edition.

The power of world history lies in its 'inclusivity', its involvement; in the challenge of recounting the diversity of human history in an integrated, global yet ultimately distinctive story. That power is also its biggest challenge. How do we translate that inclusive and distinctive story into a condensed and coherent history? How do we give it meaning? The choices I made are reflected in the structure of the book, which is divided into ten chapters. They are organized thematically and depart from the big questions in human history. We will search for ten parallel and integrated historical stories. They take place in a world formed by myriads of human actions and interactions. Traces of these actions make it possible to look back on where we came from.

Eric Vanhaute
*Antwerp, 2012*

# Prelude

## Cosmic history and human history

In the history of the universe, the human journey is only a small story, but it is our story and it is fascinating. Yet it is almost impossible to recount the history of humankind if we want to record the entire story. Nevertheless, stories about the fate of humankind and its environment are one of the oldest forms of collective storytelling. That need to giving meaning and significance is just as human as asking questions about the 'how' and 'why' of things. Later in this book we look at the 'what', 'why' and 'how' of world history. This prelude places human history in perspective and sketches a short historical setting based on the most recent insights. They are covered in more detail later in the book.

Against the historical background of the 13.7 billion-year-old universe, human history is just a blink of an eye. If the Eiffel Tower in Paris symbolizes the history of the universe since the Big Bang, then humankind's story represents the thickness of the paint on top of the tower. The following box relates the history of the universe to one calendar year.

| Big Bang | 1 January | 13.7 billion years ago |
| Formation of stars and star systems | Beginning of February | 12 billion years ago |
| Birth of our solar system | 9 September | 4.7 billion years ago |
| Creation of planet earth | 15 September | 4.5 billion years ago |
| Earliest life on earth | Beginning of October | 4 billion years ago |
| First worms | 16 December | 650 million years ago |
| First reptiles and trees | 23 December | 370 million years ago |
| Dominion of dinosaurs | 24–28 December | 330–65 million years ago |
| First humans | Evening of 31 December | 2.7 million years ago |
| First agricultural societies | 11:59:35, 31 December | 12,000 years ago |
| Beginning of Common Era | 11:59:56, 31 December | 2,000 years ago |

The history of planet earth only began when the universe was already nine billion years old. Earliest life appeared quite soon after that, approximately four billion years ago, but for the majority of time it was limited to microscopic small, single-celled forms of life. More complex organisms appeared 600 to 700 million years ago; on the cosmic calendar it was already mid-December. The first humans (*Homo habilis*) walked the earth at dusk on December 31.

## Evolution and progress

Evolution is a story that is too big and too grand for words. That the universe originated from nothing 13.7 billion years ago, and that living creatures originated on a small planet out of hardly anything nine billion years later is staggering to say the least. The fact that this was the beginning of a process of evolution that led, amongst others, to a species that is able to fathom this process is just astounding.

The miracle of evolution does not make it a predestined tale. The British evolutionary biologist Richard Dawkins expresses it as follows:

> Evolution has reached many millions of interim ends (the number of surviving species at the time of observation), and there is no reason other than vanity – human vanity as it happens, since we are doing the talking – to designate any one as more privileged or climactic than the other. ... The historian must beware of stringing together a narrative that seems, even to the smallest degree, to be homing in on a human climax.
>
> (Dawkins 2004)

Paleontologist and evolutionary biologist Stephen J. Gould explained it even more sharply.

> Homo sapiens are neither representative nor the final outcome of the process of evolution. Evolution is not a pre-delineated theory of phases that would always have the same outcome if it were replayed like a movie. There is too much coincidence involved or, from our point of view, call it luck. The chance that something like a human being would develop if evolution started from scratch once again is negligible.
>
> (Gould 1996)

This coincidence or luck is determined by extinction. In the evolution of life, extinction is the final fate of nearly all species. About 99 per cent of all species that once lived on earth are now extinct. This did not occur uniformly: there were various periods of mass extinction. At the end of the Cretaceous period (65 million years ago), the dinosaurs and approximately half of all existing species became extinct. This 'coincidence' enabled the advancement of mammals, at that time still insignificant nocturnal insectivores, and later of human beings. Mass extinctions at the end of the Triassic period (200 million years ago) and during the transition from the Permian to the Triassic period (250 million years ago) affected an estimated 75 per cent and 90 per cent of all species respectively. According to some scientists, under the regime of Homo sapiens we are presently confronted with a new phase of mass extinctions.

Recent scientific insights reject the idea of specific, guided evolution. There is no pre-delineated pattern or rhythm in evolution, let alone something like an 'intelligent design'. That does not mean that 'progress' is not possible in evolution: not an inevitable progress in the direction of humankind, but progress in the direction of greater complexity. We must not forget that the oldest and simplest forms of life, bacteria, are still the most common. The same evolutionary discoveries have been made frequently and independently from each other (such as the development of eyes in all kinds of forms of life); this indicates a limited degree of predictability. That is because comparable problems require comparable solutions, and the number of solutions is limited. Those new solutions are a result of what Richard Dawkins calls the continuous evolutionary arms race. The battle for survival between species, between predators and prey, stimulates progressive evolutionary steps, a gradual, systematic, progressive improvement via natural selection.

> Progress in evolution is not a single upward climb but has a rhyming trajectory more like the teeth of a saw. A sawtooth plunged deeply at the end of the Cretaceous, when the last of the dinosaurs abruptly gave way to the mammals' new and spectacular climb of progressive evolution. But there had been lots of smaller sawteeth during the long reign of the dinosaurs. And since their immediate post-dinosaur rise, the mammals too have had smaller arms races followed by extinctions, followed by renewed arms races. Arms races rhyme with earlier arms races in periodic spurts of many-stepped progressive evolution.
>
> (Dawkins 2004)

When indicating periods, we avoid using Eurocentric names such as Antiquity, Middle Ages, Modern Era and Renaissance. Time designation follows the Christian calendar but is indicated in a more neutral manner: BCE (Before Common Era) and CE (Common Era).

## The history of humankind in a nutshell

The group of joint ancestors of chimpanzees, bonobos and hominids split up approximately 5 to 6 million years ago. Eastern and southern Africa remained their biotope for millions of years. A few dozen species probably developed from the evolutionary line of the *hominids*, our direct ancestors. All are characterized by walking upright and by an increased use and later a gradual improvement of (stone) tools. Many of these species became extinct; others initiated further evolution. The most important characteristic is the gradual increase in cranial capacity. *Homo habilis* ('handy-man', sometimes regarded as the first real human being, of the genus *homo*) lived approximately 2.3 to 1.5 million years ago and made complex stone tools. *Homo erectus* was the species at the basis of the first major migration out of Africa to the remotest corners of Eurasia approximately 1 million years ago. Homo erectus learned to control fire. In time, all human species but one became extinct: *Homo sapiens*.

It is generally accepted that the history of modern humankind started between 200,000 and 300,000 years ago with the appearance of Homo sapiens. Recent genetic information has revealed that all human beings today descend from a small group of African ancestors that roamed the savannas thousands of generations ago. Modern man distinguishes itself from its ancestors by more developed forms of (symbolic) communication, by passing on accumulated knowledge and by processes of collective learning, everything summarized as culture. This enabled human beings to adapt faster to changing circumstances, without changing the human genetic pattern first. Homo sapiens were able to disseminate over large parts of eastern Africa with the assistance of more sophisticated stone technology. It is estimated that there were no more than 10,000 Homo sapiens about 100,000 years ago. At that time, modern humankind started its migration out of Africa – first to Asia, then about 50,000 years ago to Australia, about 40,000 years ago to Europe and 20,000 to 15,000 years ago to America. Meanwhile, human beings were able to adapt and improve their technological knowledge. This happened very slowly compared to contemporary standards. This was due to a low population density and the small scale of the societies. For more than 200,000 years – 95 per cent of its history – modern human beings survived as hunter-gatherers (*period of hunter-gatherers, 250,000 to 10,000/8000 BCE*). During that period, humankind developed a remarkable diversity of ways of life and technical knowledge due to frequent migrations. This was combined with a steady, but slow population growth. There were only a few hundred thousand human beings 30,000 years ago. In the period just before the agricultural revolution that had increased to 6 million. This growing group applied new, more successful hunting techniques and used fire to clear forests for new plants. Weapons, clothing and various forms of artistic expression improved in the last period before the agricultural revolutions.

The first agricultural societies developed 12,000 to 10,000 years ago (*period of agricultural societies, 10,000/8000 BCE to 1750/1800 CE*). The transition was very gradual. Small forms of more permanent settlement and cultivation appeared first. Even though the hunter-gatherer period lasted 250,000 years, the agricultural age is the most important period in human history when looking at the size of the population. After all, 70 per cent of all people who ever lived on earth lived in that period (compared to 12 per cent in the period before). Agricultural societies developed in a divergent world. Regional differences were greater than in the periods before and after. Four large zones developed more or less independently from each other, at least until 1500 CE: Afro-Eurasia, America, Australia and the Pacific Ocean islands. Strikingly, agricultural societies developed in diverse regions at about the same period, followed by large-scale forms of government, cities, monumental architecture, state religions and bureaucratic management instruments like writing. The development of comparable agricultural techniques, independently from each other, points to the prevalence of similar factors such as climate changes (warming trend after the last ice ages), ecological limits (droughts, extermination of mammals) and increasing demographic pressure. More permanent settlements were able to feed and house more people. Technological changes occurred faster than in the previous period. Populations and production were able to increase at an unprecedented speed. Products derived from agriculture (such as fibres, skins, manure and milk) became trade commodities between communities. The growth of agricultural societies was often curbed by war and the outbreak of new diseases – a consequence of the transmission of new pathogenic bacteria between animals and human beings. In the long term, these communities gained the upper hand in large parts of the world. The organization of agriculture over the seasons and the management of supplies required new forms of control. That control was executed by new groups of non-farmers who supported themselves by extracting part of the harvest via tributes (or taxes). Social differences grew.

From 8000 to 3000 BCE, the early agricultural societies developed as conglomerates of villages that still often supplemented their diets by hunting and fishing. Further growth led to more specialization, new types of leadership that transcended old family ties, and new gender relationships that usually kept women away from power positions in the village. Sometimes a hierarchy grew within the network of villages, and that hierarchy was frequently legitimated by the need for protection. These earliest forms of state-building instigated the development of the first cities (3000 to 500 BCE). The oldest cities in Afro-Eurasia are 5,000 years old. Those in Central and South America are 2,000 years younger. Cities are characterized by a more complex internal division of labour with specialists in governance, religion and warfare at the top. Cities could only survive if they were able to live off progressive and productive agrarian societies with considerable surpluses. They often relied on forms of agriculture that needed a central organization, such as complex irrigation networks.

Agrarian empires or civilizations were built upon cities that developed into centres of a larger administrative system. They were all characterized by forms of formal rule, a permanent siphoning off of some of the surpluses (taxation), the development of a central administrative and military power, and by a religious state system. The first major empires or civilizations were in Mesopotamia (around the Tigris and Euphrates Rivers), Egypt (around the Nile River), India (around the Indus River) and Northern China (around the Yellow River). They were also characterized by extensive infrastructural networks, trade systems and cultural exchange. Commercial and communication networks grew between these centres of civilization, including the Silk Roads between West and East Asia.

The number of civilizations or empires increased from 500 BCE to 1000 CE, and so did their interaction: Japan, Korea, China, India, Persia, Rome, Ghana and Teotihuacán. Historians call this period (especially 500 BCE to 100 CE) 'the axial age', due to strongly similar movements in many parts of the world. Cities and more extensive states also appeared in more peripheral regions like Northwest Europe, sub-Saharan Africa, South India and southern China. Cultural exchange was fostered through increased contact between major empires like the Achaemenid empire in Persia, the Han dynasty in China, the Roman empire around the Mediterranean, the Kingdom of Magadha and the Maurya dynasty in India, and later the Islamic Abbasid dynasty. This is most apparent in the growth and dissemination of world religions. World religions all claimed universal truths, dispersed from ancient centres (Buddhism from North India, Christianity from the Roman empire and Islam from the Arabian Peninsula), and were no longer linked to one political entity. The same expansion of empires in an economic, military and cultural sense occurred on the American continent, amongst them the Teotihuacán and Maya civilizations in Central America and the Moche civilization in present-day Peru. Populations also increased outside agrarian centres, in more peripheral areas like the steppes of Eurasia, the plains of North America and on islands in the Pacific. Impressive empires also developed in these regions, such as the Mongolian empire that stretched from China to Europe in the thirteenth century. In Africa, a migration movement from the western core area to the east and south spread the languages and cultures of the Bantu.

Between 1000 and 1750 CE these trends continued, but with important changes in the background. The most important shift was a linking of the major world zones. The Vikings and Mongols played an important role in Eurasia due to their conquest campaigns and the development of trade networks. In America, the military expansion of the Aztecs (Central America) and the Incas (South America) brought a large number of people together in huge empires. The most important impulse came from a more peripheral region in the Afro-Eurasian complex, namely Europe. An extremely competitive system of small, strongly commercialized and militarized states developed in Europe after the collapse of the last major empires. In a search for new commercial opportunities outside the established Asian networks, Europe laid the foundation for a new, truly global system. Control over trade networks to the west (America) and the east (Asia via Africa) brought great material and intellectual wealth, but left a path of destruction (massive mortality, plundering and slave trade). This new network, which, grafted on to existing Asian networks, developed into a global system controlled by Europe. An integrated world system, which put Europe on the map and eventually transformed the whole world, expanded as of the sixteenth century.

The period after 1750/1800 has been the most turbulent period in world history (*modern society, 1750/1800 CE to the present*). Despite the fact that this period only spans about 250 years, the number of changes largely exceeds those of the rest of human history. The years 1750–1800 primarily refer to the start of the first industrial revolution, which drove the speed of economic and social change to new heights. The most important changes include a new economic organization (industrial capitalism), a quick succession of innovations, changing global relations, fast population growth, and major political and cultural shifts. These transformations also generated larger social and geographic differences. Agrarian societies remained dominant until far into the twentieth century in most regions outside the core states. Only at the beginning of the twenty-first century do we see more people living in cities than in the countryside. Old empires and civilizations finally gave way to modern states built on complex bureaucracies in the early twentieth century. Intensified interconnections did not lead to a more unified world. Income differences increased rapidly, both in the period of colonization (until 1960) and afterwards. This book raises many questions related to these fast contemporary changes. In the last two to three centuries there have been several 'industrial revolutions' – the first was based on coal and iron, the second on oil, petrochemistry and electricity, and the third on digital information. The economic growth resulting from these industrial revolutions resulted in a more global society, but not a more equal society. At the beginning of the twenty-first century, the growth engine of the 'modern period' seems to be approaching its human and ecological limits, and the roots of previous societies have disappeared (hunter-gatherer societies) or are breaking down quickly (rural societies). This fuels the debate about the contours of a new, different global society that is able to combine population, wealth and ecology with democratic forms of government and free social and cultural choices. Simultaneously, we must search for new international and global relationships that are not built on European and Western supremacy, unlike the previous 250 years.

## A short chronology of human history

| | |
|---|---|
| 250,000–200,000 years ago | Modern man appeared (*Homo sapiens*) and dispersed across Africa |
| 100,000 years ago | Modern man started migrating out of Africa to Eurasia |
| 30,000–20,000 years ago | Acceleration in the development of techniques and culture |
| 20,000–15,000 years ago | End of the last ice age |
| | Modern man appeared in America; first forms of permanent settlements in Eurasia |
| 10,000–8000 BCE | First agricultural communities in Mesopotamia, North and West Africa, China, Mesoamerica and Papua New Guinea |
| 3000–2500 BCE | First fully-fledged cities and states in Mesopotamia, Egypt, India, North China |
| 2000 BCE | Formation of Eurasian trade networks |
| 1000 BCE | Formation of cities and states in Central America and the Andes; start of Bantu migration in Africa |
| 500 BCE–1000 CE | Growth of cities and empires, of population and of trade networks |

*(Continued)*

*(Continued)*

| | |
|---|---|
| 500 BCE–100 CE | 'Axial period' with the flourishing of major civilizations and innovations in religion, philosophy and science |
| 200–1000 CE | Post-imperial worlds (Eurasia) |
| Thirteenth century | *Pax Mongolica* in Eurasia |
| Sixteenth – seventeenth century | Formation of global networks that link all major regions; end of empires in America; Columbian exchange |
| | Maritime empires: Spain, Portugal, Holland, Japan |
| | Continental empires: Ming China, Mughal India, Russia, Ottoman empire, Songhai in West Africa |
| Late eighteenth century | First breakthrough new industrial techniques and fossil energy |
| | Beginning of supremacy of the West |
| Nineteenth century | Expansion of Western world system under British hegemony; new wave of colonization |
| Twentieth century | Expansion of Western world system under American hegemony; decolonization |
| Beginning of twenty-first century | End of American hegemony; end of the supremacy of the West? |

# 1 World history: a history of the world?

If history is *bunk*, as car manufacturer Henry Ford once proclaimed, then world history is truly the ultimate form of drivel. If it is not bunk and we want it to be more than 'one damned thing after another', then we need to ask 'what' and 'why'. The most important reason to study world history today is to gain access to the historical background of our contemporary, globalized world. Now that we experience how complex and connected our world is, we also realize that regional and national stories are no longer sufficient to comprehend the world around us. How did the world become what it is? How did diverse social, cultural, economic and political paths develop and how do they interact? World history departs from the premise that the life course of individuals, groups, nations and civilizations only gains sense or meaning in its correlation within the overarching human story. Just like any historiography, world history gives meaning, but with a focus on comparison and interaction at a global level. This will be explained in the first chapter. We will address the perspective that world history utilizes in the areas of looking or knowledge (section 1) and in thinking or ability (section 2). This questions the identity (section 3) and the reasons for world history (section 4). We will explore striking innovations in world history over the past decennia (section 5). World history has become a distinct discipline with its own questions, methodology and theories, its own publication channels and its own finality. World history examines the story of the human race. It also explores the most distinct issues affecting contemporary society, including demographic growth, ecological limits, food security, administrative decision-making, cultural diffusion, and social and economic inequality.

## World history is a different way of looking

World history is huge and ambitious. Huge because the timeline is long and the spatial dimension is wide. Ambitious because the quantity of themes in world history are almost infinite, because the sources about and knowledge of parts of world history seem complex, and because the analytical instruments for understanding this information are very diverse. Yet world history is manageable. Time, place, themes and methods demarcate a frame of research in which large, ambitious yet clear stories about humankind's exciting journey are told. Generalizations, comparisons, connections and transformation force researchers, writers and readers to structure stories in such a way that divergence and convergence, change and continuity, cooperation and conflict are recognizable as guiding forces.

The most accepted definition of world history or global history is that *it studies the origin of, growth in and changes to human communities in a comparative perspective and within their mutual connections. Key words include communities, comparisons, connections and systems.* Human communities that have shaped the world over time are central rather than the world itself. World history studies those communities in a dual manner: (1) in a comparative perspective to detect patterns, similarities and differences; and (2) in their interaction via contacts, connections and influence.

World history looks at diverse forms of human society that have developed over time, but does not view them on their own. World history is a translocal, transregional and transnational history. Human communities are the building blocks and actors. The world is the context and stage. That world is the result of the coexistence of humankind and nature, of the interaction between human communities and the ecological environment. Within very divergent environments, human beings make choices – sometimes the same, sometimes different. World history asks which choices were and are being made, and why. World history wants to know why those choices in very divergent environments are sometimes the same and sometimes very dissimilar. World history also works out to what degree those choices influenced each other, to what extent interregional contacts have changed the course of the history of human communities. World history always places humankind's journey within the worldwide arena. This results in meta-stories, stories about the history of human beings and the human race that are embedded in local and regional experiences and that look for wider correlations, patterns, connections and systems.

World history is primarily a perspective, a way of looking that thoroughly differs from other methods of social research. Without a worldwide dimension, history remains limited to individual 'cases' (group, region, country) or individual 'development trajectories' (Europe, the West).

## World history is a different way of thinking

World history is more than knowledge; it is also an attitude, a position, a way of thinking. The image changes when human communities are studied in a comparative perspective and in their relationship with and dependence on each other. The 'big picture' lies behind every snapshot that we make. Every photograph taken with a zoom lens can and must be complemented with a wide-angle image. This global dimension causes us to ask different questions and reformulate old questions. World history covers all major domains of human action:

- people and their natural environment (including demography, techniques);
- the development and interaction of cultural systems (including religions, arts, sciences);

- state-building and conflict (including forms of government such as empires and states, wars, revolutions);
- the formation of economic systems (including agricultural systems, trade, industrialization);
- the development of social structures (including gender, family, race, class).

Big questions invite big answers. Those questions and answers redefine the three dimensions that are intertwined in social and human sciences: the spatial dimension (world), time dimension (history) and thematic dimension (world history or the history of human societies). World history explains that these three dimensions are the result of choices and therefore are the subject of permanent discussion.

1   Existing, culture-specific periodizations lose much of their meaning in a wider *time perspective*. 'Global time', since the origins of our planet, life on earth or the human race, requires different descriptions. Timescales remain relative and are constantly questioned in world history.

2   *Spatial and geographic concepts* are also culture-bound. World history makes us aware of divergent visions that exist about our own space and the way diverse dimensions overlap, from local, regional, national and international to global.

3   The *thematic dimension* is also the result of choices. World history is not the history of everything; that is not possible nor desirable. Like all historical stories, world history wants to give meaning but on a different, wider scale. This is only possible after one has determined the unit of analysis (human systems, ecological systems) and the theme being studied.

This introductory book focuses on enquiring about these three dimensions. This is covered in detail in the last chapter, which will give the reader better insight into the possibilities and limitations of world history as a signifying narrative.

## Which world history?

World history studies the origin of, growth in and changes to human communities in a *comparative perspective* and within their *mutual connections*. Attention is not paid to individual communities (family, clan, village, tribe, state, culture or civilization) but to *differences and similarities in the development* of the various communities and to the *connections* between those communities. In world history, systems of human coexistence (small and large) are given meaning in a wider perspective. We must first understand the choices that these communities have made in relationship to their environment and to each other. This interpretation becomes clearer when we look at what world history is not. World history is not (or not only):

- universal or total history: world history is not the history of 'everything';
- international history: world history is not only the history of relationships between 'nations';

- a history of (Western) civilization: world history is more than a history of the ascent of one (Western) civilization;
- non-Western history (previously called colonial or overseas history): world history is more than a history of the world outside the 'West';
- comparative societal history: world history is more than a comparative history of societies;
- globalization history: world history focuses on much more than the history of contemporary globalization.

Three questions and story lines dominate this form of world history. First is the gradual, progressive (internal) growth of human societies in relationship to (external) ecological challenges. In every human group, we see the origin of comparable societal patterns: forms of social order and cohesion, of language and communication, of leadership, of food supply, of social reproduction (fertility, child rearing, family structures) etc. Similar and very different choices are made within those patterns. The choices strongly depend on the natural context that the groups live in. Second, due to increased interaction, human groups form larger, coordinating structures, cultures or civilizations. Every culture or civilization must answer the same questions: which system of political control (state, leadership, bureaucracy etc.), which system of economic survival (agriculture, trade, industry, plundering etc.), which system of social control (legitimization, repression etc.) and which system of cultural interpretation (religion) should it choose? The choices made within every culture/civilization show many similarities and differences. Third, cultures and civilizations come into contact in peaceful or less peaceful ways, and this usually has a big impact. These contacts take place via very diverse paths and have very diverse consequences: trade (transaction of goods), migration, cultural diffusion or imitation, plundering, conquest, war, integration, or incorporation.

To understand these big questions it is not necessary to know everything about everything. It is important to make choices related to the unit of analysis (group, tribe, region, civilization etc.), the timeframe (period), the spatial framework (place) and the theme (perspective). These choices do not necessarily (or usually do not) cover the whole world, yet they always aim to transcend their own case. They aim to present a story that offers insight into the development trajectory of the entire human community.

Then a suitable research model is drawn up that relies on three pillars.

*Pillar 1* A comparative analysis in which the specific case is placed in a wider context. Comparison avoids the pitfall of absolute pronouncements about an alleged 'uniqueness' or exclusivity of human societies (comparative analysis).

*Pillar 2* An analysis of the interaction and interconnection between societies or systems, and of the way those patterns of contact change (network analysis, translocal/transnational analysis).

*Pillar 3* An analysis of human systems in which the various societies and their mutual contacts are given shape. This includes large, spanning forces that must be studied as a whole, in their systemic unit. Examples include economic systems (the current world system), migration systems, ecological systems (climate, disease) and cultural systems. Human societies are always linked together by several of these systems and act in reaction to these systems (systems analysis).

This threefold track forms one, inseparable trajectory that must enable us to answer the basic questions in world history:

- How do population groups in different contexts of time and space try to attain similar objectives with different means: the reproduction of their physical self, of their labour, their knowledge and their insights, of social and cultural patterns and, finally, of their society? Which factors (external: ecological; internal: social) determine different or similar outcomes?
- How do population groups develop their society and how do those social systems change as a result of contact, interaction or conflict with other societies? To what extent do certain social systems live alongside each other or take over other systems?

From the previous questions, we learn the following. First, it is clear that the 'world' in world history does not stand for the physical notion of 'earth' but for all of humankind, human society and the outcome of human choices in an unfamiliar, natural context. In other words, *world is not a thing, it is a human activity.* Second, this delineation does not prevent the central theme in world history from being less easy to grasp than 'national history'. The leitmotiv of national history is the political organization of a country/state/nation. Politics turns a state into a state. Economic, social and cultural analyses are inserted where necessary. World history is not built around a political story; nor is it exclusively built around an ecological (humankind/nature), demographic (reproduction), economic (survival), social (power structures) or cultural (life orientation) story. All stories come together in the question of how societal systems take shape over time and space, and how they adapt and change via connection, cooperation or conflict. Third, dates, events and persons are not central in the story. Emphasis is not placed on memorizing but on analyzing, comparing and understanding. No matter what a human being or a group of people does, either consciously or unconsciously, this always plays in the background of a global dimension. Choices are always determined and restricted by the location of the human being or group of people within the entire human community. In world history, learning that attitude and dealing with it critically are central.

Finally, postmodernists feared that world history would be a new, all-encompassing story (a *master narrative*) that departs from an exclusive, unambiguous explanative framework. It is not; it is a meta-story, a story of stories, with a vast outlook and massive ambitions, but with answers that are never absolute or definitive.

## Why world history?

World history aspires to a different form of knowledge and of insight. World history is the best way to portray, analyze and understand the story of the entire human community. Whichever historical and spatial scale is employed, it is always necessary to portray the wider context. Historical processes like family formation, cultural reproduction or state-building rarely or never occur in isolation. World history tries to give meaning to the myriads of human actions that have created our 'world' via a wide framework. As indicated above, a triple insight lies at the core of this.

1   Societies come and go, succeed or ruin each other, and are never the same. Nevertheless, they share several basic characteristics: they all develop material (economic) survival structures, political control systems, social and gender (man/woman) relations, cultural life orientation patterns, and demographic and familial reproduction systems. That is why they can be compared. *Comparative analysis* enables us to gain a better insight into the way people shape their lives within a societal group, and why certain choices are made in certain contexts while other directions are not chosen.

2   Societies do not originate, grow and change in isolation. They are always in contact with other societies to a greater or lesser degree. These patterns of *interaction/interconnection* are a second motivation for social/historical science at a global level. The impact of these interactions only becomes visible in a wider/larger analysis rather than the analysis of an individual society.

3   Societies are almost always the primary means of analysis, but the level of analysis and interpretation can seldom be limited to these societies. Human groups give shape to their existence within wider social contours that cannot only be understood in their sublevel. *Systems* of influence, exchange and migration often span many human communities and find their existence in the merger of diverse, different geographic dimensions.

Moreover, world history often makes a contemporary, moral claim. It shows the complexity of the past and present world. It shows that differences and diversity are core characteristics of the human story, and that insight into this and dealing with this are important moral qualities. Judgments are not only weighed against one's own world, they are predominantly weighed against the complexity of human history.

In conclusion, world history is important; not so much for global knowledge, but for learning to employ a global view. That global view is not obtained by tallying up national or regional events, but by zooming out so that you see the world and the way human contacts and interactions have taken place in one large image rather than in fragmented images. Consequently, world history is both a historical story and a contemporary story. The global perspective links humans, peoples and cultures. It links diverse places, various periods and the former world with that of today and of tomorrow.

We can translate these insights into a collection of world history aims that can be divided into *knowledge* (passive insight) and *ability* (active application).

*Knowledge*

- An insight into the 'what', 'why' and 'how' of world history. An 'introduction to' is more important than a 'summary of'. The three dimensions of time, space and thematic interpretation are central in their mutual connection.
- Understanding that questions in human sciences often get different answers within a global context, and that those answers are frequently ambiguous. Students must be able to explain and substantiate this, and must be able to discuss this critically based on examples. In other words, they must be aware of the fact that the employed perspective (time, location and theme) determines the answers that are given. Moreover, they must always evaluate and question the perspective from which the answers are formulated; for example 'Eurocentric' compared to 'global'.

*Ability*

- Formulate how the global perspective is related to diverging scales in time and space.
- Explain how processes of interaction and diffusion shape global society.
- Assess how one can judge via comparative analysis processes of change versus continuity.
- Understand how connections and systems constantly change human societies.
- Critically evaluate universal presumptions and generalized statements about human beings and their society.

## World history as tradition and innovation

The history that is taught today is still mainly 'national' history. It is still mainly the history of a nation, a cultural space, a group of people busy building their own society, in modern terms: a nation/state. The story of the construction of one's own society is important. That specific society is the social-political and often cultural and economic context in which each of us tries to shape our lives. However, the national story does not take place in a vacuum; it is always part of a larger story. Nevertheless, so-called national histories are not very old. They were created together with the appearance of modern nation states. The roots of this process lie in the *Ancien Régime*, but it climaxed in the 'romantic' nineteenth century. Nationalistic and Eurocentric historiography were children of their times, and therefore took advantage of a need for legitimization (the nation state, European hegemony). Other forms of historiography originate also as a reaction to a specific need for knowledge and justification. The following short summary should clarify this.

### Ethnocentric world histories

Historical stories with a perspective outside their own spatial, ethnic and political boundaries have a long tradition in China, Japan, Southeast Asia, the Islamic world and parts of Europe (Greece). In other parts of the world, few or no traces of such 'universal' histories have been found for the period before Western colonization. Sub-Sahara Africa did not leave its own texts; consequently, we know almost nothing about the way Africans viewed the world outside their own physical and mental boundaries. This is also true of the people on the American continent and in Oceania. The Hindu world left behind very few testimonies in which interest is shown for the outside world. This is surprising because for a long time the Indian subcontinent was the central link in a wide African-Asian trade system and was the birthplace of a new universal religion – Buddhism.

The oldest historiographic surveys with universal pretensions aim to summarize their own world – Jewish, Greek, Hellenistic, Islamic, Arabic, Chinese, Japanese – in their own story or genesis. Moreover, these histories often conjure up an image of the desired world order and the way the people in the known world relate to each other or should relate to each other. These historical stories give meaning to their own world, in its historical roots and in relationship to the known outside world. Their impact is always teleological and the superiority of one's own civilization is the logical departure point and destination. Curiosity about the outside world only occurs when those people play a role in their own story. Historiographies from the Islamic world pay a lot of attention to the surrounding world, while the Hindu world is much more inward looking. Every social group fosters its own genesis story, a story of the group's origin. Major religions often record their origination story (Judaism, Christianity and Islam). These stories combine myth, divine predestination and meaning with actual events in their own past. They aim to present a general, universal and often timeless truth. In Christianity, the 'historia universalis' builds on this tradition. It relates the teleological and timeless tale of two cities (the City of God and the City of Man) as originally recorded by *Saint Augustine* in the fourth century CE. An example in this tradition of universal history is J. B. Bossuet's *Discourse on Universal History* (seventeenth century), which is a mix of theology, myth and historical stories.

In diverse cultures, a more 'worldly' historiographical activity appears and looks at the world known at that time. *Herodotos* was not only a historian of the Greek world; he was a historian of the entire world known to the Greeks in the fifth century BCE. To understand the differences between Greeks and non-Greeks (*barbaroi*), he searched for geographic and ethnographic differences and connections. He went on study tours through the world known to the Greeks at that time. His masterpiece, *The Histories* (*historiès apodeksis*), is a voluminous bundle of books that are a cross between the memoirs of a traveller and a historian's attempt at historiography in a detached manner. Historiography was also a traditional part of Chinese and Japanese culture. This historiography consists of annals, biographies of leaders and other exemplary figures, calendars and chronicles of political and cultural life. This knowledge serves the government and the empire as an example or as aura. An interest in people outside the empire was limited to their own interests, trade or conquest. Chinese historians saw the world in sinocentric terms until the nineteenth century. The world was divided into zones depending whether the people were closer or farther away from the Chinese civilization. The superiority of the Chinese centre determined the image of the other regions and people, just as European or Arabic writers they called others 'barbarians'. The most famous historian in ancient China was *Sima Qian* (or *Ssi-ma Ch'ien*, second to first century BCE during the Han dynasty). He combined impressions from the many trips he took with historical stories and data, which he examined with a critical mind. In his work *Shiji* (The Historical Events), he recorded the story of China from the time of the mythical Yellow Emperor to the Han dynasty – 3,000 years of Chinese history. *Shiji* consists of 30 chapters of general political, dynastic, economic and cultural history, followed by 100 chapters with a biographical approach.

The tradition of universal history was strongly present in the Islamic world (in Arabic, Persian and Ottoman languages) until the nineteenth century. This was related to the 1,000-year history of trade, expansion and conquest, and with the tradition of incorporating new peoples under Islamic rule. The Islamic world was not an empire in the formal sense of the word; it was much more of an ecumenical community. Therefore, knowledge about diverse parts of the world had a practical and a legitimating objective. The focus of the historiography was wide: stories about rulers and events, chronicles of the government and histories of cities and provinces. The most important period in their own history was the origin and expansion of Islam. Although the texts were written under the rule and approval of religious and worldly authorities, everything was portrayed as accurately as possible. Also in Islamic historiography, their own chronography was often central (*Ja'far al-Tabari*, ninth to tenth century CE, with a history of prophets and kings from Adam to the prophet Mohammed). The work of *Ibn Khaldoun* (fourteenth century CE) has a real 'universal' pretense; his ambition was to write a history of civilization. His life's work was *Kitab al-Ibar* (Book of Lessons). In this work he combined three histories: the *al-Muqaddimah* (known as *Prolegomena* in Greek) is an introduction to his world history project; books two to five relate the history of mankind (as he knew it); and books six and seven are a history of the Berber people. His work has a very modern sociological slant because he searched for the impact of social and political cohesion on the rise and decline of tribes and civilizations. He also paid a lot of attention to geographic and climatologic factors, which makes him the real precursor of later world historians.

### A European universalism

The secularization of 'eschatological, universal history' started in Europe under the eighteenth century enlightened philosophers (Voltaire and Kant). In the nineteenth century, this led to a search for 'general laws' that shape the history of humankind, such as the 'idealistic world views' of Georg Wilhelm Friedrich Hegel, the 'historical materialism' of Karl Marx and Charles Darwin's evolution theory. This universalism was coloured in a very original way by two centuries of Western triumphalism. The nineteenth century was a European century, with an absolute economic, political, military and ideological hegemony. The economic growth and imperialistic expansion were unseen. A large majority of European intellectuals subscribed to an introspective world image in which Europe was the norm. They followed Hegel's adage, which stated that only people who have formed a state and achieved a certain form of spiritual development can have their own history. He added that history travels from east to west and that Asia is the beginning and Europe is the end of history. Modernization and progress, revolution and development according to the European path; this became the canon in historiography and in all social sciences. The European path was the norm, whatever fell off the path (the East) deviated from the norm. Mapping the European development trajectory was the central aim of new scientific disciplines like sociology, economics and history. The non-European world became the object of research for ethnographers and anthropologists looking for an explanation of 'the other'.

This resulted in a division or 'disciplining' of the sciences: the social sciences split off from the physical sciences and the social sciences were divided into subdisciplines with their own codes, jargon, publication channels, schools and courses (history, anthropology, sociology etc.). More general, trans-discipline approaches declined, as did attention to the wider image, the large scale and the long term.

The breakthrough of a Eurocentric modernization perspective with universalistic presumptions went together with the triumph of nationalistic historiography under figureheads like Jules Michelet, George Bancroft and Henri Pirenne. This is where the new standards of the *historic métier* (heuristics, analysis, argumentation, synthesis) were established. Attention was paid to so-called 'universal histories', but they focused almost exclusively on the rise (and sometimes the predicted decline) of the West (August Comte, Leopold von Ranke). This national and Eurocentric approach remained the norm in history and in the social sciences until late in the twentieth century.

At the edge of dominant historical activity, two traditions or paradigms preserved the wider, global view. The first was the paradigm of the civilization history, written in the older tradition of historical philosophy. Famous examples include Oswald Spengler (*Der Untergang des Abendlandes*, 1918–1922), H.G. Wells (*A Short History of the World*, 1922) and Arnold Toynbee (*A Study of History*, 1933–1961). In these works, civilizations are analyzed as more or less independent units; autonomous organisms with their own life cycles (emergence, growth and decline). Separate from this was the paradigm of the capitalistic world economy (emergence and decline of a global, all-encompassing economic system; see Marx and Engels). For several authors this was the inspiration for large-scale historical analyses. Examples include Vladimir Lenin (*Der Imperialismus als höchstes Stadium des Kapitalismus*, 1916), Karl Polanyi (*The Great Transformation: The Political and Economic Origins of Our Time*, 1944), Maurice Dobb (*Studies in the Development of Capitalism*, 1946) and Fernand Braudel (see below).

### A new world history

A new, global world order grew due to the economic reconstruction and decolonization after World War II. World history got a new impetus in the 1960s. It completely changed objectives and content. The most important stimuli for the development and transformation of world history came from outside academic histiography. Since the 1960s there has been a growing awareness that societies do not have independent life cycles; they are shaped by *processes of mutual interaction*. As a result, we need to comparatively analyze group and society formation, and we need to utilize a wider time and space perspective. In addition to the local setting (in which people shape their lives), more attention is paid to the global dimension (in which societies grow or languish). Examples include: research into trade relations and migration movements, such as the work of Philip Curtin (*The Atlantic Slave Trade*, 1969; *Cross-cultural Trade*, 1984); the study of the political economy as a (unequal) global system: Andre Gunder Frank (*World Accumulation, 1492–1789*, 1978), Immanuel Wallerstein (*The Modern World-System*, 1974, 1980, 1989, 2011; *Historical Capitalism*, 1983); and the history of the world outside Europe: Eric Wolf (*Europe and the People without History*, 1982). There is also an increasing historical interest for processes on *an ecological scale*, such as the distribution of diseases, plants and animals, and the impact of changes in geology, climate and flows of energy on humanity. Pioneers include William H. McNeill (*Plagues and Peoples*, 1976), Alfred Crosby (*The Columbian Exchange. Biological and Cultural Consequences of 1492*, 1972 and *Ecological Imperialism: The Biological Expansion of Europe, 900–1900*, 1986) and later Jared Diamond (*Guns, Germs and Steel. The Fates of Human Societies*, 1997). The stimulating influence of non-historians like the sociologists Frank and Wallerstein, the ecologist Crosby, the anthropologist Wolf and the evolutionary biologist Diamond, is striking.

Within the historical world, the paradigm of the state as the primary unit of analysis was brought up for discussion in the 1960s. In *La Méditerranée et le Monde Méditerranéen à l'époque de Philippe II* (1949), Fernand Braudel analyzed the Mediterranean as one *économie-monde*, one world system in which the traditional borders of nations, cultures and civilizations were breached. This integrated analysis of human interaction established a new standard in historiography. In his pioneering work *The Rise of the West: A History of the Human Community* (1963), William H. McNeill focused on civilizations as interacting systems rather than as independently-existing entities. Four paradigms take over from each other in McNeill's world history: the urban paradigm (origin of civilizations); the ecumenical paradigm (interaction between civilizations); the European expansion paradigm (creation of the 'modern' world); and the Cold War paradigm (twentieth century). In this book, McNeill opened up the borders of state-linked history. Braudel broadened his analysis of early capitalism as a world system in *Civilisation Matérielle, Economie et Capitalisme, XVe–XVIIIe siècle* (1979) and McNeill has since published *Plagues and Peoples* (1976) and *The Pursuit of Power: Technology, Armed Force, and Society since A.D. 1000* (1982).

The impact of the new world history grew in the 1980s. This is reflected in a further professionalizing of the field via specific publication channels, professional organizations, scientific meetings and debates, specific courses, degree programmes and textbooks, and via the development of specific norms, argumentations and jargon. According to Patrick Manning (2003), this is not only logical, it is also necessary. After all, world history is not the sum of local and/or national knowledge. That is why modern world history cannot simply adopt the norms and methods of the existing human and social sciences. According to Manning, a further professionalizing of world history must go hand in hand with a further exploration of the possibilities and limits of:

1   Sources and data. They are usually formulated in the context of a community or, more recently, a national state, and therefore must be 'reread'.
2   Methods. For the reinterpretation of data, new or adjusted methods of data collection and data analysis are needed. These methods include comparative techniques and systems analysis.
3   Analyses. The interpretation framework is no longer exclusively the local community or the national state; it integrates a wider scale.
4   Theory formation. World history looks at other social and physical sciences (like chaos theory) to give meaning to 'global knowledge' outside the local/ national framework.

## Civilization history versus world history

The reorientation of the content of civilization history into a modern and integrated world history is a crucial process. It implies a fundamental paradigm shift. In the words of the Bangladeshi historian Dipesh Chakrabarty, European history is 'provincialized' (*Provincializing Europe: Postcolonial Thought and Historical Difference*, 2000). This switch is not linear; histories of civilizations are still published. Moreover, this process gives rise to intense ideological debates about the contents of world history and about the place and role of the wider historical perspective.

Peter Stearns (2003) sketched the troublesome merger of the concepts 'civilization' and 'world' in recent world history. This led to a long and intense debate in the American academic and educational world in particular. The wisdom or folly of a Western civilization perspective, summarized as *Western civ*, is at stake. In the United States, Western civ, or the history of Western civilization, developed from an older national historiography. When searching for the roots of the American nation, historians searched for equivalent partners with a similar value system embedded in a Western civilization model. The story of Western civ propagates a strong message of superiority and progress. It focuses on European and American history. Other people and parts of the world are only covered when they come into contact with Western society.

Criticism of the narrow interpretation of the civilization concept and of the 'imperialistic wrong-doings' of Western or American society at that time fuelled objections to the content of Western civ courses in the 1960s and 1970s. The criticism concentrated on (1) the homogenizing notion of 'civilization' in which differentiation, internal differences and mutual conflicts of interest received too little attention; (2) the progress idea that departs from a Western 'mother' civilization; and (3) civilization as an ideological concept that leaves no room for other types of society. That criticism gave rise to world history concepts that departed from an equality of civilizations and cultures, and that focused more on the inter-action between diverse human systems. Civilization history received a new impulse in the neoliberal 1980s, mainly from the motivation that one's own his-tory should remain the first and foremost frame of reference. From this point of view, Western values received renewed attention; this was combined with the alleged uniqueness of a Western civilization model. It seems paradoxical that this reaction, which returned to a more particularistic historiography that emphasized differences, was situated in a period of accelerated globalization. That is why the call for a real world history has been growing in many scientific milieus, espe-cially since the 1990s. This history must not depart from one type of society; it should pay attention to the diverse ways that people have lived together, and this in a comparative and integrated manner. The debate about civilization history versus world history, which is ongoing, shows how sensitive content choices are within a global perspective, and how closely they are linked to normative visions of world events, so-called *world views*.

A new world history is an answer to new questions in a new era in which glo-bal knowledge, global interaction and global challenges increasingly determine the agenda. The West, not to mention Europe, is no longer the norm. Development via the Western path is no longer self-evident. New knowledge should anticipate the new need for insights on a global scale, which no longer departs from alleged universal claims from one region. The historical story must be separated from the private interests of one group, nation, religion or people. It should provide a meta-story that is aware of the diversity in human history, and that simultaneously assembles that diversity in a human journey that is determined by global interac-tions. The circumstances for a new world history are favourable. Not only has our knowledge of the history of human communities from all eras and all places increased tremendously, our methods and interpretation models have been refined and adjusted. We have also learned from the insights and the errors of introspec-tive, Eurocentric and national historiography, and from their frequent use of concepts that are too narrow (such as civilization, the West etc.). After two cen-turies, the absolute hegemony of the Western society model and of Western think-ing comes to an end. A dialogue with knowledge and insights outside the West obliges us to broaden and deepen our view of human history.

The structure of this book illustrates this idea: an 'introduction to' and not a 'summary of' world history. The chapters are constructed around the major ques-tions in world history:

- A human world: how humankind developed from a threatened to the most successful species.
- A natural world: how nature helped shape human history.
- An agrarian world: how agricultural societies gave human history a new twist.
- A political world: how humankind got organized into increasingly more complex administrative systems.

- A divine world: how humankind developed new religious and cultural life orientation patterns.
- A divided world: how the paths of the 'West' and the rest of the world separated over the last centuries.
- A global world: how the world became more global at the same time.
- A polarized world: how the world became and is marked by diverging patterns of wealth, poverty and inequality.

# 2 A human world
## Humans and humankind

A dramatic encounter took place on 16 November 1532 in the city of Cajamarca on the Peruvian Highlands. Francisco Pizarro, *conquistador* of the largest empire in the western part of Eurasia (Spain under Charles V), and Atahualpa, Incan sun god and absolute ruler over the most extensive and most developed empire on the American continent, met for the first time. Atahualpa received the Spaniard on familiar territory, escorted by an army of 80,000 soldiers that was feared far beyond the Incan empire. Pizarro had no more than 168 men with him, in the middle of hostile territory and cut off from the rest of the Spanish troops. Nevertheless, Pizarro was able to capture Atahualpa a few moments after their first contact. The Incan emperor was held hostage for eight months. The Spanish promised to set him free after receipt of one of the largest ransoms in history. Once they received the gold, enough to fill a room that was 23 feet long by 16 feet deep and 8 feet high, Atahualpa was executed.

What does this event tell us? The kidnapping and execution of the Incan emperor symbolizes a turning point in world history. The contact between Pizarro of Spain and the Incan ruler Atahualpa was the first meeting between peoples that grew apart some tens of thousands of years before. The Incas are descendants of migrating hunter-gatherers that crossed the Bering Strait roughly 13,000 years ago, then gradually populated the American continent. Prosperous communities and large civilizations arose in diverse regions, most notably in Central and Southwestern America. After millennia of isolated development (except for a few sporadic contacts with migrants), two of the most developed civilizations on either side of the Atlantic Ocean stood face to face in 1532.

Why was that confrontation between two powerful, centrally-ruled and expansionist empires so unequal? What explains the sudden collapse of the large civilizations on the American continent? Why did Europeans depart for America and why didn't the Incas disembark on the coast of Europe?

First, the Amerindian people did not have seaworthy ships. In contrast to the Europeans, they did not need them for their expansion plans. Second, both groups had different intentions. While Pizarro, Cortés and the other Spanish adventurers had direct confrontation in mind, the natives were mainly led by curiosity. The sudden appearance of Europeans (which the natives knew very little about) caused great and deliberate confusion. Neither the Incas nor the Aztecs suspected that the troops led by Pizarro and Cortés were only the vanguard of a true colonization project. The Europeans' intentions were completely misjudged. Third, the Spanish made optimal use of tools and weapons that were unfamiliar to Amerindian peoples. These included horses, steel swords, body armour, helmets and firearms. The ensuing chaos was often sufficient to capture or kill the leaders. Only this can explain the enormous panic that broke out amongst the Inca warriors after the unexpected attack of Pizarro and his 168 soldiers, of whom 62 were on horseback. Within a few hours, they are reported to have killed 7,000 Inca soldiers without one Spanish casualty. Fourth, Pizarro and Cortés were able to destabilize the very hierarchic-minded civilizations, thanks to the kidnapping of the Inca and Aztec emperors. They engaged the help of hostile tribes. The continent was further explored, reinforcements were sent in and the central junctions were taken under control. The final blow came in the form of epidemic diseases such as smallpox, measles, typhus and the flu, introduced by the Europeans. These diseases undermined the economic and social fabric in a short period of time, and ultimately killed up to 95 per cent of the pre-Columbian population.

This disastrous contact between human civilizations tells the story of the human journey in which expansion and conflict, growth and annihilation go hand in hand. The pre-Columbian civilizations did not disappear because they were less developed; they were simply in a much weaker position vis-à-vis the Europeans. They were completely unprepared for the felonious intentions of the 'gods of the west'. They did not have large pack and riding animals, nor did they have strong steel armour and gunpowder. Most importantly, they were defenceless against the diseases to which Europeans had already built up immunity.

This reversal in world history is an illustration of the impact of the sometimes similar, sometimes divergent paths that human communities have followed. Sizeable and strong civilizations based on progressive farming, a centrally-governed state and a repressive religious and cultural model developed in the Eurasian and American continents completely independent of each other. The strong position of the European civilization can be explained by its position in the much larger Eurasian-African world. Knowledge, technology and immunity were acquired through interaction with other peoples in this region. The more isolated American empires did not have that advantage. To be able to interpret this, we must first understand the diverse paths that the human race has followed in its expansion across the earth's surface.

## Ever more people: population growth

Recent and current DNA research creates an increasingly clearer picture of the contours of the *human journey*. It confirms that the current world population (7 billion) descends from a small group of African ancestors (no more than a few thousand, part of the Homo sapiens group) that roamed African savannas 70,000 to 80,000 years ago. Descendants of this group dispersed 'out of Africa' and slowly colonized the whole world. A consequence of the geographic bottleneck that the human race travelled through is the striking uniformity of the population.

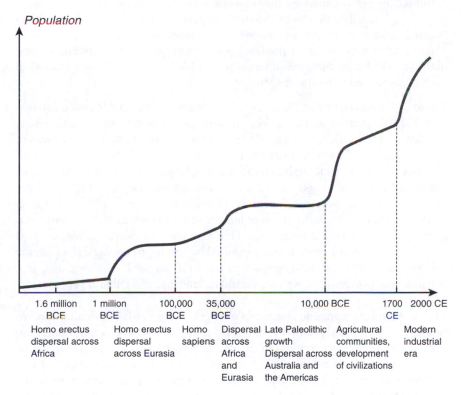

Population

| 1.6 million BCE | 1 million BCE | 100,000 BCE | 35,000 BCE | 10,000 BCE | 1700 CE | 2000 CE |
|---|---|---|---|---|---|---|
| Homo erectus dispersal across Africa | Homo erectus dispersal across Eurasia | Homo sapiens | Dispersal across Africa and Eurasia | Late Paleolithic growth Dispersal across Australia and the Americas | Agricultural communities, development of civilizations | Modern industrial era |

*Figure 2.1* Long-term cycles of demographic growth.

Source: P. V. Adams *et al.*, *Experiencing world history*, New York University Press, 2000, p. 33.

The extraordinarily small difference in DNA structure (99.9 per cent is the same for all human beings) contradicts the idea that human biological subraces exist. Moreover, there are hardly any 'homogeneous' population groups. All of us have accumulated genetic material from very diverse origins. Twenty per cent of the population of the Iberian Peninsula has Jewish ancestors and 11 per cent has an Arabian bloodline. This is a result of the massive conversion of Jews and Muslims during and after the Catholic Reconquista in the fifteenth and sixteenth centuries.

The human race spread over the face of the earth in diverse steps, and the growth of the population was not a continuous process. We are able to distinguish four phases in the long term.

*Phase 1* Human history commenced between 9 and 5 million years ago when African anthropoids split into four species: gorillas, chimpanzees, bonobos and 'proto-man'. *Homo erectus* appeared between 1.7 and 1 million years ago and differed from its human ancestors in that it had a larger body, comparable to ours, and increased intelligence (a brain size of 800–1,050 cm³ compared to

1,400–1,500 cm³ in modern man). A first phase of accelerated population growth coincided with Homo erectus' dispersal across Africa and Eurasia (from 1 million to 100,000 years ago). Using simple stone technology and fire, Homo erectus was the first colonizing population group. The population grew until it reached from 1 to a maximum of 1.5 million, then halted due to technical limitations related to food and protection.

*Phase 2* The ancestors of modern man, *Homo sapiens*, appeared between 250,000 and 200,000 years ago. For a long time it was assumed that multiregional development took place, in which Homo erectus developed into Homo sapiens in diverse locations. Recent evidence such as DNA research points in the direction of the 'out of Africa' hypothesis. Homo sapiens began their advance in African savannas 100,000 years ago and were the motor behind the second 'global wave of colonization' across Africa, Eurasia, Oceania and America. Modern human beings ousted or assimilated all older human species (such as Neanderthals who disappeared about 18,000 years ago). This new wave of migration was coupled with new population growth. It was supported by striking technological, economic and cultural advances: hunting and gathering equipment, clothing, housing, collaboration between groups, trade relations, language and cultural patterns.

The tempo of demographic and social changes that preceded agricultural revolutions was particularly slow in comparison, but they were crucially important for human history. The survival of diverse ecological bottlenecks, in which the human species were often at the brink of extinction, and the dispersal and exchange of genes, enabled Palaeolithic man to spread across large parts of the world. The most important achievement is entirely unique to the human species: cultural exchange. Over many tens of thousands of years, modern humankind learned the art of collective learning or: the accumulating and passing on knowledge. The use of fire, improved hunting methods, new technologies, learning (symbolic) language – all of this would have been impossible without collective learning. The first 150,000 years of the history of modern humankind, Homo sapiens, took place on the African continent. When this species appeared 250,000 to 200,000 years ago, it developed new techniques and colonized new areas. As indicated above, all contemporary human beings descend from a small group of Africans that possibly survived an ecological threat successfully. Descendants reached Asia 70,000 years ago, Australia 60,000 to 40,000 years ago, Europe 40,000 years ago and America 20,000 to 15,000 years ago. Human beings were able to adapt to the most diverse ecological conditions, something that no other animal species had ever done before. After the last ice ages, 16,000 years ago, humankind travelled further north both in Europe and in Asia.

For 95 per cent of our human history we have lived in small, mobile groups of up to 50 members. For the majority of this time there were no more than a few hundred thousand of us. In the run-up to the agricultural revolutions, the population increased faster. There were up to a few million Homo sapiens 10,000 years ago.

*Phase 3* The establishment of agricultural societies in diverse locations around the world about 10,000 BCE initiated a third phase in population growth. Because agrarian, pre-industrial societies could only support limited population growth, this acceleration did not continue. Nevertheless, world population in this period grew from a maximum of 10 million 12,000 years ago to 1 billion in 1800. After 1500, long before the industrial revolution, the population started to increase more strongly in several, very diverse regions. Between 1500 and 1750 the population doubled in England (to 5.75 million), Russia (to 35 million) and China (to 200 million).

*Phase 4* The fourth acceleration phase was a result of the industrialization process that started in Europe after 1800. Population growth continued to accelerate until the late twentieth century, when it seems to shift. Population growth continues to decelerate in the twenty-first century and zero growth is expected between 2050 and 2070.

Before the Neolithic revolution and the development of agricultural societies, world population growth was extremely limited. It is estimated that less than a million people lived on earth up to 50,000 years ago, and less than 10 million people lived on earth up to 10,000 years ago. There was hardly any growth, up to 0.001 per cent per year. The growth rhythm accelerated 15,000 to 10,000 years ago. The total population increased from 5 to 10 million in 10,000 BCE to 7 billion in 2012.

---

**Doubling time**

We estimate the effects of population growth by calculating the *doubling time*. The period in which the population doubles can be calculated by dividing the number 70 by the annual growth rate. For example:

| Annual growth rate (per cent) | 0.001 | 0.01 | 0.1 | 0.5 | 1 | 3 |
|---|---|---|---|---|---|---|
| Doubling time (years) | 70,000 | 7,000 | 700 | 140 | 70 | 23 |

---

Population numbers are based on estimations until the twentieth century. Table 2.1 outlines the general picture.

Accelerated growth is a recent phenomenon. On average, the world population grew between year 1 and 1750 by 0.05 to 0.07 per cent per year (a doubling in 1,000 to 1,500 years). Between 1750 and 1950 growth accelerated to 0.6 per cent per year (doubling in 117 years), and to 1.8 per cent per year between 1950 and 2000 (doubling in barely 40 years). The first billion was achieved around 1800, 2 billion in 1918 (118 years), 2 billion in 1960 (42 years), 4 billion in 1973 (13 years), 5 billion in 1987 (14 years), 6 billion in 1999 (12 years) and 7 billion in 2011 (13 years). This is called exponential growth. It means that the growth is proportional to the size of the population. The impact of the growth of the current population is at least three times as large as 50 years ago.

*Table 2.1* Population growth over time

|  | Population (millions) | Growth rate (per cent) | Doubling time (years) |
|---|---|---|---|
| 10,000 BCE | 5–10 | 0.008–0.01 | 8,000–7,000 |
| 400 BCE | 153 | | |
| 1 | 252 | 0.04 | 1,750 |
| 600 | 208 | | |
| 1000 | 253 | | |
| 1200 | 400 | | |
| 1400 | 374 | | |
| 1600 | 579 | | |
| 1750 | 770 | 0.07 | 1,000 |
| 1800 | 954 | | |
| 1850 | 1,241 | | |
| 1900 | 1,634 | | |
| 1950 | 2,520 | 0.6 | 116 |
| 2000 | 6,236 | 1.8 | 38 |
| 2010 | 6,909 | | |

It is estimated that about 82 billion people have been born since the dawn of humanity. Almost 8 per cent of them are alive today. Due to their size and increased life expectancy, the generation born in 2000 will absorb almost a fifth of all the tallied years (the years lived by every person since the origin of the human group).

Tables 2.2a and 2.2b summarize the distribution of the world population across the continents.

Asia's large share of world population (not including Russia) is striking. After a decline in the nineteenth century, it rose to 60 per cent once again after 1950. The European population (including Russia) grew strongly in the nineteenth century, then its share more than halved between 1900 and 2000. Africa's share of world population declined very sharply between 1500 and 1900, a consequence of the slave trade, internal disputes and colonization in the nineteenth century. Its growth after 1950 is striking. The American population almost halved between 1500 and 1800, a consequence of the decimation of Indian population groups. Massive immigration explains the fast growing share in the nineteenth century and beginning of the twentieth century.

Projections predict an increase in the world population to 9 to 10 billion in 2050. It is certain that the speed of growth will continue to decline, possibly even to stabilize after 2050 (previous projections to 15 billion have been adjusted). This increase will take place almost exclusively in the poorer parts of the world. Populations in the 50 poorest countries will more than double in the next 50 years (from 0.8 billion to 1.7 billion). Africa's share of world population will increase

*Table 2.2a* Distribution of world population (millions)

|          | Asia  | Europe/Russia | Africa | America | Oceania | Total |
|----------|-------|---------------|--------|---------|---------|-------|
| 400 BCE  | 95    | 32            | 17     | 8       | 1       | 153   |
| 1 CE     | 170   | 43            | 26     | 12      | 1       | 252   |
| 600      | 134   | 33            | 24     | 16      | 1       | 208   |
| 1000     | 152   | 43            | 39     | 18      | 1       | 253   |
| 1500     | 245   | 84            | 87     | 42      | 3       | 461   |
| 1800     | 631   | 195           | 102    | 24      | 2       | 954   |
| 1900     | 903   | 422           | 138    | 165     | 6       | 1,634 |
| 1950     | 1,376 | 575           | 224    | 332     | 13      | 2,520 |
| 2000     | 3,736 | 807           | 832    | 830     | 31      | 6,236 |
| 2010     | 4,110 | 784           | 1,040  | 939     | 36      | 6,909 |

*Table 2.2b* Distribution of world population (percentage share)

|          | Asia | Europe/Russia | Africa | America | Oceania | Total |
|----------|------|---------------|--------|---------|---------|-------|
| 400 BCE  | 62   | 21            | 11     | 5       | 0.7     | 100   |
| 1 CE     | 67   | 17            | 10     | 5       | 0.4     | 100   |
| 600      | 64   | 16            | 12     | 8       | 0.5     | 100   |
| 1000     | 60   | 17            | 15     | 7       | 0.4     | 100   |
| 1500     | 53   | 18            | 19     | 9       | 0.7     | 100   |
| 1800     | 66   | 20            | 11     | 3       | 0.2     | 100   |
| 1900     | 55   | 26            | 8      | 10      | 0.4     | 100   |
| 1950     | 55   | 23            | 9      | 13      | 0.5     | 100   |
| 2000     | 60   | 13            | 13     | 13      | 0.5     | 100   |
| 2010     | 59   | 11            | 15     | 14      | 0.5     | 100   |

from 15 per cent in 2010 to 21 per cent in 2050. Europe's share will decline further from 11 per cent to 7 per cent.

The most important cause for decelerating population growth is a drop in the number of surviving children per woman, from five in the 1950s and 4.5 in 1970–1975 to 2.65 in 2000–2005. It is estimated that this number will be 2.1 in 2050. The proportion in most developed countries is already 1.56; considerably lower than the replacement level (2.1 children per woman). For the least developed countries, experts predict a decline from five children per woman today to 2.6 in 2050. The life expectancy of infants will continue to increase from 65 years in 2005 to an average of 75 years in 2050. Progress will be most spectacular in the least developed countries, from 51 years today to 67 years in 2050. The world's population will be much greyer in 2050 than it is now, even in the poorest countries.

## Demographic transitions

The phases in population growth suppose several 'demographic transitions', periods in which demographic behaviour (the way that people deal with their fertility) changes fundamentally. These changes are shaped by the interaction of two forces: external limitations and internal choices. Under limitations we imply climate, disease patterns, the supply of land, energy and food, and settlement patterns. These factors are 'structural' and change slowly. The choices that are made gear one's own reproductive behaviour (family formation, births and migrations) to the external limitations. If the relationship between limitations and choices changes, we speak of a demographic transition. The two most important transitions in human history are the Neolithic transition and the contemporary transition.

Slow population increases and an exhaustion of natural resources amongst Palaeolithic hunter-gatherers stimulated the search for larger food yields on smaller plots of land. This meant that nature no longer provided enough food for the human groups so they had to manipulate their natural environment, domesticating plants and animals. About 10,000 years ago the world population began to grow at an unseen tempo to 250 million people at the beginning of the Common Era. This was only possible because the difference between births and deaths became larger. Until recently, this was attributed to the success of the Neolithic Revolution, the ability to maintain more people on a smaller surface area. Recent research points to several new uncertainties related to the transition to agricultural cultures: dependence on a more lopsided range of foods (based on grains) and an increased risk of transmitting contagious diseases (less mobility, more interaction between (tame) animals and people, increased population densities). Mortality, also amongst children, seems to have increased rather than decreased. Yet the number of births continued to increase at a faster pace than the number of deaths. The 'cost' of raising children shrank considerably in sedentary cultures. It is more difficult and riskier to raise children in mobile hunter-gatherer groups. That is why births were spread out more amongst those groups. Moreover, the 'proceeds' of a child are greater in agricultural cultures. They can be deployed in the economic process more quickly. On balance, growth in the number of births in agricultural cultures is greater than the number of deaths, with a higher excess of births resulting in increased population growth.

The current demographic transition started in Europe in the eighteenth century. Mortality decreased at first (resulting in increased life expectancy) and this was followed by reduced fertility (fewer surviving children per woman). There is always a gap between these two movements, resulting in accelerated population growth.

Again, demographic theory explains this transition via the 'cost' of raising a child. In traditional agricultural societies, having a large number of children is a way to address high infant mortality, ensure hereditary succession and continuous production, and to guarantee that aging parents are looked after. In new, industrial-urban societies, children gradually lose their 'economic benefit' (abolition of child labour, introduction of compulsory education etc.). Infant mortality decreases quickly and new cultural patterns appear in which parental investments in the child become a long-term project. In the Western world (richer countries) this transition

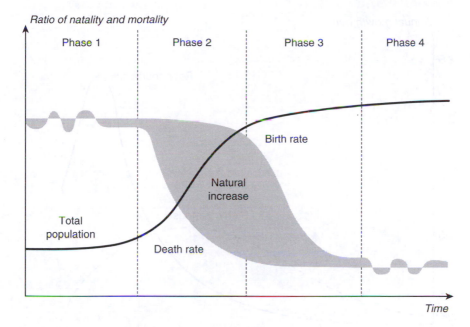

*Figure 2.2* Contemporary demographic transition.

process gradually moved from high birth rates and high mortality to low birth rates and low mortality. Average growth figures seldom rose above 1 per cent. In the non-Western world (poorer countries) this transition was much more abrupt, resulting in a much larger surplus of population.

In less rich regions, the growth rate has been dropping since the 1980s. The average number of children per woman has fallen from 5.4 in 1970–1975 to 2.7 in 2005–2010. Fertility rates continue to grow towards one another, as shown in Figure 2.4.

## Demographic growth as an impediment or a stimulus

The relationship between population growth, economic development and welfare is still an open question that cannot be answered without qualification. A growing population forces societies to look for different and better forms of food provisioning. On the other hand, uncontrolled population growth consumes the available resources at an accelerated rate, resulting in shortages.

### Population growth as an impediment

The most famous theory relating to the tension between population and economic resources is due to the rural English minister Thomas Robert Malthus (1766–1834). When looking for an explanation and a remedy for the fast growth in population in the early years of the First Industrial Revolution, he predicted a growing gap

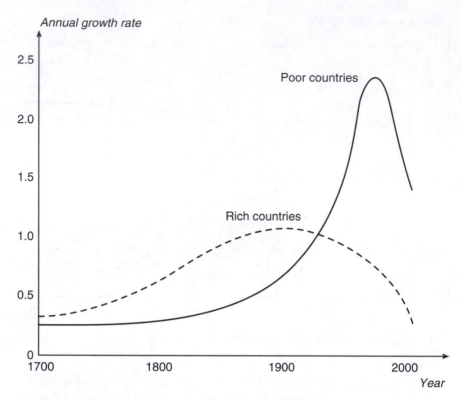

*Figure 2.3* Demographic transition in rich and poor countries.

Source: *World Population Trends* (http://www.un.org/popin/wdtrends.htm).

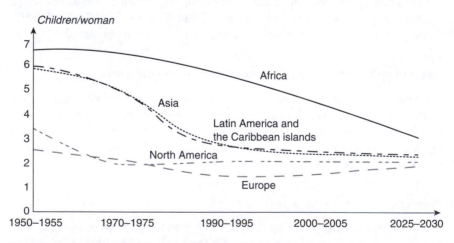

*Figure 2.4* Number of children per woman, 1950–2030.

Source: *World Population Trends* (http://www.un.org/popin/wdtrends.htm).

between the speed of population growth and an increase in foodstuffs. While the population appeared to grow at an exponential rate (a doubling every 25 years: two, four, eight, 16 etc.), Malthus predicted that the available foodstuffs (actually the cultivated land) would only increase at a linear rate (at equal increments: two, four, six, eight etc.). A catastrophe (famine, war, an epidemic: *positive checks*) could only be avoided by adjusting reproductive behaviour (celibacy, abstinence: *preventive checks*). Figure 2.5 shows the impact of demographic growth and reduction according to the Malthusian model.

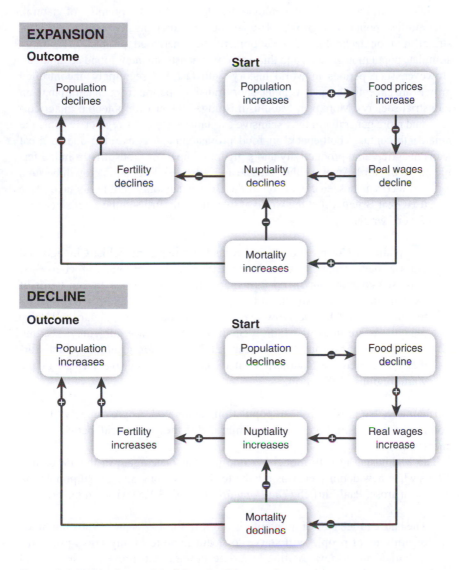

*Figure 2.5* Malthusian model of demographic growth.

Population growth increases the demand for food and food prices rise as a result. This causes real wages to decline (decreased purchasing power and increased cost of living). In turn, this influences mortality (more deaths), nuptiality (fewer marriages) and fertility (fewer births). More deaths and fewer infants result in a population decline so the demand for (and price of) foodstuffs declines. The diagram also shows the choice, according to Malthus, that the (world) population is confronted with: either limit one's own fertility (preventive check) or head for a demographic disaster (positive check). The reverse process occurs during a population decline.

This Malthusian vision of demography departs from a premise of natural, uncontrolled population growth. Human beings' attempts to remove the constraints put on technological development and increased productivity simply stimulate population growth, and this quickly exhausts any new-found advantages. However, such periods in world history with fast and seemingly uncontrolled growth are exceptions (such as in the short transition period from an agrarian to an industrial society). Moreover, Malthus misjudged the growth potential in agriculture, and more generally in the expansive capitalist system. As regards Europe, the nineteenth century 'bottleneck' in food provisioning was avoided due to great leaps in agricultural productivity and a gigantic import of foodstuffs from the fertile plains of North America, the Ukraine and Australia. Economic growth became a global fact. The unseen expansion of the British economy could only take place because Great Britain ruled the world at that moment. In 1865 the English economist Jevons wrote:

> The plains of North America and Russia are our corn-fields; Chicago and Odessa our granaries; Canada and the Baltic are our timber-forests; Australia contains our sheep-farms, and in South America are our herds of oxen; Peru sends her silver, and the gold of California and Australia flows to London; the Chinese grow tea for us, and our coffee, sugar, and spice plantations are in all the Indies. Spain and France are our vineyards, and the Mediterranean our fruit-garden; and our cotton-grounds, which formerly occupied the Southern United States, are now everywhere in the warm regions of the earth.

Furthermore, 'surplus' European populations emigrated. Approximately 20 million Britons and 55 million Europeans migrated to the 'new world' between 1815 and 1940.

The Malthusian growth model became popular once again in the 1960s and 1970s when new doom scenarios related to the impending and global population explosion arose. Paul Ehrlich (*The Population Bomb*, 1968) wrote in his preface:

> The battle to feed all of humanity is over. In the 1970s and 1980s hundreds of millions of people will starve to death in spite of any crash programs embarked upon now. At this late date nothing can prevent a substantial increase in the world death rate ...

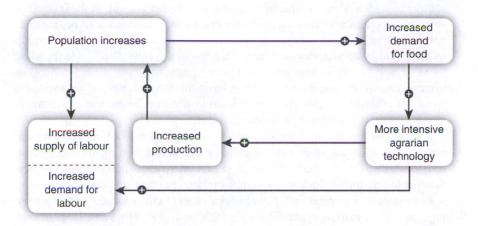

*Figure 2.6* Intensification model of demographic growth.

The growth figures of the world population decreased from the 1970s and 1980s faster than expected due to generalized family planning and contraception (China) and the AIDS epidemic in Africa. Experts believe that global agriculture currently has the technical ability to feed 9 to 10 billion people.

### Population growth as a stimulus

Before Malthus launched his pessimistic vision, the most accepted belief was that population growth was a condition for economic development. European states strived for the largest possible population in the belief that a growing population was a symbol of and the basis for national wealth. The idea of demographic growth as a motor of development gained influence in the past decades. Figure 2.6 summarizes the paradigm.

A larger population causes an increased demand for food. This stimulates the agricultural sector, which invests more and experiments with new techniques: intensification. This leads to higher production and an increased demand for workers. The extra supply of labour, created by a population increase, can be absorbed in the economic circuit. The premise is that the agricultural sector only modernizes and becomes more productive when confronted with the required demographic stimuli. Examples of intensification include the disappearance of the slash and burn culture, the disappearance of fallow fields due to crop rotation, the use of better tools and fertilizers, the introduction of irrigation and the permanent stabling of cattle. In addition, people work together more, divide up the work and thereby profit from better division of labour.

When interpreting the causes of population growth or decline, it is important to distinguish between stable cultural systems and periods of disruption, transition or instability. In more or less stable social structures, homeostatic mechanisms are always at work to keep the size of the population under control. In the interest of survival, a population group must always ensure that the number of people does not increase or decrease too quickly or too much. In principle, every human group has the ability to outgrow the maximum possible yield that its tools offer. Consequently, every human group tries not to exhaust those tools too quickly, because that would undermine their own basis for survival. Several demographic tools are available to this end. They include limiting births and expelling or allowing part of the population to leave (migration).

Controlling and limiting female fertility is a central concern in every human community. Most societies control or have controlled fertility through moral, religious or legal rules. They often limit sexual intercourse, permit forms of abortion (including infanticide), invoke taboos related to etiquette etc.

For example, European agricultural societies were characterized by an increasingly restrictive marriage pattern between 1000 and 1800. The average age at marriage was over 25 and many men and women never got married. This kept birth rates low and eased the pressure on increasingly scarce land. It also enabled women to offer their services on the labour market for longer, which gave them a more independent status than in regions where women married young (such as China).

## Family, gender and fertility

Throughout human history, children have been born within a family unit. Families and households are central organizational forms in human societies. That makes them universal. At the same time, the configuration and makeup of families and households changes constantly. These changes are related to changes in economic life, to changes in ideals and ideologies related to the role of the family, and to changes in legislature and government. Relationships between men and women, both legally and in the real world, play a major role in family formation. The relationship between family and household shifts at the same time. The family represents all kinship bonds, while a household refers to the place of residence (cohabitation). Except for extensive households, family and households do not usually coincide.

Hunter-gatherers lived in small groups, ordinarily limited to a few dozen members. These extensive family relationships were the dominant societal pattern during the largest part of human history. During the great wave of Homo sapiens migration over the continents, several groups formed larger communities thanks to more efficient methods of hunting, gathering and accommodation. They lived on semi-permanent campsites, sometimes with dwellings. Even though females gave birth to their first child at 16 or 17 years old, fertility remained low. A long suckling period meant that intervals between births were long. Before a woman died at 30 to 40 years of age, she gave birth to an average of four or five children. High child mortality meant that only half of these children survived to adulthood. This hardly exceeded the replacement level of 2.1 children per woman. Even with limited births, children weighed heavily on hunter-gatherer communities. A group of 40 people with eight or nine fertile women having two children younger than seven equated to 16 to 18 young children. This strongly limited the community's mobility and flexibility. Food was provided via hunting (mostly men) and gathering (mostly women). In the literature, there is no consensus about the distribution of tasks, except that they were performed flexibly and in consultation. Tools were made both by women and men. Most researchers assume a great equality between the sexes in these small communities. On average, five hours per day were sufficient to provide the necessary calories for the group. Because they did not need much, could usually feed themselves easily and had lots of spare time, some anthropologists label Paleolithic communities as truly 'affluent societies'. On the other hand, people died young due to sickness, violence or during childbirth. Up to 40 per cent of the male skeletons have traces of a violent death.

Agricultural revolutions drastically changed people's way of life. The population increased, people lived together in larger groups, a limited diet and a greater susceptibility to diseases (including those originating from contact with cattle) all meant that life expectancy decreased at first. In agricultural communities women gave birth to more children on average, by limiting the breastfeeding period (and using replacement milk) and because a sedentary community can raise more children. New patterns of knowledge, society and property grew in these communities.

This revolution also had a big impact on male/female relationships. Women probably selected and planted the first seeds, thereby increasing their grip on the most important plant-based part of the diet. In many parts of the world, tilling the soil with a stick and hoe remained a woman's responsibility. The relationship between the sexes changed thoroughly once communities became entirely sedentary and cattle breeding played a greater role. After ploughing was introduced, men took over the farming. Female labour was linked to organizing the household, including spinning and weaving. This agriculture with a plough and cattle breeding was at the foundation of more large-scale, more differentiated and stricter sex-defined societies. Opinions differ as to why the growing difference between men and women arose: from an unequal access to means of production in agriculture, to a new, more dual appreciation of nature (women and children) and culture (working the land). Women became more tied to the housekeeping sphere (rearing children, domestic tasks), while men controlled the public sphere, and therefore the important economic, political, social and cultural positions.

Smaller family ties became more important in new civilizations. They became increasingly more formalized via legislation (marriage and sexuality) and legitimated via ideology and religion. Families determined the status of men and women (at a much younger age than for men), drew the boundaries of sexual relations, gave legitimacy to descendants and brought possessions together. This was the case in Confucianistic China, the Islamic world and in the Roman-European and Christian worlds. The family (in diverse connotations) always held a central place in social structures, and this was almost always linked to a confirmation of male dominance inside and outside the home. Households were organized predominantly along patrilineal lines, and the family line was carried on via sons. In many societies, the status of daughters was lower than that of their brothers. They often did not have any economic or property rights. Women earned their respect via marriage and motherhood. Of course there were big differences. Hard economic needs often prevented the domesticity ideal, and women had to contribute just as much or more to the family income. Moreover, women could often take up prominent positions.

In all civilizations, the family became a central and formally organized link in society. A large difference remained between leading social groups that put the cultural ideal into practice and the majority who had to rely on daily survival. That majority lived on small farms where the labour of men, women and children was divided proportionally.

Families were not organized the same way everywhere. An important change took place in northwestern Europe between 1000 and 1800 in the relationship between community and individuals. This change translated into different marriage and fertility patterns. More and more families started new households after marriage. The new couples took over the parental business or took up residence in a new location (neolocality). This strategy required sufficient savings and the prospect of a family income. Consequently, marriage was usually delayed until the age of 25 or later. Many adults, sometimes up to a fifth, remained unmarried. This restricted marriage market was characteristic of European marriage patterns after the Middle Ages until the nineteenth century. Families were more complex in southern and eastern Europe. In general, young married couples did not settle in a new location. Since they did not need their own independent income, there were fewer obstacles to marriage. In China, recently-married couples, primarily the oldest son, continued to live in the parental home. In this system, where parents retained authority, men and women could marry young. Girls got married from the age of 12. Almost everyone married.

These diverse forms of family formation induced diverging strategies to limit the number of children. If fertility is unlimited between puberty and menopause, a woman can have 16 to 18 children. In practice, this was limited to five or six births. An average of three children per couple reached adulthood. In northwest Europe, restrictive access to marriage was the most important obstacle to the number of births. A late marriage age and large number of adults who never got married cut the potential fertility in half. Within marriage, female fertility was not limited and women were encouraged to remarry if their husband died. Different strategies were applied in societies where people married young and where most people got married. In China, men often lived and worked elsewhere, usually in cities, for several years after getting married. Moreover, customs like abstinence and negligence (even infanticide) were more accepted. Women had their last child at a younger age. That is because women were often widowed and remarriage was much less accepted.

The development of a peculiar European marriage pattern in the second millennium was linked to changes in familial matrimony and inheritance laws. Space for marriages without the interference of parents or families grew in Latin Christianity. New households were only formed once income prospects were favourable. Women were able to inherit more often, own land and accumulate wealth. This simulated participation in the labour process and increased the supply of available and flexible labour, especially in the regions around the North Sea. In China, marriage remained much more a collective affair in which a contract was concluded between two families. Parental authority remained very strong and women were not entitled to inherit. Individual freedom was not central like it was in Western Europe; family and clan interests were central. They guaranteed more protection in periods of need and wiped out social discrepancies.

Major economic shifts after 1500 had an important impact on the organization of families and on relationships between men and women. The changes were greatest in Western Europe, in Africa and in the American colonies.

The position of marriage and the nuclear family was reinforced in Western Europe. This was a result of an increase in urbanization, but the nuclear family became also the benchmark in the countryside. Sexuality outside marriage was denounced more frequently, and fertility was restrained by means of an older marriage age and a larger number of celibatarians. This limitation of fertility was also a result of increased land scarcity, which was a restraint on a family's future prospects. This went together with greater female subordination, which was strongly promoted by the church and state via morals related to sexual control (and punishment of 'deviant' sexual behaviour) and by restricting women's rights within the family: the loss of a right to personal property and women's so-called legal incapacity. In urban economies, women were increasingly kept out of the official labour circuit (guilds and trades) so they had to resort to more informal forms of (insecure) labour.

Changes in family and sexual relations in Europe were mainly a result of internal transformations. That was very different in Africa and America. In general, one can say that the scarcest product in Europe was land, and in Africa and America it was labour. Africa mainly participated in the world economy as a supplier of (bound) labour until the nineteenth century. This intensified the tensions associated with control of female fertility. Fertility was increasingly protected by the extended family or clan via customs and rituals. Polygamy was often an answer to the imbalance between men and women (a majority of the slaves carried off were men). Ritualized access to sexuality and fertility was the basis of latent tensions between generations in African societies.

In the American colonies, a great disparity grew between the rich top layer, in which marriage within one's own extended family was common, and lower social groups, in which marriage and cohabitation was not free. 'Frontier families' in North America followed European ideals related to the family (including the unequal rights of women), but in a much more supple manner. Labour was scarce so marriage was common and people married young. Families were the basis of social life. Control by external institutions like the church and state were weak. Due to many uncertainties, societal patterns were applied less strictly than in Europe.

In the industrial (i.e. European and North American) world of the nineteenth century, women and children regularly participated in paid labour. Nevertheless, the rhetoric and ideal of the breadwinner/housewife model persisted. This model rested on the man's so-called family wage, pushing female labour back to the domestic sphere and reserving the public domain for men. In most industrialized countries, paid female labour was limited to specific feminine sectors (until marriage) and to more informal labour circuits like cottage industries. At the end of the nineteenth century, new forms of birth control limited the number of children. Children became less a source of income (child labour) and more of an investment (schooling). At the same time, child mortality decreased, life expectancy increased, the marital age dropped and the government provided better social protection.

In the context of smaller and more sustainable families in the West, the breadwinner/housewife model, supported by the legislative and financial politics of national governments, experienced its peak in the first half of the twentieth century. The dual-income model became more dominant (once again) in the second half of the twentieth century and it becomes the norm in the twenty-first century. Despite the fact that legal forms of discrimination against women were lifted, a de facto inequality remains between men and women with regard to career structure, salary and share of the housekeeping. Families are becoming even smaller (fewer children per couple) and the number of new types of families is increasing sharply.

The impact of economic and political transitions in the nineteenth and twentieth centuries were at least as drastic outside (Western) Europe, North America and Japan. On the one hand, urbanization, colonial politics and new forms of labour on plantations and in mines stimulated a reproduction of the European family model, with smaller family ties and a dominant place for male breadwinners. Moreover, the number of children per family decreased in the twentieth century and women were given more opportunities to get an education. On the other hand, income uncertainty increased, many more families were broken up due to long-term migration, and farmers' ability to survive was undermined. Women remain the centre of small family businesses, especially since men increasingly work away from home. The disappearance of small farms undermines the position of women, who often can only find employment in new forms of informal labour. Moreover, strong cultural and formal forms of inequality often continue to exist in these areas. The share of women in paid labour in Muslim countries in the Middle East is lower than 10 per cent.

## Disease and death

The risk of death was very comparable before 1800. The greatest risk of death was in early childhood. Life expectancy was low at birth (35 years), but if a person reached the age of 20 they lived another 35 years on average. In addition, there were regular mortality peaks resulting from disease and deprivation. Once an adult reached 45, they had been confronted with death frequently: the death of their own parents, the majority of their brothers and sisters, at least half of their own children and often that of their partner.

Peaks in mortality disappeared in Europe as of the eighteenth century. The course of death obtained a flatter pattern. This was because survival crises had a smaller impact. The last European famines were those of 1816–1817, 1846–1849 (potato blight) and 1917–1918 (war). Infant mortality decreased strongly. This was a result of improved hygiene: personal hygiene (bottle feeding), water supplies and sewer systems. By the middle of the nineteenth century, big investments had been made to control death. This was done without any scientific certainty that these investments would be cost-effective. Only at the end of the nineteenth century, medical insights such as the discoveries of Robert Koch (1843–1910) and Louis Pasteur (1822–1895) offered the ability to limit mortality in a scientifically-substantiated manner. Mortality also decreased outside the Western world in the twentieth century. The figures are spectacular: in India the mortality rate decreased from 50 deaths per year per 1,000 residents in 1900 to 27 deaths per year per 1,000 residents in the middle of the twentieth century and 15 deaths per year per 1,000 residents in 1970.

In the very long term, average life expectancy at birth increased from approximately 20 years in the Neolithic period, to 30–35 years in pre-industrial agricultural civilizations, to 50 years in the Western world at the beginning of the twentieth century. A substantial increase in life expectancy only occurred in the West in the last quarter of the nineteenth century. Other parts of the world followed in the twentieth century. Global averages increased from approximately 50 years in 1950 and 67 years in 2010 to an estimated 75 years in 2050. The main determining factor in increased life expectancy is the reduction of infant and child mortality. As a rule, half of the babies did not reach the age of 10 in earlier societies.

Average mortality figures do not offer insight into the intermittent course of death. This was caused by hunger, diseases, disasters and war. Even though natural causes are often underlying, many disasters are manmade. Making an inventory of human 'disasters' is very perilous. What should one do with structural factors like contemporary malnutrition? Counting the human toll is also very perilous. The relative impact differs strongly. More than 90 per cent of the original population disappeared with the death of 20 million Indians (a very rough estimate) resulting from European colonization in the sixteenth century. Caesar's campaign against Gaul (first century BCE) probably claimed more than one million lives; a fourth of the population of Gaul. The 20 million casualties during Mao's Great Leap Forward (1959–1961), in absolute terms the largest 'local' mortality crisis, represented less than four per cent of China's population.

Despite the fact that the past was marked by many large mortality crises (the fall of the Roman empire, the Mongolian wars of conquest, the African slave trade, civil wars in China etc.), the twentieth century was the most murderous century in human history, especially in absolute figures. The twentieth century was also the worst in recent history with regard to war casualties.

In addition, the last century tops the list of genocides (planned 'cleansings'): China (1958–1961, 1966–1969: 20 million casualties), Soviet Union (1934–1939: 13 million), Germany (1939–1945: 12 million), Japan (1941–1944: 5 million), Cambodia (1975–1979: 1.7 million), Turkey (1915–1922: 1.5 million), Rwanda (1994: 1 million). The figures are indicative, but striking.

Deaths resulting from food shortages are not only a feature of past, non-industrialized societies. Scarcity is a structural fact in agricultural societies, but this

*Table 2.3* War casualties, sixteenth–twentieth centuries

|  | Total casualties (millions) | Casualty rate (per thousand population) |
| --- | --- | --- |
| Sixteenth century | 1.6 | 3.2 |
| Seventeenth century | 6.1 | 11.2 |
| Eighteenth century | 7.0 | 9.7 |
| Nineteenth century | 19.4 | 16.2 |
| Twentieth century | 109.7 | 44.4 |

seldom leads to massive mortality. For that to happen, you need a succession of failed harvests; usually the consequence of a combination of disease and/or war. History shows that famines do not inhibit population growth. Famines in which more than 10 per cent of the population dies are exceptions (like the Irish 'famine' in 1845–1848 with 1 million casualties, one eighth of the population). Every excess mortality resulting from a famine is quickly followed by a remarkable increase in births, so the balance is restored quickly and there is often new growth. After all, it is the weakest portion of the population that dies first.

The nineteenth century saw massive mortality resulting from famines in Ireland (1845–1848: 1 million), India (1876–1900: 12 to 20 million) and China (1876–1900: 20 to 30 million). The twentieth century list is headed by the USSR (1921–1922: 9 million), Northwest China (1927: 3 to 6 million), the Ukraine (1932–1934: 2 to 8 million), China (Henan) (1943: 5 million), India (Bengal) (1943: 2 to 3 million), China (1958–1962: 15 to 25 million), and North Korea (1995–1999: 3 million). This list does not show the actual impact of malnutrition, a daily reality in major parts of Africa. There are currently 25,000 deaths per day, some 9 million deaths per year. This equals a massive famine every year.

The biggest killers in human history, at least in agricultural societies, are infectious diseases. Human beings contracted almost all contagious 'civilization diseases' (malaria, smallpox, measles, flu etc.) from domesticated herd animals. Pathogenic organisms transmitted to human beings almost always had a devastating effect because, at the onset, immunity had not yet been acquired. It takes an average of five to six generations before pathogenic organisms can be tolerated by human beings in a stable manner. In the meantime, this disease can lash out viciously. Increased contact between cultures and people involved a risk of infection because germs were transferred for which no immunity has been acquired. As a result, massive mortality occurred more frequently in periods of more intense human interaction:

- The fall of the West Roman empire coincided with the outbreak of diverse deadly epidemics resulting from the spread of new microparasites from the Middle East and Far East (smallpox and measles).
- The plague bacterium was endemic amongst diverse rodent populations (Mongolia) long before it arrived in Europe. It was transferred via the rat, which 'established' itself in European cities during the Middle Ages. Healthy people became infected with the very deadly plague after being bitten by an

infected rat flea. A plague epidemic broke out in China in 1331. The disease reached the Crimea on the Black Sea in 1346 via the caravan routes. It is estimated that the 'black death' killed a third of the population of Europe between 1347 and 1350. The plague reappeared many times in later years, and disappeared as an epidemic disease in the late seventeenth century (due to increased immunity and better hygiene).

- Upon arrival in America, the Europeans brought contagious diseases such as smallpox, measles and typhus, against which the indigenous population had no resistance. The continent lost more than 90 per cent of its population in one century. The population of the Caribbean islands fell from one million inhabitants when Columbus arrived to only a few thousand in 1650.
- Nineteenth century urbanization stimulated new epidemic diseases. Cholera, caused by a microbe in stagnant water, was originally endemic in Bengal. An outbreak in 1817 infected the British soldiers who were in the area, and the disease was able to spread across land and sea over the next few years. The disease was only halted in large cities once water distribution systems and sewer networks were constructed.
- The Spanish flu caused 20 to 40 million casualties in 1918–1919; that is more deaths than all the casualties in World War I. The flu was a worldwide pandemic, but the majority of the victims died in Russia and India.
- Since the discovery of AIDS in the early 1980s more than 25 million people have died from this infectious disease (2 million in 2009). Thirty-three million people are currently infected with HIV (Human Immunodeficiency Virus). Seven per cent of the adult population in sub-Sahara Africa is a carrier of the virus.

## Mobility and migration

Since the origin of the human species and the migration of Homo sapiens, people have remained mobile creatures. The global migration history of the past tens of thousands of years is a story of divergence and convergence. It starts with the diffusion of modern humankind across the whole world; a migration that commenced 100,000 years ago in Africa. Modern humankind fanned out of Africa, heading east first via the coastline of Southeast Asia to Australia (80,000 to 60,000 years ago). Between 60,000 and 30,000 years ago, humankind travelled to East Asia and via the Bering Strait to North America, as well as to Central Asia and Europe. South America was inhabited 20,000 years ago, Micronesia 19,000 to 9,000 years ago and Polynesia 9,000 to 7,000 years ago. Even though this migration initially lead to a process of great divergence in languages and cultures, increased contact between Asia, Africa, Europe and (from the end of the fifteenth century) the American continent, slowly but surely ensured a process of convergence.

Convergence commenced as of 1000 BCE due to the development of systematic trade networks over long distances. A network of direct trade contacts developed and tied large parts of the world together, with the major exception of the American continent. Silk routes linked China with the Mediterranean Sea and Africa, while specialized trade diaspora of Armenians and Wangara and later

Jews established permanent connections between the Mediterranean Sea and the Indian Ocean. Vikings later played a crucial role in the trade between Northern, Eastern and Southern Europe. Even though a relatively small number of traders were responsible for this, the gradual expansion and intensification of commercial networks at the beginning of the Common Era enabled a vast area, from Japan to the western coast of Africa, to be linked together. We can speak of a slow convergence on several grounds. These networks expanded even further in the European Middle Ages due to the large-scale migration of 'horse peoples' from the East, the Arabian expansion in North Africa and that of the Vikings in Western and Eastern Europe. Simultaneously, contacts within South and North America increased. A result of that intensification was increased migration over large distances and a growing dissemination of goods, knowledge, techniques and diseases (such as the bubonic plague in the fourteenth century). In the fifteenth century, the only remaining barriers on a global scale were the Pacific Ocean and the Atlantic Ocean, which meant that America and most islands in the Pacific remained isolated from the rest of the world.

The scale of global migration increased in the period 1400 to 1700. Improvements in maritime technology made intercontinental travel possible. This had far-reaching economic, cultural and social consequences. The 'discovery' of the Americas at the end of the fifteenth century and Vasco da Gama's successful circumnavigation around the Cape of Good Hope were crucial. Portuguese and Dutch traders came into direct contact with Asia. This not only led to increased trade and the distribution of new products on a global scale, it also ensured that migration got started between the continents. This included both free and forced migration. The most famous and largest relocation is that of millions of slaves from West Africa to the Caribbean, Brazil and, to a lesser extent, the southern states of the later United States: approximately 300,000 in the sixteenth century, 1.9 million in the seventeenth century and almost 7 million in the eighteenth century. In addition, the 'Columbian exchange' stimulated the migration of millions of free and indentured migrants from Europe, mainly from England and the German states. A third large migration flow was that of Europeans to Asia via Portuguese, Dutch and later English trade channels. Migration flows also took place from Southeast Asia to South America and Central America, and from Europe to Siberia and North America (fur trade). Recent studies estimate the number of Europeans that left their own country (temporarily or permanently) per ten-year period at 2.3 million in the sixteenth century, 3.8 million in the seventeenth century and 4.7 million in the eighteenth century (respectively an average of 2.7 per cent, 3.9 per cent and 3.5 per cent of the total population per decade). The majority were soldiers and sailors; a minority migrated to the colonies. Three to five thousand Spaniards settled in the New World every year between 1500 and 1650. The accumulated effect was immense in the long term. About 8.5 million 'whites' lived on the American continent by 1800. The migration of Chinese people was quite stable in the same period; it is estimated at 4 million per ten-year period, less than 2 per cent of the total population.

The years between 1850 and 1930 are characterized as the period with the most intensive migratory flows so far. Excluding large-scale labour migrations within

Africa, Europe and America, the number of long-distance migrants is estimated at approximately 150 million. The number of European migrants per ten-year period rose to 20 million, or more than 6 per cent of the total population, in the period 1850 to 1900. The largest group – more than 40 per cent – left the continent in that period. Tens of millions of Europeans crossed the Atlantic Ocean to settle in North and South America. A similar number of Chinese found work in Northern Asia in Manchurian mines, and Indians found work in Southeast Asia in Burmese rubber plantations. The main causes of this growth in worldwide long-distance mobility are the transport (steamboat) and communication (telegraph, telephone, post) revolutions, the expansion of colonial empires (with the British empire in the lead) and the establishment of an integrated world market. As a result, capital and labour could be mobilized on an unequalled scale. We can distinguish three regional systems in this global wave of migration: (1) the trans-Atlantic migrations from Europe to the west (55 to 58 million migrants); (2) migrations from Northeast Asia (China, Russia) to Eastern Siberia, Manchuria, Japan (46 to 51 million migrants); and (3) migrations from India and Southern China to Indonesia, Malaysia and Burma (48 to 52 million migrants). Three important growth centres with a shortage of labour (North America, Northern Asia and Southeast Asia) mobilized almost as many immigrants in the period 1850 to 1930. They display striking convergence, with high numbers in the 1870s, around 1900 and at the end of the 1920s, and a decline in the beginning of the 1890s and during World War I.

A new period of increasing international migration became apparent as of the 1960s. Several patterns can be discerned, such as the direction of the migration (to Europe, in Eastern and Southern Asia etc.) and its form (free and indentured migration). This new wave takes place in a different world, with more people, more prosperity and with wider disparities in wealth. Current globalization lacks the nearly unlimited freedom of migration seen in the period 1850 to 1914. The capacity of the twentieth century state to control human mobility is a new phenomenon in world history. States received a lot more power to control migration after 1914 and to determine whether migrants were allowed on their territory and under what conditions. The Gulf States in the Middle East are a good example. They have recruited millions of Asian migrants since the 1970s, but have only given them limited rights and do not hesitate to deport them. This turned out to be much more difficult in liberal democracies, as demonstrated by the history of 'guest workers' in Western Europe. Yet national states have been able to control migration by influencing the volume, direction and selectiveness of migration. Migratory flows are frequently labelled 'illegal' because they are not recognized by a state. The wave of migration between 1850 and 1914 was an important motor for economic growth and increasing convergence, but today's migration patterns seem to reinforce the differences and global divergence. Nevertheless, the new wave of economic globalization continues to generate new migratory flows from poor to rich parts of the world. New forms of regulation and repression do not seem capable of stopping this movement.

# 3 A natural world
## Ecology, energy and growth

The human journey takes place in an area of permanent tension between human-kind and the natural environment. The reproduction of human life occurs in cir-cumstances that humankind did not choose. They are usually hostile. Consequently, the groups that were able to adapt to natural circumstances have been able to survive.

During the longest part of the 'journey', human beings have been mobile, migrating creatures that lived from what nature provided. If circumstances became unfavourable or the supplies were exhausted, the human roamers moved to a different area. About 10,000 years ago, one of the most important – if not the most important – transition in human history commenced: the shift to more stable agricultural societies. The most successful tribes in the most fertile areas developed a more complex social organization with new elites in new cities. The first agricultural centres were established in the plains of southern Iraq, the land of Sumer. Kings reigned over a complex of city-states. The oldest known literary epoch in world history is that of Gilgamesh, the (mythi-cal) king of the city of Uruk. The story dates from about 2000 BCE and is pos-sibly much older than that. The Epic of Gilgamesh recounts the battle between the old and the new way of life, the battle between nature and culture. The story conveys a message about the advantages and disadvantages of the new civilization.

The citizens of Uruk admire the great strength, wisdom and beauty of their ruler, the demigod Gilgamesh. Stories about his battle against monsters, the con-struction of walls and temples, his travels and glorious conquests fill the inhabit-ants of Uruk with pride. Gilgamesh's delusion pushes his ambitions even further, which leads to his people being oppressed, their sons being killed and their daughters being seduced.

> He walks around Uruk-Haven, like a wild bull he makes himself mighty, head raised. No rival can raise a weapon against him. His fellows stand alert, attentive to his orders. The young men of Uruk become anxious; Gilgamesh does not leave a son to his father. Day and night his tyranny becomes more frightful. And that is Gilgamesh, the ruler of humanity! He is the shepherd of Uruk-Haven; but Gilgamesh does not leave a girl to her mother!

The population complains to the gods, who decide to teach Gilgamesh a lesson. They create Enkidu. Enkidu is just as strong as Gilgamesh, but he lives in the wild amongst the animals. Enkidu stands for the power of nature, Gilgamesh for that of the new civilization. Gilgamesh discovers Enkidu's existence in a dream. He invents a scheme to tempt Enkidu. He sends Samhat, 'she who gives, receives and is sexual pleasure', to greet him. She seduces him in an unmistakable manner.

> Samhat unfastened her loincloth exposed her sex, and he took in her volup-
> tuousness. She was not restrained and took his energy. She spread out her
> robe and he lay upon her; she performed for him the task of womankind. His
> lust caressed and embraced her; for six days and seven nights Enkidu stayed
> aroused and had intercourse with Samhat until he was sated with her charms.
> But when he turned his attention to his herd, the gazelles saw Enkidu and
> darted off; the herd distanced themselves from his body. Enkidu was utterly
> depleted of strength, his body was limp; his knees went rigid while the herd
> ran off. Enkidu was diminished and could not run as before, but his under-
> standing had broadened!

Enkidu was no longer a creature of the wild. Samhat brings him to Uruk, where he meets Gilgamesh. Enkidu was the only one who dared to speak out against Gilgamesh and the two musclemen wrestled each other. Because they were equally strong, there was no winner. The two heroes became friends and hung out together during most of the story.

In this epic Gilgamesh symbolizes culture, as well as power, authority and delusions of grandeur. For his subjects, glory and wealth are at the expense of freedom. The new elites bring glory to Uruk and Sumer, but simultaneously they make old family and societal relations subordinate to a new social hierarchy. Labour and income are placed in the service of the city via taxes. Rules and laws replace old agreements. The new city, a new society is born.

## An ecological world history

A large-scale investigation at the beginning of the 1990s tried to measure the impact of human history on nature. Human beings' total impact between 10,000 BCE and the middle of the 1980s was traced out on a scale of 100 (the total impact in 1985) for 10 key indicators. For each indicator, researchers calculated when 25 per cent, 50 per cent and 75 per cent of the change was achieved.

Table 3.1 illustrates the enormous acceleration in the process of ecological change. Fifty per cent means that at that time (only) half of the change was achieved compared to 1985. For seven variables, there was more change in the period 1945–1985 than in the previous 10,000 years. The variables include water shortage, population growth, and sulphate, phosphate, nitrogen and lead emissions. As for deforestation, carbon emissions and the extinction of vertebrates, more than half of the increase occurred in the past 150 years. Without unquestioningly linking disaster scenarios to these changes, it is clear that the enormous acceleration process of

*Table 3.1* Ecological change caused by humanity 10,000 BCE to the middle of the 1980s

| Type of change | Date of quartiles (compared to 1985 levels) | | |
| --- | --- | --- | --- |
| | 25% | 50% | 75% |
| Deforestation | 1700 | 1850 | 1915 |
| Diversity terrestrial vertebrates | 1790 | 1880 | 1910 |
| Water shortage | 1925 | 1955 | 1975 |
| Population growth | 1850 | 1950 | 1970 |
| Carbon emissions | 1815 | 1920 | 1960 |
| Sulfate emissions | 1940 | 1960 | 1970 |
| Phosphate emissions | 1955 | 1975 | 1980 |
| Nitrogen emissions | 1970 | 1975 | 1980 |
| Lead emissions | 1920 | 1950 | 1965 |
| Carbon tetrachloride production | 1950 | 1960 | 1970 |

Source: B. C. Turner II *et al.* (eds), *The earth as transformed by human action: Global and regional changes in the biosphere over the past 300 years*, Cambridge University Press, 1990, p. 7.

the twentieth century is unique in human history. It still is not clear what the long-term consequences of this acceleration (in time and scale) will be.

Unsurprisingly, in such times of turbulent change and increased uncertainty about the strength of the ecosystem, many 'world histories' are told from an ecological point of view; from the constant area of tension between culture and nature. Some authors link the rise, success and disappearance of peoples and civilizations to ecological factors (Diamond). Others study the way that some peoples/civilizations have passed their ecological system on to other cultures, often with disastrous consequences (Crosby). Recent syntheses link the story of 'the rise of the West' to the conversion from an old, biological regime based on renewable solar energy to a new regime that uses fossil energy sources (Marks).

Jared Diamond (1997) summarizes his ecological vision of world history in Figure 3.1. From the presence and distribution of plants and animals (ultimate factors), we pass through cause and effect (domestication, sedentary societies, technology) to derived factors (horses, weapons, boats, state organization, diseases) which, in turn, explain why some human groups can rule over others and why some societies disappear.

Diamond also questions which ecological circumstances helped form humanity's divergent development paths on the five continents and, in particular, why Eurasia was able to develop a lead. He distinguishes four sets of explanations:

1    Differences (per continent) in the presence of plants and animals suitable for domestication. Due to extinction, large mammals that are suitable for domestication were no longer present on the American continent.
2    Differences in the speed of diffusion and migration. Diffusion and migration occurred faster in areas with similar climate zones (therefore on an east–west axis)

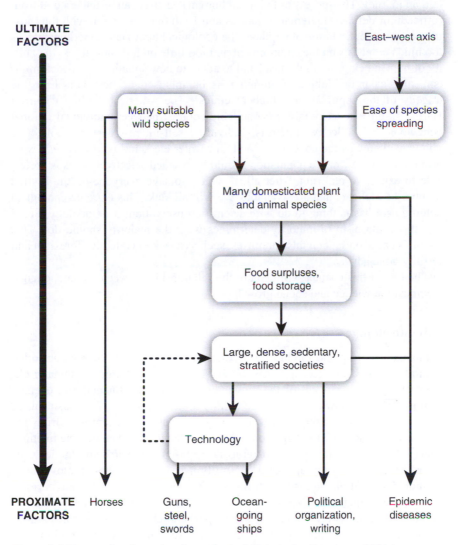

*Figure 3.1* Factors that determine the ecological-historical pattern in world history.

Source: J. Diamond, *Guns, germs and steel: The fates of human society*, Norton, 1997, p. 87.

and with relatively small ecological and geographic barriers. The difficulties were much greater in Africa and especially in America (both on a north-south axis).

3    Differences in interaction between continents, whereby America and Australia remained cut off for a long time.

4    Differences in population size. There was more interaction, competition and pressure to change where larger population groups lived. That is especially clear in core areas in Eurasia.

This ecological approach adds an essential dimension to understanding the human journey. The success or failure of human societies can be understood from (efficient or deficient) internal structures and from our interaction with the (hostile) environment. On the other hand, the ecological approach sometimes places too much emphasis on the environment and too little on human actions: the ability of human beings to think ahead and to adapt to new situations. This determinism, also clear in Malthusian thinking, is paraphrased in metaphors like 'the tragedy of the commons' or 'lifeboat ethics'. The American biologist Garrett Hardin assumes a seemingly irreconcilable contrast between individual rational behaviour and collective interests. Individual self-interest destroys collective goods we know as the commons (food, air, water etc.). In his *lifeboat ethics* he proposes that the world's population should be rescued selectively; this is preferable to expected total ruin. After all, if we try to save everyone on the limited number of lifeboats that are available, we will all sink. This extreme ecological determinism has nothing to do with scientific observation; it is ideology. Some call this ecofascism (a minority determines what the majority should do). This vision is based on several false premises, such as a lack of collective foresight and fertility gone adrift.

The rest of this chapter will explore the relationship between climate, energy, technical knowledge and social growth.

## Climate changes

Humankind is first and foremost a product of nature and of climate-controlled natural cycles. Climate change has always been around. Large, systematic climate changes are a result of the movements of large continental and oceanic tectonic plates and of changes in the earth's orbital geometry. This has enabled the earth to change from a freezer to a greenhouse, for example during the Cretaceous period 147 to 65 million years ago. Due to a gradual decline in atmospheric $CO_2$ concentrations, temperatures decreased afterwards and the ice caps formed (Arctic ice only appeared 2.7 million years ago). Shorter movements include those of the transition from glacial periods to interglacial periods. During these intervening periods, the average temperature was a few degrees higher. These shifts are caused by small, periodic changes in the earth's orbit around the sun. This has an impact on solar radiation and on the presence of atmospheric gas concentrations (such as $CO_2$ and methane). Since the end of the last ice age, approximately 15,000 years ago, the earth has been in a period of relative warmth.

Climate changes have a global impact, especially when they coincide with social changes. Decreased temperatures during the start of the 'little ice age' in the fourteenth century caused longer winters in the north (Europe, China) and more severe droughts in the south (Central America and Central Africa). This climate change has also been linked to the outbreak of the bubonic plague and the cessation of Mongolian expansion. In the last quarter of the nineteenth century a specific climate change – El Niño or the disruption of wind and rain patterns – was the underlying cause of large-scale famines. El Niño's impact was the greatest in Asia (China and India), Africa and South America; regions that were seriously weakened by colonial rule. Deforestation, plantation economies and large migration movements undermined the ecological and economic strength of agricultural societies. The colonial regimes reacted late or not at all. Thirty to fifty million people were casualties of famine between 1875 and 1900.

Anthropogenic changes, climate changes caused by humankind, are much more recent. Over the past 400,000 years, $CO_2$ concentrations in the atmosphere remained relatively stable, fluctuating between 180 and 280 parts per million (ppm). The presence of this greenhouse gas increased to 380 ppm between 1800 and 2000, an unprecedented rise in the earth's recent history. The speed of the increase, especially after 1960, is a cause for concern. The most important causes are the burning of fossil fuels and deforestation. A recent climate report by the United Nations (*Intergovernmental Panel on Climate Change*, backed up by the work of 2,500 scientists) confirmed humankind's responsibility in the matter. The increase of greenhouse gases can be attributed to human activity with 90 per cent certainty. As a result, the resistance of climate sceptics has become a rearguard action.

Increased atmospheric greenhouse concentrations ($CO_2$, methane, nitrogen monoxide etc.) cause global warming. Research on average temperatures in the northern hemisphere during the past 1,000 to 2,000 years confirms the unusual character of the recent warming. Average temperatures on the northern hemisphere during the second half of the twentieth century are very probably higher than in any other 50-year period in the last 500 years and probably the highest in at least the past 1,300 years. While temperature variations in the past 700 years can be strongly ascribed to volcanic eruptions and variations in solar intensity, human effects have mainly contributed to warming in the twentieth century. The world average temperature has risen over the past 100 years between 0.56 °C and 0.92 °C. That increase is not distributed equally over the planet: large landmasses and the polar regions are warming up faster; the oceans and tropics are warming up less fast. Climate models in which human influences are excluded cannot explain the observed increase. The world average temperature is expected to increase further between 1.1 °C and 6.4 °C (compared to 1990) until the end of this century. The large range is caused by the uncertainties in the emission of greenhouse gases and uncertainty about the downshift in the climate system, which could strengthen or weaken the effect. The consequences are known: variable weather patterns (precipitation, drought), melting of the ice caps and increased sea levels. It is assumed that if the world average temperature increases by 2 °C then the consequences will not be reversible.

The responsibility for global warming is not shared equally. With 5 per cent of the world's population, the United States was responsible for 30 per cent of carbon emissions in the period 1900 to 2000. Europe was responsible for 22 per cent, while China was only responsible for 7 per cent and India 2 per cent. The current emissions per capita in these countries are still 50 to 80 per cent lower than global averages.

## Energy

Over the course of history, almost every increase in the control over nature seems to be linked to a greater dependence on nature. The Dutch sociologist Goudsblom argues that as humankind's ability to control fire increased, its way of life was increasingly geared to the availability of fire. Humankind therefore became more dependent on fire and on the social organization and psychological discipline needed to control and use fire. Dependence increased over time: protection from the cold and the dark, making or improving tools, processing food and cultivating land. According to Goudsblom, by controlling fire human communities became more productive and efficient thereby overturning the balance of power between hominids and their greatest enemies, feline predators, to the favour of the hominids. A few hundred thousand years ago, our species developed into an ecologically dominant species that could control their surroundings (to a limited degree). Armed with this knowledge, Homo sapiens were later able to colonize all the continents using more refined technical means and closer social agreements.

In a scientific sense, world history can be described as the constant search for and control of ever-greater energy flows. Our planet's biosphere can be looked upon as one big solar energy system. Depending on the characteristics of their metabolic system, various plant and animal species are all involved in the energy flow, which uses the sun as its source (photosynthesis, biomass decomposition etc.). In the history of humankind, we can distinguish two energy regimes. Solar energy was by far the most important form of energy until the nineteenth century. Palaeolithic hunter-gatherers (until 10,000 years ago) used solar energy through non-controlled (extensive) extraction of biomass out of the environment (solar energy via the photosynthesis stored in plants that yield labour and warmth via biological reconversion or combustion). The quantity of available energy is limited. Consequently, survival must be geared to a varying supply of energy through increased mobility and limited fertility. The most important technological breakthrough was the ability to control fire. This enabled human beings to expand their diet of plant and animal food considerably. Hunter-gatherers were also responsible for the extinction of several (mostly large) animal species – for a prehistoric 'overkill'. Seventy-three per cent of all large animal species (heavier than 44 kg) on the American continent disappeared between 17,000 and 12,000 BCE. Some species were massacred in a few hundred years due to improved hunting weapons.

Agricultural societies thoroughly changed the relationship with solar energy and the process of photosynthesis. Much larger quantities of bioenergy could be produced via agriculture and cattle breeding. The controlled cultivation of plants and breeding of animals enabled humankind to monopolize part of the solar energy for its own needs, thereby changing the balance with the natural environment for good. More hierarchic societies organized and spread out energy production and consumption. Their success strongly depended on the way they were able to align the supply of energy via nature and agriculture with the demand for energy. They improved agriculture, used animals for power and invented elementary techniques like agricultural equipment, mills and forging. Agricultural communities used the solar energy system through a controlled (intensive) extraction of biomass via agriculture. Dependence on solar energy meant that the vitality of rural societies was always limited. The energy available depended on the surface area; cultivation and habitation were small-scale and dispersed. However, (small-scale) ecological disasters were possible due to overexploitation. These disasters included soil erosion and deforestation. A link can often be made with strongly hierarchically structured societies in which power perspectives were more important (in the short term) than economic strength (in the long term). An example of this tension is the Mayan civilization, which prospered in Central America between 600 and 800 CE. The many cities were supplied via intensive agriculture with ingenious and productive farming (raised fields in wet areas, terraced agriculture on the deforested hills). A growing top layer of priests, rulers and soldiers, and population growth in the cities increased the pressure on agriculture, resulting in soil erosion, silt deposits and further deforestation. The pressure on farmers increased and yields fell. In the space of a few decades, Mayan society collapsed, mortality increased quickly and cities were abandoned. The overgrown fields and cities were rediscovered more than 1,000 years later.

Agricultural societies grafted on to a biological regime of renewable energy, regulated by solar cycles. These cycles also limited these societies' ability to expand. The industrial society, which started in the nineteenth century, was built on a very different biological regime or energy system. Fossil fuels (coal in the nineteenth century; oil, gas and uranium in the twentieth century) formed the basis of this society. Growth acceleration rested on the exhaustion of large reserves of mineral solar energy that were stored under the earth's surface for millions of years. Technological revolutions followed, and they unleashed previously unseen power that could be used in production, transportation and later in households. The energy revolutions of the past two centuries followed in quick succession, starting with steam generated by burning coal (steam engines, steam trains and steamboats), followed by energy from oil and gas, electricity and nuclear power. The energy revolutions made much larger concentrations of people and labour processes possible. This much more intensive exploitation strongly increased the risk of depleting raw materials and disrupting the global ecosystem. If you take the total energy production on earth (total energy of sunlight converted into plant material via photosynthesis), then the hunter-gatherers only consumed an average of 0.1 per cent. In farming societies that increased to five per cent, in the industrial and post-industrial world that is 40 per cent. As one of the millions of living species on this planet, humankind consumes almost half of all the solar energy.

Table 3.2 shows the growth of energy consumption per capita. It increases from 5,000 calories per person per day for hunter-gatherers to 26,000 calories in mature agricultural societies and to 230,000 calories today. This is 46 times more than our oldest ancestors. All our energy requirements have risen, especially due to the growth of production and trade, and due to increased comfort. If we take into account the increased size of the world population, then today's daily energy

Table 3.2 Energy consumption per capita in a historical perspective (energy unit = 1000 calories per day)

| | Food [a] | Private and trade | Industry and agriculture | Transport | Total per capita | World population (millions) | Total consumption |
|---|---|---|---|---|---|---|---|
| Technological society (2000 CE) | 10 | 66 | 91 | 63 | 230 | 6,000 | 1,380,000 |
| Industrial society (1850 CE) | 7 | 32 | 24 | 14 | 77 | 1,600 | 123,200 |
| Developed agriculture (1000 BCE) | 6 | 12 | 7 | 1 | 26 | 250 | 6,500 |
| Early agriculture (5000 BCE) | 4 | 4 | 4 | | 12 | 50 | 600 |
| Hunters (10,000 BCE) | 3 | 2 | | | 5 | 6 | 30 |
| Proto-humans | 2 | | | | 2 | N/A | N/A |

Source: I. G. Simmons, *Changing the Face of the Earth: Culture, Environment, History*, Blackwell, 1996, p. 27.

Note
a Including fodder for livestock.

requirement is 46,000 times larger than before the Neolithic revolution and 200 times larger than during agricultural societies. Energy consumption per capita increased by a factor of five in the twentieth century. In the same period, total energy demand increased 19 times. More than 90 per cent of all energy came from biomass (mostly wood, charcoal and turf) until the nineteenth century. That was still 80 per cent in 1850 but it was less than 20 per cent by 2000. Coal was the most important alternative energy source until the middle of the twentieth century. The majority of our energy (85 per cent) currently comes from non-renewable sources (fossil fuels like oil, coal and gas). Dominion over these energy sources is one of the areas of conflict in the twenty-first century.

During the majority of history, humankind has depended on human and animal muscle power for its energy production. While humans can produce an average of 100 watts of energy, a draught animal can achieve three to six times that output (especially when the animal is harnessed more efficiently). The first important investment was to involve animal power more efficiently in agriculture. The earliest forms of large-scale mechanical energy production were via water mills and wind-mills. They produced 5,000 to 10,000 watts (period 1000 to 1800 CE). The break-through in mechanical energy production took place in the nineteenth century with steam machines (from 20,000 watts for the first machines by James Watt to 100,000 watts per machine after 1800) and later with gas turbines, combustion engines and nuclear power plants. The transition from animal to mechanical energy sources was not gradual or in phases. Sixty per cent of all energy was still produced with human and animal labour in 1900. That was only a few per cent a century later.

The great shifts in energy production and consumption concealed very diverse evolutions on a regional scale. Innovations in energy technology were primarily local and regional processes. In China under the Han dynasty (200 BCE–200 CE), important progress was achieved in knowledge related to coal and gas exploita-tion and in the production of iron and steel. The plough was enhanced, and the harness of draught animals was improved. Knowledge about sailing vessels, irrigation and windmills was improved during the first centuries of the Islamic civilization (eighth to tenth centuries). Medieval Europe (after the twelfth cen-tury) adopted the knowledge of the Chinese, Indian and Arabic civilizations, and improved the use of kinetic energy in water mills and windmills. Mills were used in all economic domains: irrigation, grinding of grain and oilseeds, fulling of cloth, energy for producing iron etc. The most powerful seafaring nation in the seventeenth century, Holland, was built with maritime technology and the inten-sive use of mills. Turf was the most important fuel. The British industrial revolu-tion and English dominion in the nineteenth century was partly built on the steam engine and blast furnace technology. Coal and cokes were the basic fuels. Oil (and later electricity and nuclear energy) is to the United States what turf was to Holland and coal to Great Britain. Europe and the United States housed 30 per cent of the world population in 1900 but they consumed 95 per cent of the fossil fuels. By 2000 they housed 20 per cent of the population and still consumed 70 per cent of the fuels.

The impact of higher energy consumption, both per capita and in total, on world history might be obvious but it is not clear-cut. On the one hand, we can point out the link between a greater supply of energy and higher production (agriculture, industry), increased population growth, more urbanization and more transport. On the other hand, potential destructive powers became greater, military strength increased, the risk of ecological degradation (extinction of animals, deforestation, exhaustion of fossil fuels, pollution) increased and inequality remained very high. Ten per cent of the world population currently uses almost half of all the available energy. On the other hand, the problem of energy conversion does not determine world history. People and societies make choices according to their needs and possibilities of use and control. Contrary to Great Britain, China did not apply its knowledge about energetic steam power in an industrial production process. Agriculture was not the object of mechanization and expansion everywhere. Human and animal muscle power is often still the prime choice.

## Knowledge and technology

The relationship between technology and the environment helped shape human history. The appearance of modern humankind meant that biological evolution was no longer the most important engine of change. That switched to the use of resources – knowledge, communication and tools – to control the natural environment. New knowledge and technologies shifted the borders of human ability. They also had an unparalleled and often disastrous impact on the environment.

The accumulation of technological knowledge made the human species' unseen expansion possible, even in places where it could not survive in the past. The 'domestication' of fire and the improvement of resources related to food, accommodation and clothing were a result of collective learning processes that were passed down to later generations. This also made early human communities dependent on knowledge and resources in order to exploit the natural environment. The transition to agriculture was a decentralized and gradual process that went hand in hand with the accelerated adaptation of new technologies. The most important new technologies were the production of agricultural tools, such as ploughs, pottery, early metalworking and the ability to control water. Successful agricultural societies were able to ensure the supply of fresh water for a long time, often by constructing irrigation networks. More centralized governments developed quicker in such areas, for example the Nile, Tigris and Euphrates deltas, and along the Yellow and Yangtze Rivers. Together with agriculture, the gradual development of metalworking changed the relationship between humankind and nature in many places across the world. Metallurgy changed the essence of natural raw materials. Metal objects made agriculture, hunting and war much more efficient (copper, bronze and iron) and supplied the new elites with wealth (silver and gold). The exploitation and melting of metals left behind large mining and deforestation scars. Due to a growing demand for charcoal, there was an acute shortage of wood in large parts of Europe and China before the end of the first millennium CE. The answer to this scarcity – coal and the development of coke technology – was the basis of the industrial revolution many centuries later.

With regard to scientific and technological knowledge, the world displayed many more similarities than differences before 1500 CE. Technological knowledge developed everywhere as a product of collective or social learning. This cumulative knowledge made it possible to increase the yields of the production factors land, capital and labour, and to create more output with less input. Social learning presumes the conversion of knowledge into transmittable forms, or so-called external memory systems. The oldest forms of learning consisted of imitation and copying. The development of language systems made a more structured transfer of knowledge possible. The capacity to transfer knowledge would have been limited without external memory systems. The development of graphic representations a few tens of thousands of years ago and writing systems a few thousand years ago made the growth and passing on of knowledge possible outside our biological memory. The formalization of storage and transmission systems accelerated the accumulation of knowledge: a multiplication of books and magazines, the development of classification systems like libraries, educational and research institutions, and, more recently, the massive growth of digital storage capabilities. The multiplication of knowledge is therefore primarily a social process. Individually, we are no smarter than our hunting ancestors were. We now have more accumulated and inherited knowledge, the result of collective and social learning.

The survival and success of agrarian civilizations was subject to the development, preservation and passing on of knowledge (collective learning). Historians have distinguished ten technological complexes or 'toolkits' that are used by every civilization to generate and store new knowledge. They are: weapon technology, textile production, support for written language (such as paper), pyrotechnics (controlling fire), water management (such as irrigation), bureaucratic organization (writing and counting), the use of animal traction (such as harnesses), maritime technology, mathematics (including cosmology and cartography) and agricultural techniques. The process of innovation and diffusion of knowledge mainly occurred via collective learning within social networks. In many places, great progress was made in architecture, shipbuilding and seafaring, military organization, industrial production and agriculture throughout the centuries. This progress occurred in diverse places and in general very slowly. It often took several centuries before elementary technological innovations like the clock or the wheelbarrow spread across Eurasia. There was no technological epicentre. Technological innovation did not occur in a linear fashion, but in spurts. Many innovations came from the East. China made large contributions to cartography, sea travel (compass, sailing vessels), irrigation and canal construction, warfare (gunpowder), printing and the traditional production of porcelain, paper, textile and silk. India developed advanced techniques in the production of cotton fabrics. The Islamic world took the lead in producing spices, wood and carpets. Russian furs, Japanese swords and gold and ivory products from Africa were also in demand. Europe developed new techniques in agriculture, the wool industry, glassblowing and brewing. These products were the foundation of an intensive Eurasian trade system.

Centres of scientific and technological progress developed and prospered in diverse places until the eighteenth century. None of these places held a dominant position for a long time. These pre-modern scientific traditions shared several basic characteristics. First, they fit in a dominant philosophical and religious world vision. Acquiring scientific knowledge helped substantiate the metaphysical belief system. This did not impede new insights in many cases. However, if there was a risk of conflict, the prevailing religious and political order was chosen. Over time, scientific progress was stuck in movements that placed orthodoxy above innovation. Second, pre-modern sciences almost always distinguished between mathematical and natural sciences. Mathematical sciences included numerology and geometry, but these were not considered useful for knowledge about the concrete universe in the Greek, Medieval European, Arab and Chinese worlds. Natural sciences and theology tackled the workings of nature and humankind. Experiments and mathematical calculations were infrequently linked together. Real progress was sought through logic and argumentation, with roots in the dominant philosophical and theological worldview. Mathematical reasoning could not question the insights derived from the dominant worldviews, let alone challenge them. In conclusion, every civilization tried to reconcile scientific knowledge with philosophical-religious legitimization until a few centuries ago. This occurred by respecting a specific order. First and foremost, tradition (the past and ancestors as justification), religion and revelation (holy texts as justification) were the important roots of knowledge. This was followed by reason, knowledge acquired via logical argumentation or deduction, then finally by observation and experimentation.

Consequently, various scientific traditions developed in the world before 1500 CE, with direct observations of the sky and the earth, and many insights into the workings of nature. World history refutes the still popular vision that modern science originated in Europe as a direct successor of the Greek tradition from the period 500 to 200 BCE. Greek thinking was largely indebted to knowledge built up in earlier Egyptian, Babylonian and Indian societies. Many rules of mathematics, such as the number system, have Indian and Arab roots. The ninth century Iraqi mathematician Al-Khwarizmi laid the foundations of modern *algebra* with his work about *al-jabr*. Around 1500 CE scientific knowledge was mainly concentrated outside Europe, primarily in the Muslim dominions that stretched from Spain in the west to central Asia in the east. Knowledge related to mathematics, natural sciences, geography and astronomy was compiled and amassed here. It was assembled in the lingua franca of the time, Arabic. Modern science would not have been possible without that knowledge. The first universities were established as centres of knowledge and research in Egypt and North Africa. Both Islamic and Christian scholars (such as Pope Sylvester II, who introduced the Arab number system in Europe) studied at the university of Al-Karaouine in Fez, Morocco. More books were produced in the Islamic world than were produced anywhere else. Cordoba, the capital of Islamic Spain, had more than 70 libraries and the largest library contained more than 400,000 manuscripts.

Growing friction and discord in the Islamic world, and wars waged against external attackers like the Mongols and Christian crusaders, curbed the development of science and culture after 1000 CE. However, the most important centres of scientific knowledge remained in the Islamic world for quite a long time. Three large Muslim empires formed in the sixteenth century: the Ottoman empire in the west, the Safavid dynasty in Iran and central Asia and the Mogul empire in India. The regime became hardened in the three empires, which resulted in less tolerance and more emphasis on orthodoxy. Innovation gave way to stability or, more negatively, to rigidity.

European scientific thinking made little progress between 200 and 1400 CE. Indeed, much of the knowledge accumulated in the Greek-Roman world was lost. A true reversal occurred and the scientific knowledge centre shifted to Europe between 1500 and 1800 CE. In the era that Islamic innovations diminished strongly, a new scientific climate developed in Europe. A revival of the 'classical tradition' signified an escape from established Aristotelian notions about geography, anatomy and astronomy. Many of the new concepts, e.g. the work of Copernicus and Galileo, met with resistance and reprisals from defenders of the dominant, inflexible religious worldviews. Cracks started to appear in this structure as of the seventeenth century. A competitive European society generated several new spaces for less restricted research. The infallible authority of classical, Greek or Christian texts was abandoned time and again. In other words, scientific knowledge was no longer justified by referring primarily to tradition or revelation. It was justified by using reason, observation and experimentation. This gave space to new knowledge systems that were first and foremost based on rationalism (see Descartes) and empiricism (see the Royal Society of London and scientists like Bacon and Newton). The fact that there was no central political structure that could modulate, block or even turn back innovations was new in world history. This new scientific thinking went hand in hand with important technological breakthroughs, such as the large-scale application of steam power. That helped give world history a new direction after 1750.

Blast furnace technology based on burning coke was developed in England in the eighteenth century. It gave metal production, mining and steam engine techniques a huge boost. New materials and production techniques were the basis of England's industrial revolution. That revolution gained a global dimension due to economic and political-imperialist expansion in the nineteenth century. Steam power released massive amounts of energy and revolutionized mining, factory production and transportation. Trains and steamboats opened up large parts of the world for European interests after 1850. A fast modernization of military strength magnified the differences between the West and the non-West even more. The latter areas mainly ensured food supplies (grains and meat) and supplies of new raw materials like palm oil and rubber.

Households were 'industrialized' in the twentieth century thanks to the Western consumption revolution (electricity, cars and other consumer goods). The growing impact of increasingly faster, subsequent waves of technological innovation became apparent in the form of increasing environmental problems. This 'ecological imperialism' has had a very large impact on our quality of life (biodiversity), on the air, the water and the climate (global warming). The growth cycle based on the extraction of fossil fuels clearly reached its limits at the beginning of the twenty-first century.

## Limits to growth?

In order to survive, agricultural societies had to take into account the ecological limits that they operated in at all times. Those limits shifted slowly, primarily due to technological innovation (plants and animals, tools, cultivation and fertilization techniques etc.). If the limits were exceeded too abruptly, this was followed by overpopulation, soil degradation, deforestation and the extermination of animal species. Except for the extinction of large mammals and local deforestation, the effects of this remained limited. The intensification of worldwide contacts after 1500 accelerated the processes of ecological change. European 'ecological imperialism' introduced new animals, plants and micro-organisms into the 'new worlds', often with disastrous consequences for the local populations. Furthermore, land was seized, plantation economies destroyed local ecosystems, and forests were cleared.

At the same time, this was the beginning of an era of unseen economic expansion. It is not easy to measure the economic and ecological impact of this growth. The most frequently used indicator is gross national product (GNP). GNP measures the total market value of all goods and services that are produced in one year in a national economy. The relative economic performance between countries is usually expressed in GNP (total and per capita). This arithmetic model has many deficiencies. GNP is a bad indicator for demonstrating the actual wealth of a national economy. The GNP model emphasizes monetary added value, whereas social and ecological values (which cannot easily be translated into money) are ignored. GNP adds up all formal economic activities without distinguishing between positive and negative activities. According to GNP, we become richer from all the costs arising from a multiple car collision or an oil spill. GNP also ignores a whole range of activities that stimulate wealth, but are not part of the formal economy. Reproductive, care-giving tasks – which are essential for all societies and upon which 'productive' economic functions are based – are ignored. It also ignores environmental services that ecosystems deliver free of charge, such as clean water, clean air, a stable climate and nutrient recycling. GNP figures also neglect the way that national incomes are distributed. A country with high growth figures, but whose rewards belong to a small minority, will score well in the GNP ratings even if its social inequality is very great.

National GNP-thinking nourishes the idea that global economic growth is the only answer to poverty in the world. Studies show that the trickle-down effect of economic growth is very small on a global scale. Moreover, it often concerns economic growth that entails enormous environmental costs and that has a disproportional effect on the poorest citizens. Approximately 80 per cent of the total environmental impact is caused by the richest 25 per cent of the world population.

On the other hand, the principle of ecological sustainability demands that the total biophysical scale of the world economy does not grow any further, because global capacity has already been exceeded. For this scenario (global justice + ecological sustainability), scientists have calculated that the flow of materials and energy through Western economies will have to drop by a factor of 10 (that is 90 per cent less). This scientific fact is difficult to reconcile with endless GNP growth in rich countries. A different calculation model is needed for measuring national and global wealth; a model that does more than simply considering monetary transactions. We need to work with a set of indicators that emphasize the various dimensions of sustainable development: actual economic affluence, ecological sustainability, human wealth and subjective well-being. The *ecological footprint* model is an example. The ecological footprint measures humankind's use of natural resources. It is expressed in global hectares. A global hectare measures the biologically productive area; this includes cultivated land, forests, fishing grounds and fuels. Humanity's ecological footprint grew by 150 per cent between 1961 and 2007 – faster than population growth in the same period (+120 per cent). The footprint for energy (most importantly, fossil fuels) rose by almost 700 per cent in that same period. The total footprint consumed half of the planet in 1961. In the 1970s and 1980s, this surpassed 100 per cent and in 2007, the global footprint was 150 per cent of the earth's annual capacity. This means that the current impact of cultivation, exploitation, production and consumption exceeds the earth's capacity by about half. Moreover, the total footprint is distributed very unequally across the world. If we take into account the current world population and available reserves, then there is 1.8 global hectares available per person. The average total use is currently 2.7 hectares per person. An average inhabitant of India uses half of the available space, while North Americans use 8 hectares. This exceeds the sustainable average by more than four times. An average European consumes twice as much as the sustainable average. If the inhabitants of the non-Western world had the same consumption pattern as the inhabitants of the rich North then we would need five extra planets.

The current world economy is an economy of unpaid costs. Ecological damage, natural degradation, and limits to mineral and fossil fuels are seldom or never factored into the prices that we pay. The transition from an old (solar energy) to a new (fossil energy) biological regime has strongly increased the pressure on the earth's ecological capacity. Twenty-four per cent of all mammals are currently threatened with extinction. Eleven per cent of birds are threatened with extinction, 4 per cent of reptiles, 3 per cent of amphibians, 3 per cent of fish and 10 per cent of all plants. Since the speed of extinction increases, later world historical analyses will probably regard today's short period (a few centuries) as a new phase of mass extinction. This is only one sign of the fact that the growth potential of the current social organization is limited. The quickly-accumulated ecological debt can be translated as an overuse of the global ecosystem. Again, the regional impact is very unequal; that inequality is reinforced by asymmetric ecological trade. The growth of a world system led by Europe created unequal zones. Core countries could import non-renewable riches and could export ecological degradation via mining and plantation agriculture. In other words, the profit of the growth flows in a disproportionate degree to the rich core countries, and the harmful consequences of the growth weigh disproportionately on the periphery.

We have come to realize that growth, as we currently know it, is limited. This realization is the result of a more complete view of the causes and effects of economic growth. Costs that were never 'paid' in the past (pollution, degradation, loss of raw materials), are more frequently integrated and therefore included in the overall costs. To make a complete cost-benefit analysis of our production system and to predict the sustainability of this system, all costs must be known, including exploitation, transportation, energy and waste costs. Consequently, the price of the goods will increase drastically. Accepting this premise means that, at some time in the not too distant future, fundamental choices will have to be made in connection with our economic growth model. The question is how much deceleration or contraction our economic capitalist model can bear. An 'ecological' variation of capitalism presumes a pressure on growth figures and much more control and regulation. This calls into question the primacy of contemporary economic organization (the individual profit principle). These ecological limits also put the ambition for greater equality under pressure. One of the founding myths of our modern society is that participating in the consumption market makes greater equality possible. Capping growth primarily blocks the entry of new consumers. The outcome can be a greater 'apartheid' between the North and South, or the rich and the poor. This gap can only be maintained via greater control and repression (eco-totalitarianism). An alternative is a fairer distribution of the benefits (now mainly in the North) and the costs (now mainly in the South), and the development of more regionally-coordinated and controlled production systems.

# 4 An agrarian world
## Farmers, agriculture and food

A new fish was introduced to Lake Victoria, one of the lakes in the Great Rift Valley of East Africa, in the 1950s. That fish was the Nile perch. It was introduced to help start up commercial fishing. The introduction of this predator had a catastrophic effect on the local fish population. Many hundreds of local species became extinct in the lake. Although the Nile perch was useful for large fisheries in the short term, the long-term damage is much greater. The fish has disturbed the lake's ecological balance. The lake is being overfished and local communities around the lake have been disrupted. Industrial fishing yields millions of export dollars but many small fishermen have lost their traditional income. The fish need to be dried, so the demand for firewood has grown, resulting in deforestation and erosion.

The Nile perch story illustrates current global food relations. Demand from the West for boneless fish filets stimulated a flourishing export industry on the banks of Lake Victoria. This export transformed local societies and disturbed the ecological balance resulting in uprooting, migration, poverty and famine. The fish symbolizes lopsided trade relations, which are portrayed so superbly in the documentary film *Darwin's Nightmare* (Sauper 2004). Cargo planes filled with frozen fish fillets return to Africa empty, except when they transport food aid or (illegal) weapons.

In addition to oxygen and water, food is one of the few things that human beings need every day. This simple observation is dwarfed by a staggeringly complex story of searching for, trying and swapping food, of experiment, beliefs and mysticism, of distribution, power and inequality. In our common history, daily food is a reflection of internal and external relations, of local and global relations. The use of land, exploitation of resources and distribution of the yields are all expressions of the way humankind has constructed its societies. That is why food is also identity and multiculturalism. Food is what the world is. World history is also a history of food and food production. This history was shaped by eight 'revolutions' or major transitions:

1   the accumulation of knowledge of how to cook food;
2   the ritualizing of the nutritional process;
3   the pastoral revolution and domestication of cattle;
4   the farming revolution and domestication of crops;

5    the use of food as part of social stratification;
6    the diffusion of food crops;
7    the exchange of food crops on a large scale (the Columbian exchange);
8    the industrialization of the food chain (agro-industry).

With regard to the global diffusion of agriculture and food production, three pivotal moments are crucial: agricultural revolutions during the Neolithic period, the
exchange of agricultural crops during European expansion, and the globalization
of agricultural questions and food issues today.

## Humans became farmers

Science has shaken human beings' self-image several times over the last few
centuries. Astronomy taught us that the earth is not the centre of the universe.
Biology showed that man was not a creature created by God, but the result of a
very long evolution. Palaeontologists pointed out the unpredictability of this evolution - man as a 'splendid accident'. Archaeologists and other scientists, in turn,
have recently questioned the story of human progress. The introduction of agriculture – the most important step in the human journey up to date – was not
always a story of success. Some scientists even call it a catastrophe because,
together with agriculture, we introduced social repression and sexual inequality,
despotism and – lest we forget – a long chain of deadly illnesses. What about the
spectacular increase in food supplies, in productivity and population? What about
the origins of civilizations, the development of culture and the rise in standards
of living? Questioning the long-term results does not change the fact that the
transition to agricultural systems was not a 'logical' step in the history of humankind. Recent research shows that hunter-gatherer cultures had a more varied diet
and more free time than agricultural societies. It is estimated that hunter-gatherers
needed 15 to 20 hours per week to secure their food supplies. This is considerably
less than a farming family. A prehistoric hunter of big game yielded many more
calories per hour of labour than an early farmer. The meals of these people were
also more varied and contained more protein. The threat of food scarcity and
famine was lower due to large variations in diet (every group ate at least a few
dozen wild plants) and extensive mobility. Early farming societies depended on a
very limited supply of plants, had a diet that was mainly based on starch, and
were therefore much more vulnerable to scarcity. Due to more intensive contact
with animals and lower mobility, they were also more exposed to the spread of
parasites and contagious diseases. Research done on skeletons confirms this.
Hunter-gatherers were generally taller than their farming successors (heights
have only increased substantially in the last few centuries). Farmers display much
more damage resulting from illness and malnutrition. Life expectancy also fell
initially. For example, archaeologists studied a North American Indian community and found that life expectancy fell from 27 to 19 years.
    Not only did farmers have to work longer and harder to yield the same calories,
the distribution of agricultural work also created important gender differences,

and the distribution of the yields created larger social differences. Once the transition was made, farming societies could produce much more food and support many more people (100 to 1,000 times as many) per surface unit. That was offset by a high toll: poorer health, greater vulnerability and greater social and sexual inequality. We must not forget that the 'standard of living' in hunter-gatherer cultures also took a high social toll: a long time between births (maximum every three to four years), infanticide and the banishment of less mobile members (the elderly and the weak).

Therefore, the core question remains: why did several human communities – independent of each other in diverse locations around the world and in approximately the same time period – switch from the hunting-gathering strategies that had been successful for so long to a livelihood as a shepherd and farmer? Why didn't this happen 20,000 years earlier or 10,000 years later? Five factors played a role in this.

1   A growing scarcity in the supply of wild plants and animals. Palaeolithic hunters exterminated mammals and birds in many locations around the world. This was the result of slow but persistent population growth and better hunting techniques. For example, large mammals disappeared in North and South America, mammoths disappeared from North America and Eurasia, and the moa disappeared from New Zeeland.
2   Climate change resulting from the warming of the earth and the retreat of the ice fields after the last ice age, starting 16,000 years ago. New plants (such as wild grains) had a better chance of survival.
3   Technological knowledge, accumulated during hunting and gathering, but essential for agriculture: how to harvest food (sickles, baskets), process it (fire) and store it (in pits).
4   Slow population growth, which accelerated with the development of agricultural cultures. This was a process of action/reaction, after which there was no way back.
5   The numerical and physical predominance of agricultural and pastoral cultures forced the remaining hunter-gatherer groups to adapt, defer or retreat even further (to geographically or ecologically protected areas like Indian tribes in California, Khoisan in Southern Africa and Aboriginals in Australia).

## The origin and diffusion of agriculture

During the majority of its history, human beings were hunter-gatherers. This is in sharp contrast to the duration of our agricultural society (about 10,000 years) and of the industrial and post-industrial society (two centuries). Where did the first big changes take place?

Let's go back in time and look at the world about 13,000 years ago, before the creation of the first agricultural civilizations. New inhabitants travelled through the American continent. This virtually completed humankind's colonization of the world, except for a few island groups and remote locations. What would a fictitious observer be able to predict about the future of human history at that moment? What would the colonization patterns of that moment tell the observer? First, the observer would point out the African continent's head start. Human history goes back the farthest here, and genetic diversity between the tribes is the greatest. On the other hand, the last newcomer (America) might display more dynamism. The colonization of America only took a few thousand years and the continent is more ecologically diverse than Africa. Eurasia had the advantage of being the largest continent with a long human tradition and a few highly-developed (for that time) communities of hunter-gatherers. Australia/Oceania does not enter the picture because it was too far away and often too inhospitable; human colonization was slow here. Where would human development start accelerating first? The observer would only be able to guess, because there were good arguments for each of the three large continents: Africa, America and Eurasia.

As stated above, the origin of agriculture was not a 'natural' or unavoidable part of a huge modernization process. After the climate changes at the end of the ice ages (from 12,000 BCE), humankind's settlement pattern changed, as did the distribution of (large) game and plants. Human beings started experimenting with the domestication of plants and animals on all continents, except Australia, as from 8000 BCE. Via a slow process of learning and (seed) selection, the first agricultural tribes were able to improve a few grasses. This was followed by fruit, olives and vegetables like peas and beans. The so-called Neolithic agricultural revolution was a chain of several regional revolutions. Forms of agriculture developed independent of each other in at least four regions between 8,000 and 10,000 years ago. These regions were:

- The Middle East, the 'fertile crescent' from the Mediterranean coast to the Anatolian Plateau and the alluvial plains of Iraq; all bread-based civilizations owe their most important products to this region (wheat and barley).
- The Far East, the Yellow River and Yangtze River valleys (rice, millet, soybeans and yams).
- Central America, the area around present-day Mexico (corn, beans, pumpkins, amaranth and tomatoes).
- The Andes in South America (potatoes, pumpkins and peanuts).

In addition to these four large zones, there were smaller core areas with crops like banana, coffee, cassava, sorghum and sunflowers in tropical Southeast Asia, Ethiopia, the Amazon area and the eastern part of North America. The impact of this revolution was enormous. The seven billion people alive today still feed themselves with the crops of about ten prehistoric tribes. Despite centuries of scientific progress, not a single new crop has been added to the basic diet since that time.

In most locations, agriculture was 'mixed' from the outset. People used a combination of farming and cattle breeding. Goats, sheep, donkeys and geese were domesticated in the Middle East, cows and pigs in Southern Europe, horses and camels in Central Asia, pigs, chickens and water buffalos in the Far East, and lamas, alpacas, guinea pigs and turkeys were domesticated in America. Livestock was used for carrying and its pulling power, for its wool and skins; its manure was used as a fertilizer and the meat and milk was a source of protein. The Eurasian continent was clearly in a favourable position. A total of 72 mammal species were eligible for domestication. Sub-Sahara Africa had 51 species, America had 24 and Australia only had one. Twelve of the 14 large animal species that humans domesticated before the twentieth century came from the region that stretches from the Middle East to China (such as sheep, goats, cows, pigs, horses, camels, donkeys, reindeer, water buffalos and yaks). The lama and the alpaca were the only exceptions.

The process of domestication was based on trial and error. Only a small percentage of the hundreds of thousands of plants in the world are fit for human consumption. A few hundred of them were more or less domesticated. Barely a dozen of these plants provide 80 per cent of present-day harvests: grains (wheat, rye, rice, barley and sorghum), legumes (soybeans), tuberous plants and root crops (potatoes, cassava and sweet potatoes), sugar plants (sugarcane and sugar beet) and fruit (banana). The same applies to cattle. Fourteen of the 148 large mammal species were eventually domesticated for cattle breeding. The other species are less suitable or unsuitable (carnivores, difficult to breed and slow-growth, solitary animals).

The new plants and cattle species all saw the light of day from 8000 to 3000 BCE. After that, they spread across large parts of the earth. The population ceiling of 5 to 10 million people was breached. The world's population increased to 60 or 70 million around 4000 BCE; this was 5,000 years after the advent of agriculture but before the rise of the great civilizations. Agricultural communities lived together with wandering groups of hunter-gatherers, fishermen and herders for a long time. The transition from gatherer and hunter to farmer and herder was very gradual indeed. Recent research shows that agriculture spread through Europe as from 7000 BCE via immigrants and farming communities that spread out. These 'milk drinkers' had a physical and technological edge on the original groups of hunter-gatherers and took their places. Çatal Hüyük in Turkey was the largest settlement in the 'fertile crescent' between 7000 and 5500 BCE. Some call it the first city. It had 5,000 inhabitants and was only thirteen hectares in size. The residents still largely depended on hunting for their protein needs. Herders remained dominant in certain parts of the world (northern and eastern Africa, central Asia) for a long time. Sometimes powerful military empires grew out of these herder communities, such as the Arabs with camels and the Mongols with horses.

## The 'Columbian exchange'

In different parts of the world agricultural societies developed into large civilizations. For thousands of years domesticated plants and animals were swapped in Eurasia and North Africa. The rapid acceleration in global contacts after 1500 put these exchanges in a new gear. The 'Colombian exchange' marks an important shift in the global history of ecology, agriculture and society. This expression (coined by A. Crosby) refers to the large-scale migration of agricultural crops, cattle species, diseases and cultures between the 'Old World' and the 'New World' after 1492.

This migration of plant and animal species had an immense impact on life in Europe, America, Africa and Asia. Crops that people had never seen became (in time) popular foods: wheat and rice in America, potatoes and tomatoes in Europe, corn and sweet potatoes in Africa and Asia. Very few human societies were not influenced by this large-scale ecological exchange. It transformed the cuisine of regions all over the world.

The first European export product – horses – changed the existence of many American Indian tribes on the Great Plains. These plains later became a 'granary' of European wheat. Coffee, bananas and sugarcane, originally from Asia, became intensively cultivated crops on Latin American plantations. The new crops also supported social changes in other parts of the world. The modest potato, descendant of a wild and poisonous tuberous plant high in the Andes Mountains, became the cheap, high-calorie basic food of the working class in industrializing Europe. The potato also made accelerated population growth possible. Dependence on this crop became so great that the last European famine in 1845–1848 was caused by failed potato harvests (one million deaths in Ireland, a few hundred thousand in continental Europe).

New contacts between the Old and New Worlds also resulted in an exchange of diseases. Because the Old World traditionally experienced lots of epidemics and built up a strong immunity against them, the effect of this bacteriological migration was most devastating in the New World (with unknown diseases such as smallpox, measles, cholera, typhus and tuberculosis). America 'gifted' the rest of the world a new form of syphilis.

Commerce became more global after the sixteenth century. Products that we wear and eat are made by people that we will never know. Commodity chains explain how the 'modern world' was created via a network of transactions across the globe. Agricultural products were the first bulk goods to be traded this way. The history of the modern world can be told as a 'history in eight glasses' containing popular beverages that tell the story of a world of increasing connection and interaction:

1    Beer. Beer was a direct product of the domestication of grains in the first agricultural societies in Mesopotamia and Egypt. It was the most popular beverage in urban communities for a very long time because water quality was unreliable. Beer became a truly global beverage in the twentieth century.
2    Wine. Wine symbolizes the Mediterranean Greek and Roman cultures, and was the preferred beverage of the elites in the West for a long time. Later wine became part of global trade and it figured in the 'westernization' of non-European elites.
3    Spirits. Distillation is an Arab invention. Many types of spirits spread during European expansion, primarily sugar cane-based rum.
4    Coffee. Introduced to Europe by the Arabs, coffee houses popularized this exotic beverage, first amongst the elites. Coffee replaced beer as the most

popular beverage in the nineteenth century. Together with tea and chocolate, coffee is responsible for increased demands in another 'exotic' product: sugar.

5   Tea. Imported from the East by the British and the Dutch, this beverage became very popular in the eighteenth century.

6   Cocoa. Cacao trees are native to Central and South America and were planted in Southern Asia and Africa in the seventeenth and eighteenth century. Cocoa became a really popular drink in Europe in the eighteenth century.

7   Coca. Like many other popular drinks, Coca Cola was originally a medicinal beverage (with extracts from the coca leaf and kola nut). As the 'national beverage' of the United States, it symbolizes the twentieth century: Americanization, consumerism and globalization.

8   Water. Until recently, water was a 'common', non-commercial product. Bottled water is now the fastest growing commercial beverage. One of the themes of this century will be the battle for potable water, both as a generally-available good and as a new source of profit.

The story of an expanding world system from the sixteenth century can be told with the history of one agricultural product – cane sugar. When the Arab empire expanded in the seventh century, cane sugar began to spread as a sweetener. Due to its status as an expensive luxury product, many regions wanted to produce their own sugar. Sugar plantations were established near the Persian Gulf and on a few islands in the Mediterranean, but cultivating and processing sugar remained difficult and labour-intensive. European interest in sugar grew in the fourteenth and fifteenth centuries, and new plantations were established in Spain and Portugal. The plant and knowledge about it travelled with the earliest Portuguese colonists, first to Atlantic islands (Sao Thomé) then to South America (Brazil) and the Caribbean. Experience with black slave labour on islands off the coast of Africa formed the basis of the successful plantation system: black labour, white sugar. The enormous success of sugar, large profits and control of the trade by the Dutch, British and French turned sugar into an integrated production and trade system that linked three continents into one global, trans-Atlantic economy. In the eighteenth century, sugar became a product for mass consumption due to the popularization of rum (based on cane sugar) and of coffee, tea and cocoa (bitter beverages that must be sweetened). Sugar became the binding agent in two types of three-way trade that supported the trans-Atlantic system from the sixteenth to the nineteenth century:

• black slaves from Africa to American plantations, plantation products like sugar and tobacco to Europe and finished products like hardware and clothing from Europe to Africa;
• slaves from Africa to Caribbean islands, molasses to New England, rum to Africa.

Plantations cultivated the sugar cane and processed the sugar; this made them very labour-intensive. As consumers of 'foreign' labour and suppliers of new global products, they were the central link in a new globalizing trade and labour system. This trade network reflected the contours of the new world system: a combination of trade and industry, core-periphery relations (cultivation and basic processing in the periphery, finishing and sales in the core; the largest profits were made in the core by refining the sugar, packaging and marketing), violence and repression, and extremely high inequality. J. H. Bernadin de Saint-Pierre, a French traveller, visited the 'sugar islands' in 1773. He described the trans-Atlantic trade network as follows:

> I do not know if coffee and sugar are necessary to the happiness of Europe, but I do know that those two crops have accounted for the unhappiness of two other parts of the world: America has been depopulated so as to have land on which to plant them; Africa has been depopulated so as to have the people to cultivate them.

The Columbian exchange, a previously unseen process of ecological interaction and exchange, thoroughly changed global relations and helped create today's modern world.

## Agriculture and food today: the big escape or the big trap?

Scarcity, malnutrition and famine seem to be structural characteristics of agrarian, pre-industrial societies (incorporated in the metaphor of seven fat and seven lean years). Europe was able to escape from this 'Malthusian' trap of an imbalance between population and foodstuffs in the nineteenth century via strong increases in food production and by ensuring long-term food security. The basis of this 'big escape' was increased production and productivity (mechanization, artificial fertilizers), further globalization of food production (massive European imports of grains and meat thanks to the new steamboat shipping industry and new cold storage techniques) and development of an agro-industry (the industrial processing of foodstuffs, mainly vegetables and meat). However, this notion of the 'big escape' as a European success story is challenged by a few fundamental objections.

1   Famine was not a catastrophic or fatal inevitability in agricultural societies. There was often food scarcity and insecurity, but that was generally more the result of human intervention (war, plundering or taxation) than of natural circumstances. Moreover, famines in these societies were limited in time and space (temporary and small-scale). Excess mortality resulting from famines was usually counterbalanced quickly (higher birth rates) unless a society collapsed completely.

2   The European success story only partially rested on the transformation of its own agricultural sector after 1850. Fields produced more, farmers became more productive, and agriculture became completely integrated in the market sector. Despite this success, Europe was no longer able to feed its fast-growing population on its own. The import of grains and meat increased

strongly in the second half of the nineteenth century (the *agricultural invasion* from the 'New World' and Russia). Great Britain, undisputed leader amongst the industrial nations, had to import 70 per cent of its grains and 40 per cent of its meat in 1900. Industrializing Europe was largely fed by non-European farmers.

3   Despite the economic success story, Europe struggled with structural over-population in the nineteenth century. This was partly 'exported' to the New World. Between 40 and 50 million Europeans left the Old Continent for 'new worlds' in the nineteenth century.

4   The subjection and integration of large areas of Africa and Asia into European empires was sometimes accompanied with a catastrophic collapse of local societies. The Congolese Crown colony of the Belgian King Leopold II lost an estimated two to four million inhabitants, mainly due to starvation (forced harvesting of rubber). There were huge, successive famines in British India with tens of millions of victims at the end of the nineteenth century.

Europe's *big escape* was largely possible because the continent was the backbone of the world system in the nineteenth century. It was therefore able to import food and export excess citizens cheaply and without many hindrances. Consequently, Europe's exemplary role for the rest of the world only applies to a limited extent. Much can be learned with regard to making agriculture more productive, but this also had it limits. In spite of several successes (like an enormous increase in rice production), differences in soil and climate were and remain severe obstacles when trying to imitate new techniques. Moreover, the southern hemisphere is currently in a very different position than Europe was in the nineteenth century. By no means can it import foodstuffs or export surplus labour in the same (cheap) manner.

Famine and malnutrition remain endemic in the modern world. This has less to do with the survival of earlier agricultural societies than with increases in scale, lopsided trade relations and new uncertainties in the new global economic order. There is no shortage of food in absolute terms. The population grew by a factor of 2.4 and agricultural production by a factor of 2.6 between 1950 and 2000. This is an increase in the supply of calories per person of 22 per cent (from 2,280 kcal per day to 2,800 kcal per day). The number of undernourished people did not decline; it was 580 million in 1980, 840 million in 1990, 820 million in 2000, and 925 million in 2010. The large regions with structural malnutrition remain Central Asia, part of Latin America and sub-Sahara Africa. China, with a sixth of the world population, is the greatest success story: the average supply of calories per person rose between 1960 and 2000 by 66 per cent, compared to 21 per cent in India and a mere 7 per cent in Africa. The distribution of consumption patterns is also unequal. In many places, the products and models promoted by large western distributors displace the local supplies.

The greatest threat nowadays comes from a decline in food security. Food is increasingly produced and distributed by integrated and export-oriented companies and chains that follow a capitalistic logic. Four fifths of the countries with high childhood malnutrition are net food exporters. Small-scale peasant agriculture – the most important buffer against large-scale famine – is disappearing quickly. This is due to massive dumping of cheap food on the world market by Europe and the United States. The functioning of a modern trade triangle involving soybeans and milk illustrates global relations. Millions of farmers in Brazil have lost their farms to large agricultural-industrial groups that focus on the production of soybeans for export. Soybeans arrive in North America and Europe as cheap food for cows and chickens. Agricultural surpluses are dumped in African countries like Senegal in the form of cheap milk powder, among other things. This import destroys the livelihood of small, local herders. It also stimulates the collapse of the countryside and migration to cities and overseas.

This dumping makes prices more volatile and small farmers lose potential markets. Mexico, the preferred market for American surpluses, is a striking example. Between 1994 and 2004 Mexican livestock decreased by 30 per cent while the import of meat grew by 113 per cent. The value of corn dropped by 64 per cent, wheat by 54 per cent, beans by 46 per cent and soybeans by 68 per cent. In these years the rural population in Mexico decreased by 20 per cent. Some 3.7 million small farmers went bankrupt and 1.5 million had to leave their land. Many of them tried their luck in the United States. The price of basic foodstuffs has been on the rise since 2007. On average, world food prices were 2.5 times more expensive in 2011 than in 2001. Growing demand, poor harvests, speculation and the production of biofuels have dislocated the food market and caused new waves of food riots. A further unbridled liberalization of world trade in agricultural products will only accelerate these processes.

## The end of peasant societies?

The production and consumption of food was locally anchored until the second half of the nineteenth century. Transport over long distances was technically impossible or too expensive, except for a few luxury products like wine. Products, techniques and markets were part of local chains of knowledge; managed by and passed down on family farms. The first crack in this system appeared after 1850 when supplies outside Europe were linked to growing European demand. This was achieved thanks to the enormous expansion of farmland in the so-called Neo-Europes (the 'new world'), strong growth in agricultural productivity (mechanization, new fertilizers) and new modes of transport (shipping) that resulted in sharply-decreased transportation costs. A second revolution in globalizing food chains took place after the middle of the twentieth century. It was driven by science-based production methods (technological innovations related to production such as synthetic fertilizers and new preservation systems: freezing and canning). The agro-industry became a leading force. Commercial fertilizers made monoculture possible. Harvesting food and raising cattle became increasingly detached from the production of daily food. This resulted in a third revolution in the global food regime at the beginning of the twenty-first century. Breakthroughs in biotechnology (genetically-modified crops) and a further monopolization of food

*Table 4.1* Rural population between 1950 and 2030

|  | World population | | Proportion of rural population by region | | | | |
|---|---|---|---|---|---|---|---|
|  | *Total (billions)* | *Rural (billions)* | *Africa* | *Asia* | *Central and South America* | *North America* | *Europe* |
| 1950 | 2.53 | 1.80 (71%) | 86% | 83% | 59% | 36% | 49% |
| 1970 | 3.69 | 2.35 (64%) | 76% | 77% | 43% | 26% | 37% |
| 1990 | 5.29 | 3.03 (57%) | 68% | 68% | 30% | 25% | 30% |
| 2000 | 6.12 | 3.27 (53%) | 64% | 63% | 24% | 21% | 29% |
| 2010 | 6.91 | 3.42 (49%) | 60% | 58% | 20% | 18% | 27% |
| 2030 | 8.31 | 3.41 (41%) | 50% | 47% | 15% | 13% | 22% |

Source: *UN World Population Prospects: The 2010 Revision Population Database* (http:\\esa.un.org).

production by vertically-integrated multinational companies further marginalized local food systems and family-based peasant agriculture. Increased output could feed a swelling world population. However, detaching a majority of the world population from food production entails new risks. The problem of the undernourished 'bottom billion' remains unsolved, and food security is under increasing pressure due to volatile markets and increasing prices.

Rural societies have been the most important survival networks for the world's population. Small-scale peasant agriculture still represents half of world food production. The beginning of the twenty-first century is a turning point. For the first time since the agricultural revolutions approximately 10,000 years ago, a minority of the global population lives directly from the proceeds of agriculture. Seventy per cent of all world citizens lived in the countryside in 1950; by 2010 that had fallen to less than 50 per cent. The share of the actual agricultural population fell from 65 per cent to 40 per cent in the same period. Barely a quarter of the world's population will obtain their main income from agriculture by 2030. No continent will have a majority of rural citizens by 2030, as Table 4.1 shows.

The impact of this change cannot be overestimated. Global food provisioning is now concentrated in long, international and vulnerable chains that are controlled by large capital-intensive groups. Moreover, family agriculture – the traditional basis for survival – has become inaccessible to a fast-growing majority of human beings. As a result, a cheap reserve of labour is disappearing in the global economic system, and consequently so has one of the foundations of worldwide economic expansion in the last few centuries. The consequences of this change will undoubtedly provide some of the greatest challenges of the twenty-first century. These challenges include the massive urbanization and multiplication of megacities with more than ten million inhabitants (30 in 2025 and half of them in Asia), the growth of slums (a sixth of the world population currently lives in urban slums), tensions between ecology and agriculture (represented in the question of biofuels), the impact of rising standards of living (resulting in higher meat consumption in 'developing' regions) and the impact on the regional and global distribution of incomes (among others resulting from rising prices of agricultural products and from precarious living conditions in large cities). The loss of small-scale peasant agriculture threatens local and regional forms of food provisioning, communal property, common knowledge about plants and animals, and essential biodiversity. It is becoming increasingly clear that daily food cannot simply be subject to the laws of the global free market. It must be protected with a view to regional food security.

# 5 A political world
## Governance and rulers

The empire of Ghana in West Africa grew and flourished from the eighth to the eleventh century CE. This empire was dominated by the Soninke, which placed diverse tribes and cities located in a vast region (present-day Mauritania and Mali) under one government. The Soninke called their empire Wagadu, land of herds. The *Ghana* (king-warlord) resided in the capital Kumbi Saleh on the border of the Sahara desert. At its peak, the city had 30,000 inhabitants. It was constructed around a royal centre with ramparts. The empire flourished as a trading centre. It was part of a larger commercial system in which trans-Saharan trade with the Arabs (and Berbers) played a major role. The most important commodities were gold and ivory from the south, and salt from the north. Due to growing wealth and power, the kingdom's influence was enlarged via a tribute system. Islam was not the state religion, but it was tolerated. Ghana was one of the strongest and most prosperous empires in the world in the eleventh century. It started to decline after the eleventh century due to a combination of factors: the advancing desert and increasing food provisioning problems, a drop in trade and the *jihad* by Islamic Almoravids advancing from the north.

What is the strength of ancient Ghana's political organizational model? The empire was centrally controlled and led by a royal family. Control was indirect outside the vicinity of the capital. Remote cities and tribes became members of the empire by paying tributes, but they had a lot of autonomy. Governors were responsible for contacts with the centre. Control was efficient, as was the system of taxation. This enabled the king to keep the multi-ethnic empire together. Legitimacy and cohesion were guaranteed thanks to economic success. This rested on a well-developed agricultural system that concentrated on cattle breeding. Ghana also extracted a lot of wealth from the flourishing trans-Sahara trade, which was accelerated by the introduction of the camel in the first centuries of the Common Era. Ghana did not have any gold or salt fields; it simply organized and protected trade between the south and the north. This strong relationship with an external trade system was also the cause of Ghana's decline. When the empire lost control of trading, its internal cohesion disappeared.

The Soninke were able to develop the kingdom of Ghana as peoples did in many other places: by incorporating many smaller units into a new, larger organization model. This model had a better chance of survival due to the introduction of new forms of control and taxation, and due to integration in a wider regional system. At the same time, this is also often the weakness of such an administrative model. How can we explain this within world history?

For a long time, knowledge of the past was dominated by the political story. History was an instrument used by rulers. The historical story told the tale of the growth and success of their own empire or state. The emergence of national historiography in the nineteenth century made the nation state the most important unit of analysis, and the political past of that state became the dominant story line. A study of political systems in world history cannot depart from the state as the only or even the primary social organization model. Not only did other political control systems exist before and alongside the state, states were and still are part of wider societal structures. In this chapter, we will analyze the organization of territorial power and diverse systems of political governance. We will look for the social dynamics behind the rise, success and disappearance of political organization models. A distinction by scale divides the political systems that we have known in world history into mini-systems, empires, states and an inter-state system.

## Mini-systems

Mini-systems organize a small population of up to a few thousand people. In mini-systems the cultural-ethnic, economic and political units typically coincide. Throughout history, diverse types of mini-systems have existed: clans or *bands*, tribes and *chiefdoms*. A *clan* (or *family*) consisted of no more than a few dozen members who were generally related to each other. These small but autonomous groups were the most important cohabitation model amongst nomadic hunter-gatherers, and they were omnipresent until 10,000 to 12,000 years ago. Clans did not have a fixed abode, fixed division of labour (between men and women) or a fixed social hierarchy. Formal institutions were unknown, leadership was informal, property was communal and exchange was on a reciprocal basis. The clan or family is the cohabitation model that we inherited from our earliest ancestors. Until the arrival of more sedentary societies, it guaranteed most successfully the survival of the human species.

Improvements in hunting and gathering techniques and the first forms of sedentarism brought several clans together in a *tribe*. Limited mobility required greater control over the available territory and available resources. A few hundred people lived and worked together in one settlement (or a group of small villages). It was still managed informally but a chief (or *big man*) is appointed. Control (politics) and trade (economy) still occurred on a reciprocal basis.

Important changes only appeared when the managerial model was scaled-up to so-called *chiefdoms*. This more centralized type of society first appeared in the early agricultural areas such as the Middle East (5000 to 6000 BCE) and Middle and South America (1000 BCE). A chiefdom could group up to a few thousand people and was led by a hereditary chief (king). The decision level shifted to a central authority and property rights frequently belonged to an elite. The society was divided up socially and labour became more specialized. Separate social and economic groups developed with unequal rights. These included farmers, crafts-men, warriors, priests and administrators. Redistribution was no longer based on reciprocity but on enforced tributes (taxes). The administrators determined the rules and laws and monopolized control over the enforcement of these laws. Authority was increasingly underpinned by worship, ritualization and ideologiz-ing of the leadership.

The transition from clans and tribes to more centralized forms of authority occurred very gradually. Early forms of *chiefdom* combined reciprocity and a more centralized decision-making process. Later they could become more com-plex systems, such as city-states, or turn into a kleptocracy. This required stronger control of the subjects, more efficient skimming of the economic returns, better legitimization of the authority (ideology) and better enforcement of the violence monopoly. We can call a social organization that is moving towards 'modern' rule a 'proto-state'. Proto-states have existed into the twentieth century.

## Empires

About 6,000 to 5,000 years ago, completely independent from each other, larger administrative units originated in the deltas of the Nile River (Egypt), the Tigris and Euphrates Rivers (Mesopotamia, Sumeria), the Indus River (Harappa) and the Yellow River (China, Shang dynasty). Larger political power centers grew in Central America and the Andes about 3,000 years ago and they developed in West Africa (such as Ghana) about 1,500 years ago. In literature they are called *empires* or civilizations (see Chapter 6 for discussions about this). empires developed from a centre and gradually spread to include increasingly remote areas. These empires had a large sphere of influence and controlled tens of thou-sands to a few million subjects. The central administration was supported with its own bureaucracy (often by using writing), with formalized legislation, a compul-sory retribution system and an official state religion. These empires combined a political and an economic unity. The economic organization (always based on a successful agricultural system, the production of crafts and an internal and exter-nal commercial network) developed in symbiosis with more large-scale political structures. That is why the fall of an empire always implied a collapse of the economy. Contrary to mini-systems, there was no cultural-ethnic unity. empires were developed within expanding political and territorial borders rather than being based on former kinship bonds. Consequently, empires united people of diverse ethnicity.

In world history, mini-systems were gradually but unevenly replaced with more complex administrative systems. This raises several essential questions. First, why did more large-scale administrative systems originate in certain places in the world in certain periods? Why not somewhere else? Second, why are certain empires more successful than others?

The transition from small to larger political control systems is not a natural course of events. The variations in time and location are too great for this to be true. That is why we must analyze the conditions or circumstances in which empires develop. History teaches us that five conditions are required, and they must be viewed as a whole. The absence of one or several of the factors often explains the failure of regional empire building.

1   Population growth. empires can only develop where a population minimum is exceeded and territorial growth is not limited by narrow natural borders. In other words, there has to be enough 'critical mass' to support the economic base of an empire. Most large empires arose in Eurasia, where more than three-quarters of the world population lived and worked.
2   Efficiently organized agriculture. The organization of food production is the primordial task of every social form of organization. A growth in scale requires better division of labour, more economic specialization and more control. Larger centrally-controlled investments are often required. A popular theory about the origin of larger political units points to large-scale irrigation projects like those in Mesopotamia, Northern China and Central America. The collaboration needed to start such a project would have required a more central administration.
3   Conflict management and defence against external threats. The advantage of scale plays a role in this too. Larger population groups are protected more efficiently by a centrally-led military apparatus.
4   The transition from a reciprocal, mutual exchange system to a redistributive, apportioning system. Reciprocity is only possible in small-scale exchange. Large-scale transactions require a controlled system of collection and distribution. This coincided with the development of registration and coding systems, from which writing originated in several places around the world: Mesopotamia and Egypt approximately 3000 BCE, China about 1300 BCE and Central America approximately 600 BCE.
5   Better internal and external communication, enabling a faster exchange of people, goods and information. Successful empires always had well developed road infrastructures and trade networks.

Empires come and go. Some people call world history a 'graveyard of empires'. The world saw about 60 mega-empires of at least one million square kilometres (380,000 square miles) between 3000 BCE and 1800 CE. With the exception of the Incan empire, they all developed in Eurasia, from the African and European Atlantic coasts to the East China Sea. They did not develop in the same way. China, with its fertile river plains, is the region with the most continuous succession of empires. The most extensive territorial empire in world history was developed by a nomadic people, the Mongols, but it did not last long (thirteenth century CE). Why were some empires more successful than others? All empires were regional systems within regional economic and ecological boundaries. So what were the differences?

The oldest empires were located in *Sumeria* (Mesopotamia), where a conglomeration of more or less independent city-states formed in 4000 to 3000 BCE. This region was linked to one ecosystem: lowlands that were very vulnerable to flooding and drought. Consequently, successful control of the water resulted in the success of the Sumerian empire. The water of the Tigris and Euphrates rivers also brought large quantities of sediment and salt that remained on the fields due to irrigation techniques. Over time, this reduced the fertility of the fields, and around 2000 BCE only saltpans remained. The fertile fields in Mesopotamia were reduced to a barren plain with small villages. The political centre in the region shifted to the north, to the new power bases of Babylon and Assyria. The population of Sumeria could not avert the ecological bottleneck that they had created.

Other examples of imploding empires or civilizations are the Central American empires of Teotihuacán (near present-day Mexico City) and the Maya in northern Central America. In Roman times, Teotihuacán was the largest city on the American continent and, with a surface area of up to 30 square kilometres (11.5 square miles) and more than 150,000 inhabitants, one of the largest in the world at that time. This city was fed by an intensive agricultural system with terraces, irrigation and watering. This city was abandoned by its population in the sixth century CE. The Maya civilization, built on a centrally-governed system of city-states, experienced its peak a bit later, and quickly declined after the eighth century CE. Due to increased pressure on natural resources, the forests were pushed back and game became scarcer. When the soil lost its fertility due to erosion, internal tensions also increased between cities and between social groups. The two empires were completely ruined due to overpopulation, agrarian stagnancy and internal disputes.

The fate of Teotihuacán and the Mayas can be compared with that of the Romans. The powerful Roman empire fell apart in two centuries because of too much pressure on its internal cohesion and ecological resources. The expanding empire became more difficult to manage and provisioning became toilsome. One of the causes was the massive deforestation of the Mediterranean region. Excessive grazing and erosion reduced the fertility of the fields. Grains and other foodstuffs had to be imported from further away (North Africa and the Middle East). Rome's heritage devolved upon Byzantium.

In these four cases, the empires began to destabilize at their peak when maximum social cohesion and ecological resources were required. A sustainable response was not found for this pressure. The empires disappeared, but descendants of the Sumerians, Mayas and Romans still populate the regions that once belonged to the most important centres of the world.

The Egyptian and Chinese empires followed a different trajectory. They do not seem to have been brought down by internal implosion and ecological degradation. Egypt lived off its 'gift from the Nile' – the silted agricultural land around the Nile River. The methods of agriculture were conservative, resulting in less salinity. The population growth was markedly slow. It took 3,000 years, from the beginning of the old empire to the beginning of the Common Era, for the population to grow from two million to six million. Then the population remained constant until the nineteenth century, when new irrigation techniques were used. The maximum capacity of the ecological system was never exceeded for long. Like Egypt, China was amply endowed by nature. The deep fertile soils were not vulnerable to erosion. Agriculture was able to feed the territorial expansion and growing population without being exhausted. In both cases, the political history was written as a sequence of dynasties. The rise and fall of these dynasties did not bring down the Egyptian and Chinese empires, thanks to control of internal tensions and ecological pressures.

## States and the inter-state system

States concentrate political power like no other system was previously able to do. On the other hand, the size of the political territory seldom or never coincides with a cultural-ethnic unity (as in mini-systems) or economic boundaries (as in empires). The focus of formal political power in the world shifted to the territorial state after 1500, the same time when a new global economic system developed. States consist of a set of institutions that exercise sovereign power in a well-defined region. That sovereignty is the emanation of public power. The 'modern' state originated in Europe in the sixteenth century. Burgundy, France and England were early forms of territorial states. Empires with a strongly decentralized government, such as the Habsburg empire, the Russian empire and the Ottoman empire, lost influence and power over time.

While tribute relationships were the central binding agent in an empire, states develop control within a demarcated territory. To achieve territorial sovereignty, a state must be able to enforce a monopoly of power, control and violence within those boundaries. This requires a large administrative capacity and the centralization of knowledge in order to mobilize resources (via taxes) and people (e.g. via obligatory military service). States provide three kinds of public services with these resources: protection, physical infrastructure (transportation) and social infrastructure (education and social services). States legitimize themselves via these services in a more abstract way rather than with a leader, king or emperor. In the seventeenth century, the power of the king of England was restricted by a parliament made up of wealthy social groups. A more enforceable social-legal system controlled relationships between social groups and between the individual and the state. New forms of political revolution, such as the eighteenth-century American and French revolutions and the Haitian revolution that began as a slaves' rebellion, reinforced this changing relationship between citizens and the state. Individuals were 'emancipated' via the awarding of rights (rather than via one's place in a group as established by birth). Citizenship became the central legitimization of the state; it guaranteed a right to protection by and services from the state. Political strife enabled more sections of the population (labourers, women, ethnic and religious groups) to obtain full civil rights in the nineteenth and twentieth centuries. At the same time, citizenship (membership of a state) became increasingly more exclusive. Exclusion means the loss of rights; 'no papers' means illegality.

The growth of the state after 1600 is not a straightforward story. The state as a political organization model remained limited to Europe until the end of the eighteenth century. A *territorial state* demarcates its own territory, and within this territory it defines exclusive duties and rights. A connection was made with a 'national identity' in the nineteenth century because of the state's increasing impact on citizens' daily lives. In a *nation state,* the political space coincides with a cultural, linguistic and sometimes uniform ethnic space. This implies the 'invention' of a state's own idiom, history and collective identity. Nationalism is primarily a soliciting power; only a small minority of countries are true nation states today. The twentieth-century *social state* or *welfare state* grew out of the nineteenth-century 'social question' (the growing tension between the social classes). The welfare state multiplies the redistributive, protecting and caring functions. Citizens contribute more to the state's financing, but also receive more political and social rights. The government is an active mediator in economic (Keynesianism) and social affairs (social insurance system). The state generally withdrew and redistributed no more than 10 per cent of GDP (the value of all goods and services produced in a country) until the beginning of the twentieth century. This increased to 50 per cent in the second half of the twentieth century. At the end of the twentieth century, the *neoliberal state* wanted to alter this trend of increasing interference. The government removed itself from several social fields in favour of the 'market'. Regulations were cut back and several public services were privatized.

The new state model spread all over the world in the nineteenth and twentieth century. Well-known national revolutions include those in nineteenth-century Latin America (Bolivar) and twentieth-century Asia (Gandhi in India) and Africa (Nkrumah in Ghana). A classic example of an empire that transformed into a state is the Ottoman empire. This once powerful empire extended over three continents, from the Caspian Sea and the Persian Gulf to Budapest and Algiers. The empire weakened considerably in the eighteenth and nineteenth centuries, mainly due to growing internal social and ethnic tensions. After World War I, the Ottoman empire lost the largest part of its controlled areas. 'Young Turks' followed the example of European states and developed a modern Turkish state in the Asian heartland. This included a process of secularization (Turkey became the first secular Muslim state) and of Turkish nationalism (with the denial of rights for non-Turkish population groups). The state formation process was much more laborious in other parts of the world. In what are sometimes called 'failed states', there is insufficient infrastructural capacity to construct a fully-fledged state due to economic failure, war or corruption.

One question remains unanswered: in the ever more unified economic world after 1500, why did the earlier model of large empires become increasingly less successful, only to disappear completely in the twentieth century? The world had 193 internationally-recognized independent states (members of the United Nations) in 2010. Most of them were much smaller than earlier empires. Two factors are central: economic changes and international competition.

In territorially fragmented feudal Europe (around 1500 there were more than 1,000 different political entities of every size and shape) new, stronger yet competitive political units originated. They were smaller in scale than empires, but they could mobilize more resources from the flourishing urban and later international trade economy. They literally drew and redrew their borders, fostering an almost permanent conflict in Europe for centuries. The new, more compact state was successful on two levels. First, it was more successful in the new, internationalizing capitalist world economy. This world economy was not guided by a central command centre, but by an amalgam of collaborating yet competing states. They regulated internal and external labour and production relationships in a way that guaranteed the international mobility of capital and goods and safeguarded international competition (unlike in an empire, there is no central power that can block this). The success of the Dutch and later British state demonstrate that these political centres did not have to be territorially vast, but that they did need to be efficiently organized, militarily strong and internationally competitive. At the end of the eighteenth century, England was able to mobilize 18 per cent of its GDP for the development of its military apparatus and the Royal Navy. This was much more than any other country in the world, including China. The military recruitment of citizens grew too. France mobilized armies with tens of thousands of men until the seventeenth century. This increased to 450,000 in the eighteenth century. Napoleon recruited an army of 700,000 soldiers around 1800 and the French army was 8.6 million soldiers strong during World War I.

The economic and military success of the new state model made it superior to less coherently-organized empires. The consolidation of power in the model of the state also worked as a double-edged sword. Increasing control over the subjects turned them into citizens and therefore gave them the resources (e.g. via printing or new social media) for communication, knowledge and resistance. Differences acquired meaning; groups could inform and organize themselves, and create diverse forms of class-consciousness or nationalism. This fed a long series of social or national revolutions in the nineteenth and twentieth centuries. Groups repeatedly appealed to the state, demanding that rights be granted and consolidated.

A modern state's territorial sphere of influence is limited by its internal mobilization and control prospects. Moreover, modern states do not work independently of each other. They work in an integrated model, an inter-state system. This system is driven by a political-military balance of power and fluctuations within the global economic market. State growth is inconceivable without this new, international economic and political context. A new international political order was established in Europe in 1648 with the Peace of Westphalia. This was the first treaty to define international law: in principle, sovereign territorial states had to respect each other's borders and economy. International equilibrium was founded on the idea of non-intervention. Territory and sovereignty guaranteed mutual legitimization. The political constellation within an inter-state system differs substantially from earlier social systems. Political units (the states) have interdependent relations with each other, much more so than in the past. Moreover, their role is partly determined by their place in the larger economic system that developed in Europe in the fifteenth to sixteenth centuries, and then spread around the world in phases. In other words, the rise and decline of states cannot be explained by internal causes alone; rather it is related to tensions in the international-political and -economic arena. Because the economy is largely detached from a political unity, an economic system no longer stands or falls with the rise and decline of an individual state.

This international system does not exclude competition and conflict; on the contrary. After every large-scale struggle (after 1648, after 1815 and after 1945), the international political order grew stronger. Power relations between the states have also been unequal. Strong states have been located in economically prosperous parts of the world (the core) and weak states in more neglected areas (the periphery). These countries are almost always in a weaker international-political position.

After 1945 the political inter-state system was consolidated in a formal international organization, the United Nations. Even though neoliberal criticism of state power and discourse about the formation of a growing global identity (universal rights, cosmopolitanism) surged after the crisis of the 1970s, the national state remains the most important political player on the international chessboard. Discussions about the fall of the Soviet Union, the future of the European Union, about controlling transnational migration, changing global power relations (China) and social revolutions (the 'Arab spring') are still mainly conducted within the national state model.

## Hegemony and empire

States grow in an international system. The new inter-state system redraws the global geopolitical model and is characterized by successive hegemonic cycles (in the core) and new forms of imperial expansion (outside the core). Hegemony brings economic, political and ideological superiority together in one state. In this combination of formal and moral power, cycles have marked the inter-state system since the sixteenth century. After an initial phase, when the Italian city-states of Genoa and Venice were the guiding powers (fifteenth to sixteenth century), the following cycles succeeded each other: the United Provinces (hegemony mid-seventeenth to mid-eighteenth century), Great Britain (hegemony nineteenth century) and the United States (hegemony second half of the twentieth century). In the transitional phases, there was conflict within the core of the global system. The breakthrough always followed a 'world war': the Eighty Years' War (concluded with the Peace of Westphalia in 1648), the French–British wars (concluded on the battlefields of Waterloo in 1815) and the twentieth century world wars between 1914 and 1945.

A short comparison of American and British hegemony illustrates the similarities and differences within the successive cycles in the inter-state system. Both states conquered the first position after a battle with the closest competitor, France for England and Germany for the United States. The basis of economic power for both countries was established during the previous phase, when they were able to extend their economic power in the shadow of the strongest nation at that moment. This enabled them to grow initially into formidable rivals then into economic power centres that surpassed their predecessors in scale (Great Britain surpassed the United Provinces, the United States surpassed Great Britain). They both

*Table 5.1* Periods of stability (hegemony) and instability (world conflicts) during the British and American cycle

|  | British cycle | American cycle |
|---|---|---|
| Rise of hegemony | End 18th – beginning 19th century | End 19th – beginning 20th century |
|  | Rivalry with France | Rivalry with Germany |
|  | First industrial revolution | Second industrial revolution |
| Breakthrough of hegemony | First half 19th century | First half 20th century |
|  | Military and commercial victory | Military and commercial victory |
| Peak of hegemony | Third quarter 19th century | Third quarter 20th century |
|  | Free trade | Bretton-Woods system |
|  | London financial centre | New York financial centre |
| Decline of hegemony | From last quarter 19th century | From last quarter 20th century |
|  | International competition | International competition |
|  | Increasing rivalry | Increasing rivalry |
|  | Imperialism | Neoliberalism |
|  | (US and Germany) | (Japan and China) |

acquired political authority by being at the head of an alliance of states and by restoring international order after defeating their direct rival militarily.

A first striking difference relates to the organization of this international political order. '*Pax Americana*' is led more rigorously and directly via a network of international organizations. British hegemony ('*Pax Britannica*') followed the principle of *primus inter pares*. Furthermore, England developed its power via its own empire, while the United States championed decolonization and the sovereignty of nations. Second, the economic world order is organized differently. Free trade, unconditionally applied by the British until the 1930s, is only a means to open foreign markets for Americans. Moreover, the multinationalization of trade after World War II resulted in a new phenomenon: direct cross-border investments that remain within the company. Today they exceed the total value of world trade between nations.

The second half of the twentieth century saw the development of supranational political organizations like the United Nations. Collaboration between states was reinforced in regional integration systems such as the European Union (European Economic Community, 1958) and the ASEAN (Association of Southeast Asian Nations, 1967). Both forms of interaction are international, therefore between states as primary political units. The question is, to what extent will these collaborations replace states? It is not clear whether these supranational or international systems will become the most important political arenas in the twenty-first century. Are we experiencing a new cycle of conflict and hegemony in the inter-state system? In that case, which state will become the new hegemon and in

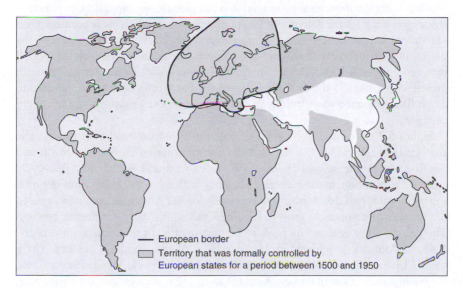

*Figure 5.1* The geography of European political control over the periphery.

Source: C. Flint and P. J. Taylor, *Political geography: World-economy, nation-state and locality*, Pearson–Prentice Hall, 2011, p. 82.

which world order? Will the political system disintegrate with regional blocks as opponents, or are we headed for a new, global empire – a multimodal government system without a real core? What will the role of the state as a political power container be? Will it remain strong or evaporate under further economic globalization? Will world cities become new power centres, as links in a global economic and social network?

As defined above, empires were large political units with overlapping ethnic and geographic borders. They form an economic block controlled by a political centre. Empires disintegrated due to gradual incorporation in a capitalistic world system. The colonial empires that were acquired by European states as of the sixteenth century had a fundamentally different character. They spanned seas and continents and were not geographically defined units. They functioned in a world with a much larger, more global economic and later political interdependence. They created and perpetuated the periphery of an expanding world system, regions that fell outside the most important decision centres and were useful for delivering cheap labour and raw materials. Imperialism is the process of political integration of these areas. Imperialism stands for the political and territorial domination of the periphery by core states. Imperialism has been perpetuating and remoulding the relations between core and periphery since the sixteenth century. We distinguish between formal and informal forms of imperialism.

Formal political control by core states over parts of the periphery has been a central characteristic of the growth of the new world system since the sixteenth century. External areas were integrated into the globalizing capitalistic production model primarily for the delivery of labour and raw materials. This is accomplished via formal imperialistic control. Almost every part of the world was under the direct authority of a limited number of European core countries for a certain period between 1500 and 1900. The Asian zone of Japan/Korea/China across Persia to present-day Turkey is the exception. However, European states were also able to assert their influence very strongly in this zone too in the nineteenth and twentieth centuries.

Figure 5.2 shows the two cycles of colonial expansion and contraction. The first cycle encompasses the rise and decline of colonial empires in North and South America, the second cycle encompasses Asia and Africa. The first cycle peaked in the middle of the eighteenth century with more than 120 colonies under European rule. Fast decolonization, especially on the American continent, caused the number of colonies to drop to less than half in the early nineteenth century. The second wave reached its peak in the last quarter of the nineteenth century. Fast decolonization followed from the middle of the twentieth century. There were 13 imperialistic core states including five large ones: Spain, Portugal and the Netherlands in the first cycle, Great Britain and France in the first and second cycles. The foundations of the Spanish and Portuguese empires were laid in the sixteenth century. They were almost completely dismantled in the eighteenth and nineteenth centuries. Great Britain and France were active from the seventeenth century and strongly expanded their colonial sphere of influence in the nineteenth century. The British empire was the largest ever. Around 1900, about a quarter of the land mass and world population was governed by the British.

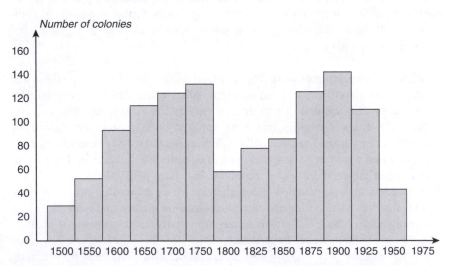

*Figure 5.2* The two long waves of colonial expansion and contraction, 1500–1975.

Source: C. Flint and P. J. Taylor, *Political geography: World-economy, nation-state and locality*, Pearson-Prentice Hall, 2011, p. 87.

The influence of the core on countries and regions in the periphery was not only translated into formal domination. The indirect influence of the three hegemonic powers of the last 400 years – the United Provinces, Great Britain and the United States – was often much deeper. Dutch and British domination of maritime trade strongly increased their sphere of influence. The United States did not underpin its global power in the twentieth century with a formal colonial empire; the imperialism was informal. Inequality in political, military and economic power relations requires large parts of the world to adapt to a world that follows rules that they did not create. Unbalanced trade relations between zones with high wages and low wages increased the dependence of peripheral areas. In addition to persuasion, the United States also resorted to hard power. Today it still has a military presence in more than 150 countries and military bases in more than 50 countries. The United States has carried out more than 40 military interventions on diverse pretexts since World War II. The most recent are the interventions in Iraq and Afghanistan as part of the 'war on terror'. These interventions did not aim for direct control in the long term; their aim was the protection and expansion of political and economic influence.

# 6 A divine world
## Culture, civilizations and religions

For one thousand years, from 600 to 1600 CE, the Islamic world was one of the most dynamic and expansive global civilizations. It originated amongst nomadic peoples in the desert of the Arabian Peninsula. The youngest of the world religions was at the base of a powerful empire that extended from India to Spain. During its growth, the Islamic civilization incorporated very diverse traditions of Arab, Persian, Turkish, Greek-Roman, South Asian and African origin. Expansion hampered a central government and the Islamic world disintegrated into diverse political units; this did not hinder the continued expansion of Islam far beyond the borders of the original Arabian empire. Despite the existence of strong ideological differences, the shared religious culture remained a powerful uniting force in what some call 'the first global civilization' (in a Eurasian context). What made this cultural force so strong? First, the faith had omnipresent networks. They nurtured a generally-shared commitment, with the same texts, the same practices and identical language tied into a truly cosmopolitan web. Second, intense exchange networks of goods, knowledge and technology connected the diverse regions and political entities. Muslim traders, especially Arabs and Persians, were dominant players in the extensive Eurasian networks, supported by new techniques in banking and business practices. Technical innovations – including water management, weaponry and transportation – spread quickly. Third, strong cultural innovations in literature, poetry, sciences, medicine and philosophy developed in this world. This triple connectedness gave the Islamic civilization great internal coherence across regional boundaries. This indicates that civilization as a cultural concept has a significance of its own. How can we explain this?

Civilizations or cultures give themselves meaning by building and maintaining memories, their own 'collective memory'. In its oldest and most widespread form, this occurred by passing on oral traditions. In more sedentary population groups, these traditions about one's own community were often ritualized and monopolized by acknowledged 'storytellers' (like the *griot* in West Africa). More complex and hierarchical societies developed more formal means of passing on cultural memory. The most complex system of expression is perhaps the written word. The ability to write remained limited to a select elite for ages. This made the medium extremely suitable for canonizing one's own stories over a long period of time. It was much less appropriate for wide dissemination. This only changed when printing became commonplace, and later with the advent of mass media. Monuments and architecture were the most powerful and politicized expressions of collective memory, ranging from the impressive pyramids along the Nile River to stone memorials in contemporary metropolises. Institutions like churches and later scientific institutes were concerned with translating (some would say inventing) the past and disseminating it. In complex societies, cultural transmission increasingly occurred through specialists like priests, teachers, academics and artists. Throughout time, regimes have made a great effort to control this construction and transmission of memory and, by extension, the guardians of memory. Only in the last few centuries has intellectual and cultural production been able to occur more freely. Increased contact (first at the speed of a horse or the wind, now at the speed of light) led to more influence and exchange of cultural systems of expression. This does not always happen on an equal basis, as the colonial period showed. The heavy-handed imposition of European values led to a so-called 'colonization of the memory' in which one's own (in this case, mainly African) traditions were obscured (Africans as 'people without a history'). On the other hand, new forms of cultural expression and interaction (from dance and language to the Internet) have created spaces for criticism and resistance. Supporters and opponents of contemporary society currently use advertising and propaganda techniques to make their case.

Cultural significance is central when building cultures and civilizations. Therefore, use of the concepts 'culture' and 'civilization' is particularly controversial. Civilization has more than one meaning. Its definition in *Merriam-Webster's Collegiate Dictionary* brings two interpretations together:

> 1a: a relatively high level of cultural and technological development; 1b: the culture characteristic of a particular time or place.

On the one hand, it refers to a general human code of conduct, to a high (perhaps the highest) form of human society. Civilization refers to unity; it is singular and inclusive. On the other hand, civilization stands for a context and culture-specific concept. The emphasis is on difference. We speak of civilizations in the plural. Civilization is an exclusive concept here.

This schizophrenic attitude towards the concept 'civilization' is also found in the past and in studies of the past. Sometimes it refers to a general development, (mostly) focusing on progress. This is often paired with evolutionary thinking, with conceptualizing history as a sequence of phases. Other times, differences are emphasized and translated as a distinction in spatial and, particularly, cultural terms. Several civilizations exist, and belonging to a certain civilization depends on cultural (and often location-based) patterns. Can the diverging concepts be integrated into one global story? In this chapter, we look at the attempts to explain the concept of civilization in the singular and the plural. We test these explanations against the issue of a 'Western civilization'. Finally, we look at religion's role in this story.

## Civilization in the singular and the plural

The term 'civilization' is derived from the Latin *civis* (citizen), member of a *civitas* (city). The term civilization in the singular received its 'modern' meaning in the eighteenth century under the influence of works by French enlightenment philosophers. The verb *civiliser* was derived from the noun *civilisation*. The verb refers to a process (acquiring knowledge, norms); the noun conveys the objective (civilization as the highest rung in human history).

The concept embraces a dichotomy due to the historical view of the process of civilizing. Civilized is the opposite of uncultured, unrefined or barbaric. In the singular definition, the dichotomy is not so much spatial (differences between groups), but chronological (differences between periods). Civilization, development, increases over time. That way everyone can be included in the civilization process. Civilization is therefore an inclusive concept. This concept of development and progress is at the base of modernization thinking, which helped legitimize and support the superiority of the West in the nineteenth and twentieth centuries. The basic assumption was that everyone can reach a higher state of well-being and civilization if they adapt themselves to Western development patterns. This way, the term 'modernization' replaced the term 'civilization'. This concept became emotionally charged with racist connotations and prejudice from the nineteenth century. Uncivilized was linked to racial or ethnic characteristics; human differences were perceived as backward.

A second cause of the waning popularity of the concept 'civilization' is the strict connotation with culture. This connection was broken more recently by emphasizing that cultures can exist without being a civilization (more 'primitive', more small-scale), and that civilization is not the same as a higher culture (or ethics). Higher material prosperity can go together with more violence or a dictatorship. As a result, the inclusive concept of civilization lost most of its popularity in the second half of the twentieth century. People now refer to more general, neutral terms like humankind, human nature, human values and human dignity.

Civilization as a plural concept supplanted the general idea of an inclusive civilization in the nineteenth century. For a long time, civilizations have been an ordering principle when analyzing the world and its history, but in Western world views civilization quickly became very popular as an instrument of analysis in the nineteenth century. By tracing out a set of characteristics for a human collective, the world and its history became the sum of a series of civilizations. Civilizations are perceived as historical societies with an origin, growth, prosperity and a decline. The history of the world … is therefore not one process of civilization, but a sequence (or cycle) of civilizations.

Textbooks and manuals about world history frequently utilize the concept of civilization to help shape the human story. They remain vague about the way they explain the concept. Their perspective can be summarized as follows. Civilizations are forms of social organization characterized by their large sphere of influence, both in space and in time. They span smaller social structures such as 'cultures'.

They can only exist if human groups are able to settle down permanently. Prerequisites for the development of a civilization are the following: a permanent agrarian surplus; economic specialization (crafts, services or trade); social differentiation (non-agrarian elites); cultural and religious hierarchy; concentrated political power; the development of cities (*civitas*); of an administrative bureaucracy and, usually, of writing; the development of new agricultural and manufacturing technologies and weaponry; and the development of contacts and networks with other groups (long distance trade). Civilization corresponds with empire, as defined in the previous chapter, but the political and cultural spheres of influence are not always the same (as shown in the example of the Islamic civilization). The rise of civilizations caused a new acceleration in human history. That is why it is useful to employ the concept as an instrument of analysis, on condition that civilization is sufficiently 'historicized' and analyzed as a cultural complex that originated at some time (together with the first empires) and disappeared at some time (with the rise of a global economy, global religions and the inter-state system).

In general world history books, authors mainly focus on so-called 'world civilizations' with great historical legacies. In a nutshell, they paint the following picture:

1   The development of early civilizations, which grew out of the first agricultural cultures (the four major valley civilizations; up to 500 BCE):

- Valley of the Tigris and Euphrates rivers (Mesopotamia);
- Nile river valley;
- Indus river valley;
- Valleys of the Yellow River (Huang He) and the Yangtze River.

Sometimes included are the early civilizations of Central America and the Andes (depending on how world civilizations are defined):

2   Great 'classical' civilizations:

- Developed out of the 'fertile crescent': Persia;
- Greece, the Hellenistic world, the Roman empire;
- China (Han);
- India (Mauryan);
- Central America (Olmecs).

Sometimes included are Africa with Ghana (fourth to eleventh century), Mali (twelfth to fifteenth century) and the Songhai empire (fifteenth to sixteenth century):

3   'Post classical' civilizations:

- The Islamic civilization;
- Byzantium and Orthodox Europe;
- China (Tang and Song);
- The Mongolian empire;
- Central America (Toltecs, Aztecs) and the Andes Mountains (Incas).

4    The world after 1500:

'Civilizations' are no longer mentioned, only 'empires' (e.g. Ottoman, Chinese, Mughal). Historians use concepts like 'a trans-Atlantic economy', 'world economy', 'state system' etc.

There is a consensus about the so-called 'great' civilizations. There is much less consensus regarding the civilizations in Central America, South America and, above all, Africa. The authors discern an independent civilization process but ask themselves whether these centres are comparable with the 'world civilizations' that influenced world history so strongly. The question remains open: what is a (great) 'world civilization' exactly? Things become even more problematic when one looks at the period after 1500. Suddenly the term 'civilization' disappears from the vocabulary. Do 'modern' societies no longer satisfy the criteria? Are we in a 'higher' phase of development once again? Is the rise of the West not compatible with 'civilization'? How does this fit the notion of a 'Western civilization'? Recent textbooks seem to distance themselves from the concept 'civilization' as an ordering principle. They speak of empires, societies and worlds, and focus more on borders, contacts, turning points and transitions.

In conclusion, several questions can be posed when defining civilization as an exclusive social structure that is clearly defined in place and time. First, how does one reach a feasible definition of civilization? What are the required conditions with regard to space (magnitude), time (life span), coherence (economic, political, cultural binding agents) and impact (on later civilizations)? Second, how does one fit civilizations into a story that emphasizes interaction and interconnection (world history)? The idea of civilizations as alternating cycles is outdated. Third, what can one do with the concept 'civilization' in the modern world? Can the historical concept still be used or are we in a different world now?

Some world historians, such as Bruze Mazlish, advocate dropping the concept completely:

> Civilization is one of those great Stonehenge figures looming over our mental landscape. Like its adjacent figure, culture, it is one of the major concepts invented and constructed in the eighteenth century and subsequently elaborated in the course of the development of the social sciences. In the new millennium, it has become a fetish. In the new time-space we have entered, it should not only be 'deconstructed' but taken down.

> (Mazlish, 2004)

## *Civilisations sont des continuités* (Fernand Braudel)

Civilizations are not eternal, nor is the concept. For clarity, we limit the concept 'civilization' to the period from the first successful agricultural societies to the expansion of the modern, globalizing world system from the sixteenth century. Civilizations are 'recognized' as distinct forms of society thanks to physical expansion (population, economy, military) and cultural expansion (norms, legitimatization, language). Consequently, they must be sufficiently 'large' in space (extensive), in time (prolonged) and in composition (coherence). They must also define themselves as coherent societies. That is why successful civilizations are always visible via their own interpretation and their own material production. The cultural binding agent is essential. There can be a sequence: an alternation of economic and political systems within a more or less coherent cultural system.

The French historian Fernand Braudel (1999 (1963)) defines civilizations as four overlapping (but not necessarily similar in location and time) spaces or arenas.

1   Civilizations are physical, ecological spaces (*'espaces'*). These are the spaces that humankind has created within its natural environment. On the one hand, these spaces are defined by natural conditions (oceans, waterways, mountains, plains, climate, fauna and flora etc.). On the other hand, they are defined by the choices that people have made to establish a society within those conditions (form of agriculture, choice of crops, type of settlements such as villages, infrastructure etc.).
2   Civilizations are cultural spaces. Specific cultural standards develop within the material forms of settlement, including 'collective mentalities' and religions.
3   Civilizations are social spaces. Social patterns, social groups and social relations (hierarchy, inequality) determine the type of society. Cities are centres of power.
4   Civilizations are economic spaces. Every civilization must create wealth and surpluses to survive. Agriculture is the basis. Systems of industrial production and trade are based on agricultural production.

The boundaries of these spaces or arenas are not absolute. Patterns – especially those of a cultural nature – are also formed via interaction with other cultures/civilizations. A civilization grows in interaction with neighbouring peoples/cultures/civilizations. These four spaces form one entity; they do not function separately from each other. A civilization connects these four spaces and provides continuity. 'Civilisations sont des continuités', says Braudel. Civilizations always have a past, and that predetermines which route a civilization follows. Civilizations exist because they define themselves as a societal pattern that outlives itself. Civilizations always have their own interpretation and legitimation, usually in the form of a dichotomy with the 'outside world'.

Even though the four spaces/arenas are linked together and overlap, they do not correspond completely. The time dimension within these spaces is not similar. Physical spaces and cultural spaces change much more slowly than social and economic spaces. According to Braudel, civilizations survive cycles in social, political and economic patterns. This is not true of the cultural basis. Braudel emphasizes cultural values as the foundation of civilizations. Cultural values are much more enduring than more fickle political or economic cycles. 'Civilization is the grandfather, the patriarch of world history. Religious values are the heart of every civilization' writes Braudel. Civilizations also come to an end. They disappear when the cultural basis is undermined (internal tensions), either by changes in the physical environment (climate, ecology) or by conflicts with other people (external tensions).

## Civilizations in conflict

The American political scientist Samuel Huntington published *The Clash of Civilizations and the Remaking of World Order* in 1996 (Huntington 1996). This remarkable book attempts to analyze contemporary global society after the fall of the Iron Curtain in 1989. The post-war cohabitation model (two blocs, Cold War) disappeared; a new paradigm was needed for global politics. Huntington builds on three premises. First, the world after 1989 is not unipolar as is often assumed, but is multipolar. It consists of several large blocs that he calls 'civilizations'. The twentieth century resulted in an intensification of contacts between these civilizations, but not for convergence. According to Huntington, the premise of a general westernization of the world is a myth. Second, the differences between these civilizations are primarily cultural and, in particular, religious. Political, social and economic models derive from this. Third, the domination of Western civilization – so prominent in the twentieth century – is waning. At the same time, the power and claims of other civilizations is increasing. These civilization blocs still mainly live next to each other peacefully, but increased differences are a source of possible new (world) conflicts.

Based on these premises, Huntington formulates the hypothesis that the twenty-first century will see increased global tensions that will mainly take place at the fault lines between the large civilization areas. One of these fault lines is between the West and Islam. This analysis generates several questions: To what degree can one classify the world population of the twenty-first century into quasi-homogeneous, geographically-delineated groups that are based on religion and culture? To what degree can all conflicts be reduced to a collision between these civilizations, and what about the conflicts related to economic resources like oil, water and raw materials? How does Huntington's divided world relate to the global capitalist economy of the twenty-first century? To what extent can such a world view have a 'self-fulfilling' character (stigmatize other population groups or translate conflicts in cultural terms)? Finally, can one still speak of separate civilizations today?

Huntington's vision popularizes the concept 'civilization' and separates it from the idea of modernization and development. Focus is placed on unity and exclusivity, on differences and incompatibility.

In his book entitled *Identity and Violence: The Illusion of Destiny* (2007), the Indian economist Amartya Sen objects to the idea that the world is heading for a war, a clash of civilizations. People are not members of one well-defined group and do not have one specific and clear-cut identity. In reality, they belong to multiple groups that constantly determine the sometimes diverse aspects of our complex identity. Those who stigmatize people into one all-encompassing identity are headed for polarization and violence. According to Sen, people are always looking for new aspects of their multilayered identity, so we must resist academics and politicians who focus only on one label such as ethnicity or religion. They are 'the prophets of confrontation, the defeatists of the clash of civilizations'. It is dangerous to categorize people based on one or a few exclusive characteristics. Many barbarian conflicts throughout history arose from the assumption that a unique and superior identity existed. Sen wants us to stop categorizing people in terms of inherited traditions, especially in terms of inherited culture and religion. He wants to get rid of *the illusion of destiny*.

## A Western civilization?

The definition of civilization as a coherent cultural pattern throughout time questions the individual character of every civilization. This discussion is visible in the question of the existence and identity of a Western civilization. If we want to know whether a Western civilization exists, then we must first determine what the West is (as a region, with a capital letter). West (without a capital letter) is primarily a direction on a compass. 'West' is derived from the Indo-Germanic word 'wespero': evening. West is the direction of the sunset. In a metaphorical sense, west is also called the Occident. When we established the prime meridian, we divided the world into a western and an eastern hemisphere. The dividing line between them does not correspond with what is felt as western and non-western. Western is different from westward.

The contrast between West and East has existed in European history for a long time. For example, take the schism between the Christian church (west: Roman Catholic; east: Orthodox), the idea of western and eastern modes of production (e.g. Marx), or way of life (e.g. Weber) and the political division after World War II (the Free West and the Eastern Bloc). In any event, the use of a term like 'the West' or 'western' always refers to a division, a dichotomy. The existence of a Western world presumes the existence of 'something different' – a non-West.

Many textbooks focus on 'Western Civilization'. They include two visions of the historical concept 'the West'. The first brings the history of the West back to the first civilizations in Mesopotamia and the Nile delta (outside present-day Europe). The suggestion is that the West is an idea and therefore not linked to a fixed location. The location of 'the West' changes throughout history:

- it starts in 'Western' urban centres outside Europe, in Mesopotamia;
- it shifts and continues to develop in the Greek and Roman civilizations;
- from the late Middle Ages, western Europe fused these traditions together, and from this point on 'the West' breaks out in every direction;
- the West currently dominates global civilization.

Western civilization is therefore the result of a process spanning thousands of years, from the origin of the first agricultural civilizations to today's global society. The core increasingly shifts – literally – to the west: Mesopotamia, Greece and Rome, western Europe, and over the Atlantic Ocean to North America.

Others call this linear vision into question. They agree that 'the West' is not a geographical notion, nor is it a specific collection of people, races or countries. The West is inspired by a set of ideas, values, habits and beliefs, such as human equality and dignity, equality before the law, democracy, rationality, religious tolerance, a belief in progress, freedom of expression and research. These values have 'conquered' the world; therefore, an examination of Western civilization is justified in their eyes. However, it is difficult to draw one line from the present back to Sumeria or Babylon. These authors place the roots of the West in the period 300 BCE to 1300 CE, with Roman expansion and the rise of Christianity. The West only gained form in the Christianized world of 500 to 1500 CE. In this vision, the West is (almost) everywhere today – as a civilization, as a cultural tradition, and as a set of moral and intellectual values.

What can we do with the concept of a Western civilization in contemporary world history? For reasons mentioned above, it is better to describe the world after 1500 with less sensitive concepts like 'society' or 'system'. Nevertheless, the idea that the contemporary world is the peak of a Western civilization path remains very popular. If this is true, what are the roots of this process? From when can we speak of a system, a *civilization* that is sufficiently *continuous and coherent*? To paraphrase Braudel, in order to speak of one civilization path it must be supported by similar principles related to social, economic and cultural organization. In historical literature, we encounter three options.

The first option links Western civilization to the early agricultural cultures in the 'fertile crescent' (from Mesopotamia to the Nile river). This option is popular because it is in keeping with the desire to put their own civilization on the historical map as clearly and dominantly as possible. Old and prestigious roots have an important legitimizing power. Extending 'the West' to the old Middle East is scientific nonsense, however. There is barely any coherence and continuity with the contemporary world. The knowledge that was passed down (agriculture, engineering, writing, money, laws and mathematics) is also shared by civilizations in northern Africa and the Middle East. Does this mean they should also be considered 'Western'? There is obvious influencing, but that is insufficient to speak of one continuous civilization path.

The second option places the roots of Western civilization in the Greek and Roman world. This option has greater scientific credibility, but problems related to sufficient coherence and continuity with the later world remain. First, the Greek and Roman world was more oriented towards the eastern than the western (and northern) world (Europe). Contacts and influence mainly occurred with civilizations and cultures from the east. Second, Greece and Rome had a great influence on European society as well as on Byzantium, the Arab world, Russia, Persia and India. Third, there is an important rift between the Greek and Roman world and the Western world after 500 CE. The West adopted many Greek and Roman inventions, not through direct tradition, but rather through rediscovery and imitation (1,000 years after the fall of the West Roman empire). There are also large differences between ancient Greece and

Rome and Europe after 1500, such as the concept of 'democracy', social relations, organization of the state and cultural patterns (differences in religion,
language etc.).

The third option isolates Western civilization to the High and Late Middle Ages
in Europe (1000 to 1500 CE). The seeds of later Europe and a Western model that
spread after 1500 grew during this period. There is enough coherence and continuity between the periods before and after 1500 regarding political and social
organization (cities, state models, and modern bureaucracy), economic organization (trade systems and new social groups), and culture and religion (Christianity,
intellectual life, technology, and science). These three fields clearly show their own
patterns that helped shape the world after 1500: politics (national states), economics
(capitalism) and culture (Christianity, Western philosophy). To speak of a civilization it is necessary to have enough internal coherence and continuity with regard
to social, economic, cultural and political patterns. The external aspect is also
important. In addition to great uniqueness, there must be sufficient openness
towards other cultures and civilizations, both in regard to the assimilation of new
knowledge and insights, and in the form of economic and political expansion. The
Western/European model after 1500 satisfies these two conditions. That is how
Europe put itself on the map in the second millennium.

## World religions

Religion is inherent to humankind. That does not mean that religion has always
been around. Religion is not older than language. Language is needed to accumulate and pass on knowledge. Language is also needed to enable a virtual world of
imagination, populated with the most important – living, dead and absent – actors
of life. Over the past ten thousand or even hundred thousand years, many forms
of proto-languages and proto-religions developed. The oldest archaeological
signs of a group-bound religion are not more than 25,000 years old. If we define
religions as social systems in which members profess their faith in one or several
supernatural beings in an organized manner, then religions are a very recent phenomenon in human history. Most religions have already disappeared without a
trace. Some are very old; others date from yesterday. Major, present-day religions
are no more than a few thousand years old.

Human beings are the only species with religion. Religions as social systems
originate where and when people develop new forms of coexistence, culture and
communication. They usually originate independently from each other, but religions all over the world show a remarkable number of similarities. It is generally
accepted that religion had and has three individual and social functions: solace in
grief and alleviation of fear (related to death), explanation of the unexplained, and
promotion of group collaboration (as opposed to affliction and danger). This does
not explain why and where religions developed, but it does indicate that religious
systems have a huge social functionality.

The transformation from informal and local folk religions into larger, organized
religions is an important step in world history. *Folk religions* are small-scale,

polytheistic belief systems that stem from the daily life of people who live together in small groups. In addition to developing agricultural systems and larger settlements, the process of domestication also denotes a process of expansion and institutionalization in religion. In the new division of labour, a separate group or class of priests or shamans (shaman: he who knows) claim a monopoly position in the organization of religious experience. Religion is 'domesticated' by this guild of guardians. These new *state religions* subscribe to a new social order of authority monopoly, violence monopoly and social hierarchy. Moreover, a shared ideology or religion helps forge new societal relations in larger groups without direct kinship, and gives them an incentive to fight (and die) for a common goal.

As indicated above, civilizations are usually defined as cultural spaces. Religion plays a leading part in this designation. Religions that underpin successful civilizations can develop into *world religions*. The major religious traditions that humankind still largely relies on developed independently from each other in four different areas in the first millennium BCE. They are Confucianism and Taoism in China, Hinduism and Buddhism in India, monotheism in Israel and philosophical rationalism in Greece. They all originated in Eurasia in centres of flourishing urban civilizations. The three major monotheistic religions (Judaism, Christianity and Islam) originated in the same region, the land bridge between Asia, Europe and Africa. These new traditions broke with small-scale polytheism. They all make universal claims via a unified doctrine. Hinduism, the oldest tradition, worships a multitude of gods but emphasizes a single 'correct path'. Buddhism developed as a reformist movement within Hinduism and is the first major missionary religion (Southeast Asia, China and Japan). The ethical teachings of Confucius and the mystical religion of Tao originated in Eastern Asia in the sixth century BCE. They remain linked to the Chinese civilization. Judaism spread away from its centre due to centuries of persecution.

World religions have three important elements in common. First, instead of an extensive pantheon of gods they propose one central source of order in the universe. Second, they all develop a coordinating religious and moral code of conduct. Third, subject to conversion, they open their faith to outsiders. Even though the roots of some of these religions are much older, the most important sacred texts (like the Bible, the Vedas and the Koran) only obtained their definitive form in the period 600 BCE to 600 CE. That is when the most important spokesmen of these religions (Jesus in Palestine, Siddhartha Gautama (Buddha) in India, Confucius in China and Mohammed on the Arabian Peninsula) lived and taught. Strong connections and interactions developed in the Eurasian area during this 'axial period'. Philosophers and prophets developed systems of ethics and morals that could transcend their own group. More general, universal claims were made based on these ethics and morals. They include the works of the founders of Western philosophy such as Socrates, Plato and Aristotle. The new world religions all originated and spread within expanding empires or civilizations. The dynamics between religious and political/military expansion largely redrew the world of the past 2,500 years. The strongest motive was the convergence of worldly and religious authority, such as in Christian Europe, in the Islamic empires or in Confucianist China. Religious movements also dispersed in a more autonomous manner via existing trade and traffic routes. The most typical example is the Jewish Diaspora after the fall of Jerusalem under the Romans.

World religions are often limited to three: Buddhism, Christianity and Islam. These are still the major proselytizing religions. Their roots are situated in a similar, dissident tradition. Buddhism originated in the fifth century BCE in reaction to and as a reformation of Hinduism. The roots of Christianity are located in a Jewish splinter movement around the beginning of the Common Era. Christianity grew as an institutionalized church as of the fourth century CE. Islam (seventh century CE) is the third monotheistic revelation religion. It reverted to the roots of Judaism and Christianity.

World religions spread from their area of origin via war and conquest, trade routes, conversion as well as adoption by elites. Medieval expansion of Christianity and Islam largely occurred by conquering new areas. Buddhism was able to spread outside India via the silk routes. In Africa, Islam followed the major trade routes through the Sahara and along the Swahili coasts. Proselytization (conversion) is an important part of these three religions. Religions achieved the greatest success when they were incorporated by the elites in large empires, such as Buddhism in India and later in China, Japan, Korea and Tibet, Confucianism and Taoism in China, Islam in Arabia, North Africa and Central Asia, and Christianity in Europe and Russia.

Over the centuries, the three major missionary religions promoted a large part of intercultural contacts, first in Eurasia, later in Africa, America and Oceania. New dynamics arose after the sixteenth century. The Reformation and Counter Reformation in Europe resulted in a new wave of evangelism, and they confirmed the role of Catholicism and Protestantism as state religions. The colonization of America and Africa resulted in new expansion. Islam was fortified in Southeast Asia and in Africa, and in many places it increased its grip on governments. Buddhism gained popularity in Central Asia, China and Japan, and became an element of political control in Mongolia and Manchuria. The world was dominated by empires and states with a clear religious profile, where political and religious leaders reinforced each other's authority until the nineteenth century. The debate about a possible causal connection between religion and political and economic expansion is still undecided. Older theses, including Max Weber's about capitalism and Protestantism, are based on an inadequate knowledge of non-European civilizations. Every world religion had its great thinkers and its periods of intellectual vitality and expansion. They often took place in times of relative religious openness and tolerance, such as during the expansion of the Islamic empires in the eighth to fourteenth centuries, Song China in the tenth to thirteenth centuries, Mughal India in the sixteenth to seventeenth centuries, and the United Netherlands and United Kingdom in the seventeenth to eighteenth centuries.

World religions are currently disconnected from political regimes for the most part. They have spread further than ever via new forms of conversion and diaspora. Despite the rise of new movements, a majority of believers still follow one of the world religions that have their roots in the six centuries before and six centuries after the start of the Common Era. Christians form the largest group (2.1 billion, 50% Catholic, the rest Protestant, Anglican, Orthodox etc.), followed by Muslims (1.3 billion, 80% Sunnis and 20% Shiite), Hindus (900 million), adherents of Chinese religions (390 million, such as Taoists and Confucianists), Buddhists (375 million) and Jews (15 million).

# 7   A divided world

## *The West* and *The Rest*

An immense Chinese fleet moored off the eastern coast of Africa at the beginning of the fifteenth century, 90 years before the Europeans arrived. This was the geographic final destination of a series of impressive expeditions. When the new Ming emperor Yong Le ascended the throne in 1402, the Chinese empire was internally consolidated. He was therefore able to campaign against the threatening Mongols and to promote ocean expeditions to areas located to the south and east. By imperial decree, an enormous fleet of 300 ships was built, with a crew of up to 28,000 sailors. Some vessels were 120 meters long and 50 metres wide, the largest wooden ships up to that time. The first expedition departed in 1405, led by the Muslim eunuch Zheng He. Seven subsequent expeditions, the last in 1433, departed in the direction of the Indonesian archipelago, Champa, Java, Sumatra, Malacca, Ceylon and Calicut on the Indian peninsula. The Chinese also sailed via the Persian Gulf to the coasts of Africa, to an area near Somalia. A fleet consisted of an average of 60 ships with a combined crew of thousands. What were the motives for this unique series of ocean expeditions? A mixture of military and diplomatic considerations (along with prestige) played a determining role. The Chinese did not explore these territories with the aim of conquering them or of establishing permanent settlements. They probably wanted to establish a tribute relationship between the visited areas and the Chinese centre. The new dynasty probably sought expansion and reinforcement of its position in several new vassal states. Thanks to the expeditions, China engaged in trade and tribute relations with Korea, Japan, Cambodia, Champa, Siam and Malaysia. These countries sent ambassadors to the Ming court laden with gifts to declare their submission to the Son of Heaven. Those gifts did not have much economic value; they were mostly symbolic.

The abrupt halt of these expeditions is very puzzling. Why did the Chinese cease all overseas exploration in 1433? At that moment, they were on the verge of rounding the Cape of Good Hope. They had excellent seaworthy ships and lots of expertise in cartographic and navigational techniques. No Chinese fleets sailed over the oceans in the centuries after 1433. Moreover, all contact with foreigners was strictly regulated. Foreign trade was subject to all kinds of limitations. This was not only for ideological reasons, but also out of fear of the undermining influence of direct relations with 'barbarians' whose customs deviated from Chinese customs and traditions.

At the same time China turned inward, Europe started its discovery of the world. A century later, Europe controlled a large area of international waters. The idea that an imperial decision could end the expeditions was inconceivable in fifteenth century Europe. China had been building a politically-unified empire (where the central authority could direct economic decisions) since the third century BCE. By contrast, fifteenth century Europe was strongly fragmented. When Christopher Columbus (Italian by birth) wanted to finance his exploration, he had to plead with European courts on five different occasions before receiving a positive answer from Spain. Thanks to intense competition in divided Europe, Columbus was able to finance his trip. After his successful discoveries, six other countries got involved in the race to the New World. In contrast with ancient China, Europe was never again a unified political unit with one central authority. The territory that consisted of hundreds of independent states around 1500 was governed by 25 to 40 nations in the twentieth century. Unlike China, Europe remained a geographically fragmented area with numerous small core regions and many irregularly-shaped coastal areas. This hindered a unified central authority, but promoted the growth of diverse, competing growth centres. What was a great disadvantage for a very long time became a driving force for the 'new' Europe after 1500.

## The Rise of the West and The Great Divergence

The period in which Zheng He and Christopher Columbus set out on their expeditions was a turning point in world history. Around 1500 CE people lived in a fragmented world. No one was cognizant of the global world. Existing world views were partitioned, despite the fact that they overlapped each other strongly in the Afro-Eurasian part of the world. Every empire, every culture or civilization had a good knowledge of its own world and an impressionistic image (via observation, tradition or reporting) of part of the outside world. At that time, no one could predict that the world would look very different after 1500 due to the spectacular *Rise of the West*.

Although vast areas of the world, more to the north and the south, were not yet linked to the centres of development, in 1500, the majority of the world population lived within the borders of large civilizations or empires. Most of them were linked together via exchange, communication and trade networks. Economic, political and cultural contact zones grew and flourished in Eurasia, as well as in sub-Sahara Africa, Central and South America. Differences in intensity, scale and success were important, but there were many similarities. Strong arable farming, intense trade relations, assertive political centres, military strength and cultural prestige characterized the expansive civilizations and empires.

World history took an important turn after 1500: the world became larger and more global. Contacts and interactions intensified across the globe. This was combined with growing regional differences in economic growth and prosperity, especially after 1800. A more integrated world was not a more equal world. A new focal point of growth – Europe and the West – took the lead: 'The Rise of the West'. Other parts of the world seemed to fall behind: 'The Great Divergence'. Why the Great Divergence occurred in the nineteenth century breaks down into three separate but related questions. First, how was part of the world able to escape the limits of economic growth, intrinsic to agrarian societies? Second, why didn't this acceleration of growth collide with its own borders? Why was it able to (at least partially) press ahead outside the borders of the first core area, namely Western Europe? Third, why did so many other countries and regions fail to adopt the growth model? This brings us to one of the most important societal questions of today: why are some parts of the world richer than others? Why is wealth found mostly in what we call the West or the North and poverty found mostly in the rest of the world? When and how did this situation develop?

Historians generally agree that the period after 1500 is a new phase in world history. However, there is much less consensus about the nature, causes and results of these changes. Was the rise (or renaissance) of Europe and the West incorporated in a long history? Was the spectacular growth after 1500 already in the genes of European society, which was rebuilt after the chaotic post-Roman period? Did ecological conditions give Europe an advantage, or did coincidence play a greater role? Did luck give Europe a (possibly temporary) comparative advantage over other 'civilizations'? Was it more related to a regression of these civilizations? Did other major cultures like the Islamic world, India and China suffer from a reluctance or inability to adapt? Perhaps the rise of Europe was exaggerated: did the continent only really take the lead after 1800? In the long term, might we speak of an interlude, a transitional phase of European/Western dominance between Oriental preponderance before 1500/1800 and after 2000?

These are only some of the questions that enliven the contemporary debate about the *Rise of the West* and *The Great Divergence*. It is clear that almost all premises and opinions about European/Western history and about world history are being confronted, leading to much disagreement and animosity. This chapter examines the most important arguments in the debate. What are the theorems? Which data are used to support these views? What are the most important explanations? First, we must determine which gap we are discussing.

## Measuring the gap

The contrast between rich and poor in the world has never been greater than it is today. It is estimated that the richest 20 per cent of the world population controls 85 per cent of all the wealth. They controlled less than 60 per cent at the beginning of the nineteenth century. That wealth is, to a great extent, geographically concentrated in the West. This lopsided ratio is a result of recent world history, especially after 1800.

We have very little reliable data for measuring the economic and welfare ratios in the long term. Data older than 1900 are usually a rough estimate, especially data from non-Western regions. Estimates of gross national product (GNP) go back to the beginning of the nineteenth century. Over the past two centuries, the value of total global production has grown almost a hundredfold. At the same time, global ratios have shifted substantially. Figure 7.1 illustrates the fast growth in Europe until the second half of the nineteenth century, and of the United States until the second half of the twentieth century. Europe and North America's share of global GNP increased from

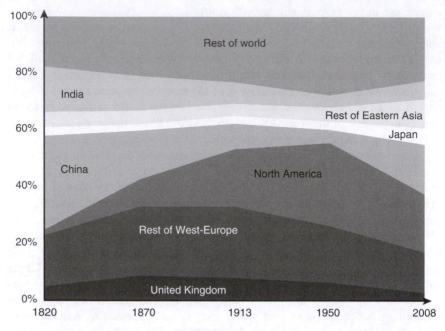

*Figure 7.1* Regional distribution of global GNP, 1820–2008.

Source: *Angus Maddison Historical Statistics* (http://www.ggdc.net/MADDISON/oriindex.htm).

25 per cent in about 1820 to 55 per cent in the middle of the twentieth century. At the same time, the share of former heavyweights China and India fell dramatically from 49 per cent to barely nine per cent. A reverse movement started in the two last decades of the twentieth century. Europe and North America represented 37 per cent of total global production in 2008. China and India were once again responsible for 24 per cent.

Figure 7.2 shows the ratio between the superpowers of the past two centuries: Great Britain and the United States, and China. The Atlantic economies only surpassed those of the East in the second half of the nineteenth century. They became dominant in the twentieth century. The ratios are once again more similar at the beginning of the twenty-first century.

The growth acceleration in the European and North American economies is largely a result of the Industrial Revolution, which started in England. The core of industrial production was located outside the Western world before 1800. The share of industrial production of the pioneers of modern industrialization (Europe, North America and Japan) increased from 32 per cent in 1800 to more than 80 per cent in the twentieth century. While China and India accounted for more than half of the global production of industrial goods in the eighteenth century, this share fell to less than 5 per cent after 1900. It is clear that the gigantic industrial acceleration in the West, which increased even further after 1950, caused an important de-industrialization in parts of Asia and extremely unequal development.

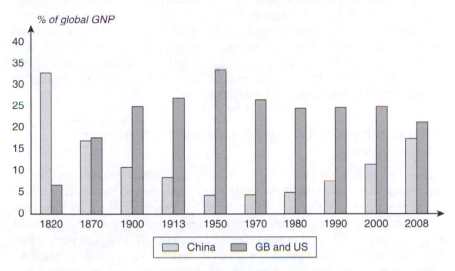

*Figure 7.2* Distribution of global GNP between GB/USA and China, 1820–2008.

Source: *Angus Maddison Historical Statistics* (http://www.ggdc.net/MADDISON/oriindex.htm).

Despite the fact that the figures are rough, the trend is clear. Somewhere between 1700 and 1900, a large gap grew between what later came to be known as the West and the non-West: The Great Divergence. This development reversed at the end of the twentieth century, especially the position of China, India and some other Asian countries. This is sometimes called The Great Convergence. What is the history of this remarkable movement? Was the great transformation mainly an internal process with roots in its own history? Should the causes be sought in global shifts? Did coincidence play a major role? In the abundant literature about the rise of the West, the following clusters of explanations return frequently in the search for possible alleged differences between the West and the East: nature and climate; religion and culture; the organization of family and labour; the state and legislation; knowledge and innovation; and trade and conquest. Without going into the discussion about the 'prime mover', there is a growing opinion that the rise of the West was a 'contingent' process (conditional, not required), a process that was not inevitable and could possibly not have happened. On the other hand, this acceleration in history could not have occurred just anywhere. It was the result of a unique cumulative process, with roots inside and outside Europe. The Industrial Revolution was indisputably a regional process (England), but with just as indisputable global roots (knowledge and trade).

This chapter distinguishes between three types of explanations. The first have a distinctly Eurocentric character. They chiefly see the rise of Europe as an autonomous process, a result of internal changes. The second model points to Asia's age-old predominance and recognizes many similarities between Western and Eastern societies until the nineteenth century. This model seeks an explanation for the divergence in a non-predestined or even accidental concurrence of circumstances. The third model distances itself from both the Eurocentric and the (sometimes entitled) Asia-centric explanations. Its point of departure is the increased interaction between the West and the East, from which European countries were able to gain the most advantage after 1500. Thanks to several comparative advantages, this increased interconnection enabled them to strengthen their position in the areas of trade, knowledge and state power.

## A world with major differences: the rise of the West as an internal process

Europe's position in the global system changed dramatically between the fifteenth and the nineteenth centuries. While Europe was – literally and figuratively – still at the edge of the Afro-Eurasian trade system in the fifteenth century, four centuries later it was the absolute dominant power in the new global system. This important change is often explained via a new internal dynamism in the European world. From this view grows the classic image of a dynamic Western society compared to a stagnant Eastern society. This explanation model relies on Max Weber's research programme, which asserts that the West distinguishes itself via a steady and systematic rationalization of thoughts, actions and institutions. As a result, a capitalist economy, a bureaucratic, legal-rational state model and modern science could develop in the West and nowhere else. The origin and dynamism of this rationalization have to be found in internal developments within Europe. The differences between Europe and the non-West became increasingly larger. Industrialization seems to flow automatically out of this Western dynamism. This vision is shared by disciples of Max Weber (rational state), Adam Smith (market economy) and Karl Marx (capitalist production relations). The central elements in this 'classic' explanation include:

- The West has been the richest and definitely the most dynamic part of the world since (the end of) the European Middle Ages. The Industrial Revolution made the gap between 'The West' and 'The Rest' even bigger.
- A capitalist market economy, state-building and rational culture are typical Western creations. So too is the development of a characteristic, Western demographic model.
- For many who adhere to the Weber premise, culture makes the difference: the development of new, Western cultural patterns related to labour, discipline, freedom, knowledge etc.
- The West was the first to develop modern, rational institutions: a modern state-system, a modern bureaucracy, an efficient military apparatus while also promoting individual property rights.
- The West was the first to develop a market economy, more or less separate from political regulation but guided by an 'invisible hand'.

In the Weberian tradition, the American historian David Landes (1998) determined the starting point and end point of the explanation of the rise of the West in Western

Europe. The new dynamism that started in the Middle Ages set off a movement that can only be explained by its own strength. The surrounding world did not play an essential role in this rise. The explanation for this can be found in the following:

- a new culture: the growth of unique European values that focus on the individual, on knowledge (science), on personal profit and on labour;
- new institutions that did not impede but adapted themselves: more compact, more efficient states, rights that protect property and individual initiative, protection of markets;
- a new market economy, the first one in the world.

The differences with the rest of the world become clear starting in the late Middle Ages. The economic and political revolutions of the eighteenth century increased the gap. This culturalist explanation model depicts Early Modern Europe as a unique experiment that grew out of a new and unique set of values. This new cultural pattern arose in a fragmented, politically and militarily competitive landscape. Landes places fragmented and progressive Europe against static, despotic Asia, where dynamism is obstructed in the self-interest of the ruling class. Openness, curiosity and flexibility make the difference.

  Until recently, the issue of the *Rise of the West* was dominated by the traditional vision in which Europe's breakthrough was seen as a result of internal emancipation, of a steady and systematic rationalization of thinking, actions and institutions. This lead to what can be considered the most rational form of: (1) economic trade: a capitalist market economy; (2) political action: bureaucratic nation states; and (3) intellectual discourse: modern science. More and more authors question this Eurocentric discourse.

- Is a Weberian cultural explanation broad enough to tell a European (rather than simply a British or Western European) story? Does a European culture exist?
- To what extent can values such as individualism and a strong work ethic be awarded to a group of people without lapsing into a racist discourse?
- How can you disconnect the growth of a market economy in Europe from the international context; more specifically, from the growth of a global economic (and colonial) system?
- Last but not least, what do we do with non-European cultures? In this perspective, they are usually the opposite of European dynamism and are, therefore, seen as static. In such studies, developments outside Europe are seldom estimated at their own value. Consequently, new research pays more attention to comparative and global analyses.

## A world with major similarities: the Great Divergence as a conjunction

New and comparative datasets undermine the image of Europe's gradual lead in the centuries before 1800. The majority of global goods production was still situated in Asia in the eighteenth century. Massive de-industrialization followed in the nineteenth century. This is a result of the Industrial Revolution in Europe, which was based on mineral raw materials and European imperialist politics that imposed unequal exchange conditions. India was the leading world exporter of cotton fabric before 1800, but it became an exporter of raw materials (cotton) and an importer of finished products (textiles) in the nineteenth century.

According to recent comparisons, the Asian continent created at least 60 per cent of the world's wealth in the eighteenth century while containing 66 per cent of the world population. In the first half of the twentieth century, the Asian continent still held 55 per cent of the world population but only 20 per cent of global wealth. Around 1700 the per capita income in East Asia (without Japan) was comparable with that of Western Europe. This was only 14 per cent in 1950. This gigantic reversal mostly occurred after 1800. Studies that distance themselves from a Eurocentric approach focus on this recent reversal. Due to China's dominant position in the early modern world economy, comparisons usually concentrate on Europe versus China. The departure point in this view is that there were more similarities than differences between the two social models before 1800. China also developed productive arable farming and intensive industrial and commercial systems. The organization of property rights and markets was not inferior to Europe, nor was the political organization less developed. Like other commercial societies in those days, growth was limited by the boundaries of organic agriculture systems. So why did Europe break this pattern?

The most influential study to date, one that assumes a reciprocal comparative perspective and that calls European uniqueness into question, is that of Kenneth Pomeranz (2000). Pomeranz departs from the viewpoint that China was the strongest economy in the fifteenth to sixteenth centuries, not Europe. The two were still evenly matched in 1800, at least when comparing the core regions: England in Europe and the Yangtze Delta in China. It was only in the nineteenth century, with the Industrial Revolution, that Europe (quickly) developed a lead (*the great divergence*). According to Pomeranz, this leap forward was not written in the stars; it could not even be predicted until the nineteenth century. Therefore, he combats what he calls false explanations:

- a different history: the core regions in Europe and China remained evenly matched until 1800;
- a more dynamic society: not more (or less) in Europe than in China;
- a technical lead: the knowledge systems in Europe and Asia show great similarities;
- a more powerful market: China is also a market economy;
- the presence of capital: China was also a match in this respect.

So what makes the difference? Pomeranz makes a case against considering the European path as 'normal'. What if Europe was the exception? What if Europe deviated from a general development route and, therefore, chose an 'abnormal' path: industrialization? In this vision, Europe did so out of necessity, because it was confronted with a double scarcity:

- Scarcity of energy: wood was in short supply and expensive, and coal had to be excavated from increasingly greater depths. This required new mining and energy delivery technologies (steam engines).
- Scarcity of raw materials: this required aggressive commercial politics and the development of an extensive trade network and colonial system. This enabled Europe to secure a relatively cheap supply of labour (slaves) and essential raw materials (including cotton and food). The European colonial empire was a prerequisite for its 'leap forward'.

Commercial capitalism and the Industrial Revolution did not arise as the result of a long progressive process; they arose from necessity. In contrast with China (which could profit from its large, united empire), the European continent was in an ecological bottleneck. The responses to this bottleneck gave Europe a considerable advantage afterwards: more efficient technical knowledge and a network of colonies (an Atlantic trade system).

Other authors such as Bin Wong (1998; Bin Wong and Rosenthal 2011) compare political and economic developments in Europe and China over the past 1,000 years. They also conclude that Europe and China showed more economic similarities than differences around 1800. Both were agricultural societies in which the market and regional specialization played an important role. The leap forward that Europe experienced with the Industrial Revolution was explained by a material necessity, not by a cultural or intellectual lead. Conversely, the differences related to political organization were significant, despite the fact that they both left room for change and growth. Europe was a system of competing states. Everything was dominated by competition, internal (between leading groups) and external (between states). Consequently, the policy of the elites in Europe was aimed at maximization of profit and power in a context of permanent rivalry. China was a unified, mainly agrarian empire; its elites were chiefly concerned with maintaining social order. The European competitive model was more suitable for fast, flexible adaptations to economic changes. The Chinese empire model was more efficient when it comes to the social protection of its subjects. The so-called 'despotic' Asian model relied on strong organization and regulations, which gave its subjects more security than in Europe. The most important message is that not one but several models of societal modernization existed. The differences were a result of long-term developments on an economic and political level in diverse regions around the world. Why one eventually triumphant over the other was not the result of providence; it was a concurrence of circumstances in which coincidence played a major role (Marks 2007).

## Growing differences due to increased interconnection: trade, technology and state

Several recent publications have labelled the revisionist image of the world before 1800 (a world of striking similarities) as too one-sided. These publications do not advocate a return to past Eurocentrism, but argue that major imbalances in economic and political power grew out of increasing global interactions in the seventeenth, eighteenth and nineteenth centuries. The imbalances were not coincidental; they sprang from different social organizations in the West and East. Europe's changing global position cannot be explained purely from an internal dynamism. Growing contacts took place between unequal partners in such a way that they helped change global relations. Contacts with the outside world changed Europe's position on diverse levels. First, its own capitalistic trade system gradually incorporated other parts of the world in such a way that the fruits of this system chiefly served the core. Second, Europe created a unique knowledge system via accumulation, import and adaptation. This knowledge system was the breeding ground of industrial acceleration in the nineteenth century. Third, Europe applied this knowledge and technology to the development of strong state systems and in unseen military strength. The result was near absolute political and military dominance in the nineteenth century.

### Growth of an unequal global trade system

The image of 'striking similarities' departs from the idea that agrarian market economies all over the world have the potential to develop into capitalist growth centres. This passes over the view (as argued by Fernand Braudel, Charles Tilly, Immanuel Wallerstein, Giovanni Arrighi and others) that capitalism is not a 'natural' result of the growth of markets. Capitalism develops where new, transnational commercial-financial elites ally themselves with assertive, mercantilist states. Capitalism is not an emanation of free markets but an exploitive economic model that grows in a competitive political system. The commercial-agrarian empires in the eastern part of the Eurasian continent were not built on such alliances between capitalist and political elites. The striking expansion of external European markets since the sixteenth century increased the impact of European trade networks and incorporated new areas in a world system dominated by Europe. The core areas colonized 'new worlds' and accumulated the profits from these new peripheries. The most important European powers before 1900 played a first-rate role in intercontinental trade and controlled a huge colonial hinterland. The import of goods in European ports from America and Asia grew quickly: precious metals, foodstuffs, raw materials and finished products, mostly obtained with violence, force and monopoly formation. They stimulated new economic activities in production and consumption, such as cotton, sugar, silk, porcelain, coffee, tea, tropical food, silver and gold. Large profits flowed into the new metropolises and the power relations in this expanding trade system shifted to new trade elites and national states.

European overseas imperialism is unique. No other empire incorporated distant areas into a core-periphery relationship in such a manner. This new world system dominated by a European centre disturbed the existing balances of power at the expense of former regional empires. The unequal exchange further deepened the differences between the core and the periphery.

This explanation model interprets capitalism as a historical world system that developed in a specific European conjunction after the late Middle Ages, in which a unique coalition grew between commercial capitalists and national states. The almost permanent competition between these actors resulted in a new growth dynamism that globalized this European model via several expansion cycles. Other authors follow the idea of capitalism as a world system, but minimize Europe's input as a fluke. Andre Gunder Frank (1998) argues that European/ Western dominance in the nineteenth and twentieth centuries is only an interlude in a long 'Asian age'. Europe was not predominant between 1400 and 1800. The world was polycentric, with several cores of development, and China was at the top. The fact that Europe was able to become the dominant region after 1800 was not due to its own merit, nor was it the result of a superior value system. In the period between 1400 and 1800, Frank sees three regions with production sur- pluses in the global trade system (India, China and Southeast Asia) and four regions with a deficit (Japan, America, Africa and Europe). America offset the deficit by increasing the export of goods (raw materials); Africa did so by increas- ing the export of labour (slaves). Europe had nothing to offer. It 'bought a ticket on the Asian train' by controlling the export trade of America and Africa and by re-exporting silver. One third (or more) of the silver extracted in the New World ended up in Asia, especially China (where the price was twice as high as in Europe).

Other authors like Hobson (2004) completely reject the idea of a specific European dynamism. Hobson claims that almost all innovations attributed to modern Europe were already applied in other civilizations, especially in the Middle East and Far East. This concerns technological knowledge as well as political and economic systems. According to Hobson, Europe was only created due to external pressure (e.g. from the Islamic world, whereby Europe got its own identity) and it remained in the margin of this global system until the nineteenth century. The power derived from the rise of Europe is that of a latecomer that worked its way up via knowledge that was developed elsewhere. The rise coin- cided with aggressive colonial and imperialistic politics and with a racist dis- course in which the world was split into unequal parts. Economic growth had nothing to do with the myth of 'laissez faire', but with the success of despotic, interventionist states supported by massive state expenditures, government regu- lation and trade protectionism.

### Growth of a dominant European knowledge system

As was stated in Chapter 3, European scientific thinking made very little progress between 200 and 1400 CE; in fact much of the knowledge accumulated in the Greek-Roman world was lost. A true reversal occurred between 1500 and 1800. A competitive European society generated new forms of uninhibited research that abandoned the authority of classical, Greek or Christian texts. Scientific knowl- edge was no longer justified by referring primarily to tradition or revelation. It was justified using reason, observation and experimentation. This gave breathing space to new knowledge systems and important technological breakthroughs – the basis of the European 'scientific revolution'.

Macro-inventions (such as the laws of atmospheric pressure) increased scientific knowledge, which was translated into a continuous chain of micro-inventions (such as diverse types of steam engines) via an uninterrupted process of research and development. In a scientific revolution, the inventors are usually at the forefront. They only realize their visions thanks to their social networks and a social climate that tolerates and even stimulates innovation. Therefore, this progress is also a collective legacy in which social learning plays a first-rate role. Contrary to previous societies, the products of that knowledge were privatized in companies or used to reinforce state power. That is why some label the economic and political revolutions in Europe as a 'free lunch' originating from knowledge systems that had older and global roots.

### Growth of a triumphant European state system

The European revolutions of the eighteenth and nineteenth centuries changed the organization of the economy, politics and society forever. They also placed large European states at the top of the global pecking order. Several authors, such as Peer Vries, have been arguing that the crushing political and military supremacy of the nineteenth century European centre has deeper historical roots.

The growth of more compact state structures in Europe was a process that took many centuries. These state structures replaced the empire's old, looser political organization. The Spanish Habsburg empire was the last empire on the European continent. This political transformation had important outcomes. The growth of a state apparatus created a rationalized bureaucracy, a modern tax system, a more efficient system for acquiring knowledge and information (administration and statistics), and a new military apparatus. This was legitimated with a specific state ideology, both economic (mercantilism with an active customs policy and protectionism) and military (struggle inside and outside Europe). The new states also made it possible for the bourgeois class to get an increasing grip on policymaking (as of the seventeenth century in Great Britain and the end of the eighteenth century on the continent). The European states developed into strong power containers, with unprecedented possibilities in the areas of commercial policy (mercantilism) and military strength.

The first modern fiscal-military state was Great Britain. With substantially higher tax proceeds than China, for example, Great Britain was able to develop a stronger 'infrastructural power' than any other country in the eighteenth and nineteenth centuries. According to calculations by Peer Vries, British taxes siphoned off up to 25 per cent of the national income around 1800, compared to less than 10 per cent in China. More than three-quarters of this tax revenue went to expanding the military apparatus, including a powerful fleet of approximately 400 ships. During the Napoleonic wars, Great Britain was able to mobilize almost one million men, much more than the few hundred thousand soldiers of the Chinese empire, which had 30 times more inhabitants. Investments in military technology and bureaucracy were many times greater. China, in the eighteenth and nineteenth centuries, showed every characteristic of a territorial empire with a limited government apparatus and great local autonomy, and particularly concerned with guaranteeing national security and maintaining social harmony. The British – and, by extension, the nineteenth century European states – were arenas of permanent political and social conflict. Growing nationalism fed the international competitive atmosphere. Increasing their sphere of influence and developing an overseas empire was combined with an endless series of conflicts inside and outside Europe. When Great Britain entered into confrontation with The Middle Kingdom in the 1840s, it immediately became clear that the Chinese state model was no match for the power of European nations.

State power is a determining factor in the growth of the world economy dominated by Europe and the inter-state system connected to it. An intense political, military and economic competition has been dominating the new world economy. Strong, more compact states in the European model had a great competitive advantage due to their far-reaching protectionism, their military strength, and their unparalleled potential to mobilize people and resources. Together with the development and application of new military technologies, this gave European countries a decisive lead in the nineteenth century battle for new direct or indirect spheres of influence.

## Europe's new global position and the transformation of European society

The *Rise of the West* completely upset relations on a world scale. The convergence of internal societal transformation and external expansion beyond its old borders propelled Europe from the periphery to the centre of global events. As stated above, opinions are sharply divided about the causes and timing of this change in the balance of power. More and more authors no longer believe in a substantial European lead before the nineteenth century. They see the period between the fifteenth and the nineteenth centuries as Europe's time to catch up. Europe was experiencing many internal changes at that time (the effects were only complete in the nineteenth century), and external expansion mainly occurred via its own periphery (South America, later North America and Africa). According to these authors, the global balance of power only changed to Europe's advantage in the nineteenth century, and this change might have been temporary. Only then did Europe achieve complete supremacy on an economic level and on a political-military and technological level. The symbolic pivotal moment was when Great Britain and other European nations were able to open up the Chinese market by force of arms (the Opium Wars 1839–1860). Until then that market had not been freely accessible to European products. At the same time, an ideology of European superiority triumphed; economic expansion was legitimized with a civilizing mission (nineteenth century) and later a modernizing mission (twentieth century).

Even though Early Modern Europe might not be richer or more dynamic than the rest of the world, it is indisputable that important social changes occurred in this region from the High Middle Ages (eleventh to thirteenth centuries), and particularly from the sixteenth century. They were the result of a combination of internal tensions and external shifts, and altered the history of this part of the world. Three processes were decisive here; in chronological order: Europe's new place in the world as of the Middle Ages; European social transformations in the sixteenth, seventeenth and eighteenth centuries; and the Industrial Revolution in the nineteenth century. In each of these processes of change, relations with the world outside Europe were decisive.

### A new global position for Europe

Europe was at the edge of the Afro-Eurasian trade complex until the Late Middle Ages. Non-Europeans were only mildly interested in this peripheral area because it had little to offer that could not be found elsewhere. The Islamic world was primarily interested in the east and the south. Nevertheless, the European continent showed the beginnings of a new dynamism from the eleventh to twelfth centuries. This became clear during the first attempts to break out of its own borders via the crusades (1096–1271 CE) and with significant emigration to the east (*Drang nach Osten*). The first centres of the newly-founded trade networks were the northern Italian city-states of Genoa and Venice. The new networks were grafted on to much older and larger commercial systems in the East. Ambition and the pursuit of profit were combined with a renewed curiosity and great respect for other cultures.

This European 'renaissance' has been central in the creation of a European/ Western identity. The traditional explanation refers to an internal rebirth, to its own resurrection. A new spirit spread across the 'old continent', with much more emphasis on a secular, earthly way of life, on human dynamism and on individual achievements. This explanation seems to have primarily a teleological function. After all, the first attempts to break out of Europe and the so-called 'discoveries' occurred long before the actual Renaissance (fifteenth to sixteenth centuries) and Enlightenment (eighteenth century). The new independent European spirit is, therefore, more of a result than a cause. A more convincing explanation for the beginning of European expansion refers to:

1    Commercial motives. The commercial network that grew out of (Northern) Italian trading interests quickly clashed with the dominant Islamic commercial world (at that time the Mediterranean Sea was Islamic territory; the crusades were not able to change this). To continue growing, Europe was forced to try western and southern routes.

2    Military-religious motives. These were important in a rhetorical sense, primarily with the intention of pushing back Islam (the *Reconquista* was launched in the eleventh century). This coincided with a reinforcement of the position of Rome and the Roman Catholic Church.

3    Technological innovations. The invention or improvement of weapons (fire power), ships and navigation made the exploration and conquest of areas outside Europe much easier (and therefore less expensive). The (initially

imported) technology determined how Europeans moored on new coasts: in Africa and Asia they stayed along the coastline as far as ships and canons could reach; in America they went on land and trampled the existing civilizations with a very small force.

Therefore, the roots of European expansion were not so much in the birth of 'the new man' but in the specific, subordinate position that Europe occupied in a larger, global perspective. We must also look for important roots of knowledge (gunpowder, compass, cartography) outside the European continent. In a certain sense, we can understand the onset of Europe's rise as a reaction by that continent to its marginal position in the world at that time. Europeans clashed with the flourishing and economically strong Arabian and Chinese civilizations in the east. Trade could not be controlled directly due to climatic circumstances (the Sahara desert) in the south. That Europe was able to break out of its borders was chiefly dictated by two necessities: a need for its own commodities and a need for its own trade networks.

As a commercial zone, Europe had very little to offer. To pay for the import of new luxury goods like silk, porcelain and spices they could scarcely use their own goods. Europe did not have the goods that were in demand in the Arabian, Indian and Chinese world such as slaves (Islamic world) and precious metals. An initial solution was plundering. The search for these commodities made Europeans explore new worlds. The gold and silver fever was mainly fed by the need for a means of payment. Second, they tried to start their own production of consumption goods: initially sugar and later cotton. Europe was only able to conquer a place in the international trade system by offering foreign commodities, especially those gained under duress.

In addition to its own commodities, the need for self-controlled trade networks grew. The routes to the east were blocked for centuries. The manifold initiatives for new trade routes were stimulated by profit motives, combined with religious rhetoric (Ottoman conquest of Christian Constantinople in 1453).

### The transformation of European societies

From a subordinate position, Europe broke out of its borders. European societies changed fundamentally from the sixteenth to nineteenth centuries. This process ran parallel with its new and stronger role in the new world economy. Three processes contributed to this transformation.

1   The growth of commercial capitalism. The process of commercialization coincided with the growth of trade networks, both international and internal. Internally, nodes of production and trade developed in cities as well as in the countryside (cottage industries). These networks were organized by a new class of merchant-entrepreneurs who employed a growing group of part-time peasant-wage labourers. Commercial capitalism developed within, in a dominantly agrarian-rural society in which the majority of the population survived via

family farming. This is how thread and linen produced in Flemish villages found buyers in the New World via Courtrai, Ghent and Spain.

2    The growth of national states and the inter-state system (see above).
3    Changing social relations. This includes the development of new social groups, like an independent bourgeois citizenry and (often part-time) wage labourers. This reinforced social polarization, with a more precarious income situation for a growing group of property-less people. This goes together with the development of new familial relations and demographic patterns. The system of 'free' (family) farmers on their own piece of land encouraged small households and controlled population growth (deferred marriages and cohabitation).

These three transformations, economic (commercialization), political (increased state control) and social (proletarianization), were the most important motors of European dynamism as of the sixteenth century. They cannot be explained without Europe's changing role in the new world economy. First, as demonstrated above, Western Europe became the centre of a world economy that it initiated and of the inter-state system connected to it. Second, the European states developed into strong power containers, with unprecedented possibilities in the area of commercial policy (mercantilism) and military strength. Third, this new world economy was dominated by a new international capitalist class that could diversify its interests according to profit motives. Since the means of production were, in principle, set free (capital, land, labour), they could have goods produced under the most profitable economic conditions. A class of free and cheap labourers grew in the wake of this economic transformation. These three characteristics are still found today in the globalized world system.

## A European or a global Industrial Revolution?

The Rise of the West is often described with a revolution metaphor. Revolution means upheaval, but it also stands for a break with the past, with tradition. The two major revolutions that are perceived as pivotal points between the (traditional) past and the (modern) present are the (political and social) French Revolution and the (economic and social) Industrial Revolution. They took place in virtually the same period, around 1800. The symbolic meaning of this twofold revolution in Western imagining can hardly be overestimated. Within world history, the concept of the Industrial Revolution has increasingly been put into perspective and brought up for discussion. The concept is currently under pressure in three areas:

• Many economic historians place the 'revolution' in a long-term perspective. They speak of a process that stretches over decennia and even centuries. The outcome is and remains a different world, so the revolution metaphor is usually retained.
• World historians abandon the classic explanation model of the Industrial Revolution that only takes into account changes within Europe.

- According to social historians, the Industrial Revolution was much more than a technological revolution with boosted production and productivity. It was also a revolution in the labour process (centralization, proletarianization), the economic process (transformation of the 'national' economy) and the societal process (new social and political relations).

Until now, the process of Industrial Revolution was mainly studied as a succession of national stories (British, Belgian, French, German, American etc.) from a strictly European and later Western perspective. In the best case, a comparative analysis was made afterwards. This approach has shortcomings because, like all historical processes, the Industrial Revolution consists of diverse and combined geographic scales:

- the regional scale, as the location of the industrial processes (British Midlands, the Belgian axis Liege-Borinage, Alsace in France, Ruhr Area in Germany etc.);
- the national scale, especially the role of national governments;
- the European scale, with a process of action (e.g. owing to scarcity) and reaction (to initiatives elsewhere);
- the global scale, with questions like: Why in Europe and not elsewhere? Why such a quick diffusion in the West and not outside? To answer these we must know Europe's place in the world at that time. In other words, how European or Western was the Industrial Revolution?

When we look at the Industrial Revolution from a wide, global perspective then an explanatory model must take into account three extra elements:

1   The history of commercial capitalism in Europe, which enabled this part of the world to develop a commercial network of power to the south and west of Europe from the sixteenth century. This Atlantic network was not yet global, but it did interact with other commercial networks (Islamic world and Eastern Asia). This commercial growth generated enormous profits for a small upper class of European trade capitalists, and the demand for new commodities grew. Import substitution – replacing imported commodities with goods produced at home – was a way to keep the trade balance positive. A famous example was the British ban on the import of Indian cotton fabric (the Calico Acts of 1701 and 1721). Increasing popularity of these light textiles resulted in the British government promoting its own textile production via those Acts (the import of cotton as a raw material was allowed). This (cotton) textile was then exported, resulting in a collapse of the indigenous Indian weaving industry. This is a typical example of a local measure with a global effect. The fact that the British were able to do this indicates that the European power base grew strongly in the eighteenth century.
2   The development of an internal market economy in several European countries. This growth was the result of a strong increase in the number of

semi-proletarians and proletarians (those who must sell part or all of their labour for wages) and of the number of consumers (those who must buy some or all of their provisions at the market). This growth of a market economy long before 1800 stimulated individual entrepreneurial initiatives.

3    The popularity of new values in Europe, such as individual entrepreneurship (due to the success of commercial capitalists), technological innovation (a wave of inventions) and an aggressive economic policy (as part of state ideology). These also predate (the end of) the eighteenth century.

Geographically, the Industrial Revolution was in principle a European phenomenon. It was 'invented' in eighteenth century Great Britain because it was worthwhile being invented there. In other words, the same process would not result in enough profit to be sustainable in different places or different periods. Recent studies such as that of Bob (Robert) Allen point to the rising price of labour in Western Europe, which made investments in labour-saving processes profitable. Moreover, the prices for capital and energy were relatively low, so labour could be replaced with steam engines and mechanical looms via investments in capital and coal. Besides supply, there was also a rising demand for new technologies that increased the productivity of labour.

As argued, this cannot be understood without involving the non-Western world. Growing international trade, colonial policy and aggressive mercantilism guaranteed the European core's rising trade volumes (like the import of cotton) and stimulated urban expansion, especially in London. This increased the demand for labour and energy. It became profitable to orient labour surpluses from the countryside to the commercial and industrial centres. Due to depleted wood supplies, it became profitable to invest in the expansion of coal exploitation.

The Industrial Revolution may have been British or European, but it did not remain a Western phenomenon. It expanded in Japan, Asia and Latin America from the end of the nineteenth century. Industrialization adapted to other cultural environments.

## Other questions, other answers

In 1831, the German philosopher Hegel wrote: 'The history of the world travels from East to West. Europe is absolutely the end of history and Asia is the beginning.' This teleological vision has dominated European thinking since the nineteenth century, and we still find it in Eurocentric explanations for *The Rise of the West*. The fundamental perspective shift in the debate surrounding *The Great Divergence* undermines old premises:

*   that the West had a lead over other parts of the world, specifically China, long before the nineteenth century;
*   that for many centuries the West had an intrinsically more dynamic society, especially compared to Asia;
*   that the West took up a pioneering role in the new world economy on its own, due to internal changes;

- that for many centuries the West had a more modern, more market-oriented economy than, for example, the Chinese, Japanese or Ottoman empire;
- that culture and institutions in the West had a unique 'Western' character.

Of course 'revisionists' do not deny that the world looked very different in 1600 than in 1900, marked by the strong rise and later dominance of Europe and the West. The question should not be approached unilaterally; a comparative view is required. We also want to understand why this shift was to the disadvantage of other parts of the world. How can one explain the decline of China and other Asian regions? Is the West's path the 'normal' path or a deviation from the general pattern? A non-unilateral explanation can only be found in a combined comparative and global perspective:

- other, non-European societies and economies must be involved in the analysis: the Ottoman empire, India, China, Japan, West Sudan etc.;
- diverse aspects of these societies must be studied in a comparative manner without taking for granted the premises of what the unique European development path might be (geography, demography, economics, social relations, political systems, cultural patterns, family systems etc.);
- embedded in a system theory, the various sub-systems must be viewed not only next to each other, but also as part of a larger system. How did the new world economy integrate the existing sub-systems?

World history teaches us that explanations for certain developments, like the *Rise of the West*, must always take into account: (1) comparison; (2) broader patterns of interaction, derivation and interdependence; and (3) the long term. Comparison teaches us that phenomena formerly characterized as uniquely Western are often present in other forms in different regions and periods. A good example is the 'Smithian' market economy led by an 'invisible hand'. Highly developed forms of market economy existed elsewhere (like China, the Islamic world, sub-Sahara Africa etc.) yet this did not result in 'modern' industrial and political revolutions.

   In addition to these variations in development paths, world history must also study the interaction between them. The new capitalist trade and production system was not national; it was European, trans-Atlantic and later global. It developed in a geographically- and socially-unequal world. World historians like Pomeranz subscribe to this line of thinking by pointing to the crucial role of the periphery (America) in the European industrialization process. England would never have been able to concentrate on the large-scale fabrication of industrial products without the import of land-intensive goods (agriculture). These industrial products were then partially sold in that same periphery.

   The most extreme position is taken by 'New Orientalists' like A. G. Frank who believe the West was only able to acquire a place of any significance in the early modern world economy thanks to precious metals from the Americas and via trade relations with Asia. Once it acquired a place, international competition and differences in comparative costs forced the West to produce goods more cheaply. It did this by industrializing during a relative 'decline of the East', when the Asian empires experienced huge problems. Orientalists see this European domination as a transitional phase, followed by a new Asian supremacy as of the twenty-first century.

However, it does not suffice to only look for a 'world of similarities' as a reaction to the Eurocentric 'world of differences'. The sixteenth to nineteenth centuries created an extremely unequal world, with a clear economic and political superiority in Europe and the West. We need to understand how the major differences were able to grow in a time of increasing interactions.

## What about Africa?

Up to now, Africa has only played a very modest role in the story of *The Great Divergence*. This continent was also incorporated in the global trade system from the sixteenth century, but almost exclusively as a supplier of cheap labour and later of cheap raw materials. Africa moved literally in the margin of the new world system. With a 20 per cent share of surface area, the continent's share of the world population fell drastically, from 19 per cent in 1500 to 11 per cent in 1800 and 8 per cent in 1900. This share is growing once again, to 13 per cent in 2000 and an estimated 20 per cent by 2050. This relative population decline is symbolic of the marginalization of Africa's economic position. Rough estimates indicate that the wealth per inhabitant (GNP per capita) were equal in Africa and Western Europe around 1000 CE. Afterwards, the ratios changed dramatically. Western Europeans were, on average, twice as rich in 1500, five times as rich in 1900 and 13 times as rich in 2000.

It looks like this de facto marginalization coincided with very little interest in the continent from a global perspective. When the history of Africa over the last millennium is discussed in a global context, it is almost always in a negative story: the slave trade, colonization and decolonization, internal conflicts, hunger and AIDS. In scenarios relating to the twenty-first century (in which Asia and China are prominent), Africa has hardly played a role (up to now).

Colonization has also colonized the history of Africa. However, as an actor, Africa can teach world history a lot, such as:

1   the successful process of internal colonization, by hunter-gatherers, by herders and farmers (Bantu migration); the development of more complex cultures and state systems;
2   processes of regional integration, with the development of regional trade and production systems (examples include West Africa and the Swahili coast); linking these regional systems to international networks like West Africa to North Africa and the east coast to the Arab world; increased cultural contacts via the spread of Islam;
3   the process of global integration, first on an extensive basis (gold, slaves) and later in an intensive manner (colonization);

4   the process of peripheralization, of marginalization within the global economy; new forms of social and economic organization to absorb the consequences of this.

In other words, the history of Africa in a global perspective confronts us with every aspect of the human journey, both positive and negative.

# 8   A global world

## Globalization or globalizations?

The Persian traveler, author and poet Sa'di wrote a collection of poems and stories entitled *Gulistan* (*The Rose Garden*, 1259 CE). The stories tell us about the cosmopolitan West Asian world in the thirteenth century.

Sa'di writes about a meeting with a merchant who was travelling with 150 camels laden with freight and 40 slaves and servants. The merchant was planning his last trip:

> I will transport Persian sulphur to China, because I heard that I will get a high price for it there. Then I will sell Chinese porcelain in Rum [Anatolia], and brocade from Rum in India, Indian hardware in Aleppo, glassware from Aleppo in Yemen, and striped Yemeni fabrics in Persia. After that I will stop trading and establish a shop.

In the thirteenth and fourteenth centuries, the Mongolian empire (one of the largest empires ever) stretched from China in the east to the Balkans in the west, and from Siberia in the north to Tibet in the south. The *Pax Mongolica* ensured strongly expanding trade on the silk routes from east to west. Caravans brought silk, cotton, pearls, jewellery and spices to the west, and silver, linen and horses to the east. People, ideas and techniques travelled over the Eurasian continent together with the goods. A maritime silk route also flourished from the Chinese Sea over the Indian Ocean to the Persian Gulf and the Red Sea. Indian cotton clothing, famous for its colours, quality and variation, was one of the most important commodities. The goods were shipped from flourishing trading cities on the Asian coasts, magnets for European merchants in later centuries.

In its most essential form, globalization stands for the expansion of trade and interaction. Some people look for the roots of contemporary globalization early in world history, especially in the growth of Afro-Eurasian trade networks. Others look at European expansion via new, overseas trade routes as of the sixteenth century, which grafted on to flourishing commercial networks in the east. The number of trade ships from Europe to Asia increased from 770 in the sixteenth century to 6,660 in the eighteenth century. 'Global' commodities such as slaves, silver, sugar, spices and fur galvanized the new expansive trade system.

Present-day world history or global history is sometimes translated as the history of globalization. But what does globalization mean and how can it be studied?

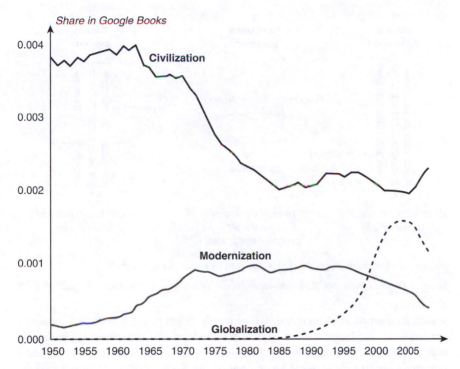

*Figure 8.1* The popularity of the concepts civilization, modernization and globalization, 1950–2008.

Note: An analysis of the use of the terms civilization, modernization and globalization in Google Books shows that the concept of civilization lost out to modernization as of the 1960s, and that modernization partially became a victim of the success of the concept globalization in the 1990s. We also see that after quick growth, the concept globalization started to lose popularity around 2003–2004 (together with a small revival of the term civilization).

The enormous popularity of the concept sometimes makes us forget that globalization is a neologism, popularized in the 1980s as a reference to the accelerated internationalization of the financial sector. In the 1990s, globalization became a buzzword, an umbrella term used to label the social transitions in the last quarter of the twentieth century. Globalization developed into a generalized container term that aimed to unite all the historical processes of increasing interaction and interconnection. This chapter further examines what we mean by globalization and, specifically, the historical scope of the concept. What does world history teach us about globalization, and is it a useful concept for denoting social changes?

## Looking for a definition

In general, the concept globalization refers to the world becoming 'smaller' or, in more scholarly terms, to a compression of time and place. Globalization implies a

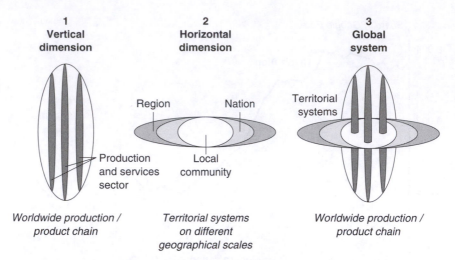

*Figure 8.2* The dimensions of interconnection in a globalizing economy.

Source: P. Dicken, *Global shift: Reshaping the global economic map in the 21st century*, Sage, 2003, p. 22.

systematic reduction of boundaries. It primarily refers to the blurring of economic borders and to the larger scale of markets for goods, capital and labour. Globalization was first used in this sense in *The Economist* in 1959. The concept experienced a breakthrough 30 years later, after the fall of the Berlin Wall and the commercial expansion of the Internet in 1989. In subsequent years, both events seemed to create a new world in which economic boundaries fell and other 'flows' of knowledge, information, ideas, values and beliefs became broader and more intense. This shrinking of the world is the seemingly paradoxical consequence of a growth process in which more and more interpersonal connections develop on an ever-growing scale. Contemporary globalization indicates the 'terminus' of this growth process: expanding markets and flows will eventually cover the earth's entire surface. Classic examples of this globalization process include increased human mobility and improved communication worldwide. Both examples immediately point to the importance of technological support for this process with regard to transport (aeroplanes, high-speed trains) and communication (the Internet, mobile phone networks).

According to Peter Dicken (2003), globalization means the integration of a horizontal (space) and vertical (production systems) expansion. Globalization is more than increased interaction (more forms of interaction, higher speed and more volume). The concept also refers to the growing impact of these contacts on social life and individual lives. One of the most popular images of globalization is that of 'the world, my village', or of a placeless world where geography (place) becomes less determinate compared to the 'global space' in which contacts take place. Once again, electronic media offer a striking illustration. The Internet in particular seems to bear the promise of a 'global village' in which everyone can develop a virtual identity while connecting with other 'internauts', in addition to the identity formed within local social networks. Contacts within cyberspace are real but less tangible. They connect people across continents via an interface, never directly face to face.

Globalization deals with interactional expansion and the increased impact of this interaction on social life and individual lives. The questions are: to what degree and why? Can we measure how much interaction and impact have increased? Can we explain why interaction and impact have increased? Regarding the measurement of interaction, a group of academics led by David Held (Held *et al.* 1999) showed that globalization can be measured in four dimensions:

1   extensity: the extensiveness of networks;
2   intensity: the intensification of relations and social contacts;
3   velocity: the speed of flows and contacts;
4   impact: the impact of interconnections.

Increased globalization implies an expansion, compacting, acceleration and a greater impact of connections and networks, up to a global level. If the four dimensions accumulate high scores then we use the term *thick globalization*. *Thin globalization* means that a spatial growth of networks is not combined with a significantly greater intensity, speed and impact. Many view Christopher Columbus' fleet setting sail in 1492 as the start of the first wave of globalization. Its speed was much slower and the scale was less extensive than the globalization offensive during the imperialistic 'scrambles' in the last quarter of the nineteenth century. The difficulty in measuring globalization has generated considerable controversy amongst scientists when assessing past and present social transformations. This applies a fortiori when discussing the last two decades, the period that started with the fall of the Berlin Wall and during which the concept of globalization created a furore.

## Globalization as a battleground

Globalization is a multidimensional concept incorporating economic, social, political and cultural processes. Globalization is a scientific concept ('what'), an ideological concept ('why') and a human process ('how'). Consequently, the concept of globalization and its interpretation is a battlefield. It is primarily about whether contemporary globalization is, in fact, new. There are three differing opinions.

*Hyperglobalists* emphasize the unique character of the current era. That value judgment is primarily determined by looking at the impact of globalization on the state. The idea is that states have a subordinate role to play in the new globalizing world. The global economy is then defined as the domain that determines the rules that states must comply with. Since money and companies are increasingly mobile, and states are not, logic dictates that states do everything they can to keep that money and those companies within their borders. In order to levy taxes, states must reduce taxes and develop fiscal and legal regimens that companies can trust and that are more favourable than regimens abroad. According to pessimists, globalization does away with the welfare state and social democracy – twentieth century national processes par excellence. Optimists point out that states are a historical relic because they are maladjusted to new, globalizing conditions.

According to them, a reduction of globalization cannot be the solution, not only since this is considered impossible, but also because national tensions are expected to disappear due to more intensive contacts between different cultures. That way, a 'global community' can be the motor towards a better and more equal world.

*Sceptics* do not believe in the alleged revolutionary character of contemporary globalization and have several arguments to support this. First, globalization is not new; long-distance trade and cultural exchange go far back in time. Second, many of these processes, both past and present, should not be interpreted as globalization but as regionalization. Creation of the European Union demonstrates this. The mobility of people and goods within Europe has clearly increased, accelerated and improved. At the same time, the mobility of people seeking a new and better life in Europe has actively been obstructed. Third, sceptics do not believe in the disappearance of the state as a regulating and organizing institution. All supranational or multinational institutions, including the United Nations, the World Bank and the World Trade Organization, exist merely by the grace of wide national support. Moreover, large states like the United States of America, Russia and China still play first fiddle internationally on geopolitical and economic levels.

*Transformationalists* choose a middle-of-the-road position. According to them, current globalization creates new economic, political and social circumstances, but it is not clear how this will affect the power of states. It is important to note that transformationalists see globalization as a historical process that changes over time. Contemporary globalization is therefore not completely new; it differs substantially from earlier phases of global acceleration. They also emphasize that globalization has an unequal impact on different parts of the world.

These different positions on the uniqueness and impact of the globalization process are not merely academic, they are also politically relevant. It is clear that the depiction of globalization as an irreversible social transformation that erodes the power of states and increases the power of companies and individuals has important consequences on political action and analysis. In several books, the influential intellectual Thomas Friedman has emphasized that individuals and states have no other choice than to adapt to the new global condition. Other intellectuals question the conceptualization of globalization as an irreversible process. This was translated into criticism of neoliberal political formulas, internationally propagated as the Washington Consensus. That neoliberal doctrine from the 1980s and 1990s championed privatization, deregulation and liberalization. According to critics, this would mostly lead to weaker states and a loss of political autonomy with regard to companies and wider financial interests. Therefore, the cause of this loss of political autonomy should not be sought in an anonymous, passive process of globalization, but in the active neoliberal formulas that are legitimized by the idea of irreversible globalization. This is an important criticism that was developed by the so-called anti-globalization movements at the end of the 1990s. Prominent voices within the movement, such as Naomi Klein, Noreena Hertz and David Korten, evaluate globalization as a discourse that supports the growth of multinational enterprises, legitimizes the drive for profit as a business principle, and allows wealth to prevail over the common good. From this point of view, globalization stands for capitalist growth and the 'westernization' of the world, two processes that are considered undesirable, but not a matter-of-course or irreversible.

The ideological battle over the interpretation and appreciation of globalization shows how careful scientists must be when dealing with the concept. Globalization cannot be a veiled concept for a combination of social transitions. That would cause the term to lose all meaning. This risk has ensured that nowadays scientists approach the concept of globalization much more cautiously and has resulted in diminished popularity of the concept. If we want to retain the concept, then it must offer explanations and reveal diverse interests in the process. In this battle to define globalization, a historical perspective might introduce new insights. In that case, the following questions must be answered:

1    When did the process of globalization start? What scale and intensity of interactions is needed in order to speak of globalization?
2    Did the historical process of globalization progress steadily or in waves? Are there periods in the history of globalization?
3    What is contemporary globalization's place in the historical story? What are the similarities; what is new? How unique is contemporary globalization?

## Searching for the historical roots of globalization

This brings us to the 'why' behind globalization. Why is there an expansion, a compacting, an acceleration and a greater impact on global connections and networks? We have already mentioned the direct role of new technological revolutions, primarily those in transportation and communication. Yet these revolutions did not come about in a social vacuum. Globalization is also – and perhaps mainly – an active process supported by diverse social actors with their own agendas and strategies. The most important actors include multinational companies, capital investment groups, states and political institutions, cultural-religious movements, and international pressure groups such as the anti-globalization movement. Individuals also play a major role by actively using technological capabilities in the 'globalization' of their social networks.

If we want to understand globalization as an active process, we need to ask 'when', as well as 'why'. Since globalization is a process, the search for its roots and reasoning are, by definition, a historical study. To ask about the beginning of the process of globalization is of primary importance in world history. The answer helps determine the way that past and present are connected together.

Academic literature includes the following four options. We will explore each of them briefly:

- globalization is 5000 years old (since the origin of the great civilizations);
- globalization is 500 years old (since the origin of a Western world system);
- globalization is 150 years old (since the spread of the Industrial Revolution);
- globalization is 30 years old (since the crisis of the 1970s and 1980s).

*Globalization is 5000 years old*

This approach departs from a neutral model: globalization as a 'self-sustaining' process of increased contacts between population groups, or more metaphorically, as a compacting of the 'human web'. Growing technological capabilities are the motor (hydropower, wind power, navigation, steam, electricity, etc.). In this interpretation, the process of globalization coincides with the 'history of civilization', and has little explanatory power as a concept.

*Globalization is 500 years old*

This approach holds that the origins of globalization coincide with the origins of historical capitalism, of a new world system that grew out of Europe. As Karl Marx expressed it:

> The discovery of gold and silver in America, the extermination of the indigenous population of that continent in the mines, the beginnings of the conquest and plunder of the East Indies, and the conversion of Africa into a preserve for the commercial hunting of black-skins, are all things which characterize the dawn of the era of capitalist production. These idyllic proceedings are the chief moments of primitive accumulation. On their heels follows the commercial war of the European nations, with the globe for a theatre.

Others summarize it thus: the global economy originated in combination with the European 'discoveries' and a global market for silver.

This new, modern world system is an expansive social system that grew out of a unique combination of the rise of commercial capitalism together with the growth of the European inter-state system and colonial expansion. The system was dominated by Europe and it rivalled other regional systems (the Ottoman empire, Mughal India, China, sub-Saharan Africa, Central America, the Incan empire). Over time, it incorporated all these imperial systems, and became a truly globally-integrated system by the nineteenth century. This globalization was not a neutral process; it was an outcome of the aggressive expansion of one specific world system. The motor of this expansion was the economic growth of capitalism, and the most important fuel was the constant search for cheap labour, cheap raw materials and new markets. That economic expansion coincided with a very specific logic of territorial expansion that was shaped within a two-fold arena:

1   A battle in the core of the system: the battle for hegemony. After competition and struggle, the core shifted from Northern Italy in the fifteenth century to Holland in the seventeenth to eighteenth centuries, then to Great Britain in the nineteenth century and finally to the United States in the twentieth century.
2   A battle in the periphery: the battle for colonies. Started in the sixteenth century by the Spanish and Portuguese empires, the seventeenth- and eighteenth-century battle was mostly fought by Holland, France and England. The climax of the colonial race took place in the nineteenth century. Formal decolonization

followed in the twentieth century under the impulse of the new hegemon (the United States), but with a new global battle for spheres of influence in the context of the Cold War.

This economic and political-territorial expansion was legitimized by a new, universalist discourse in which values like civilization and modernization were passed on as universal.

### Globalization is 150 years old

In this view, a global world only erupted in the nineteenth century, after the successful Industrial Revolution in Europe. The European development model only became the universal standard in this century. The idea that modernization can only succeed after breaking with one's own past, via several societal revolutions, fed a new belief in progress. Successful economic and political-social revolutions buoyed the self-image of the West with key words like progress, technology, rationalization. New universalism was summarized in the motto of the French Revolution: 'Liberty, equality, fraternity'.

These changes also sparked new contrasts, which were less prominent in the discourse of progress-optimism: labour versus capital, individualism versus greater government control, patriarchy versus individual emancipation (for women and children), democratic principles versus social exploitation, universalism versus racism and inequality. The economic and territorial growth of nineteenth-century Europe was prompted by strong British hegemony. After the Industrial Revolution, Great Britain became the 'workshop of the world'; it controlled large parts of the earth and, by extension, the oceans (as 'ruler of the waves'). The influence of Great Britain and Europe waned toward the last quarter of the nineteenth century. The economic epicentre slowly shifted across the Atlantic Ocean, and increased tension within the European core and periphery (the colonies) resulted in two destructive world wars in the first half of the twentieth century.

The rapid processes of change as of the 1870s are often viewed as the momentum of the 'first' large wave of globalization. This wave had four important components. The first is a new cycle of imperialistic expansion. This was a consequence of growing competition between European nations. Around 1900, Europe's direct grip on the world was greater than ever due to the colonial scramble. The second component is the wave of foreign investment spurred by economic stagnation of the Industrial Revolution in Europe (with infrastructure projects all over the world). The third is the rise of multinational companies that established branches abroad (especially German and American companies). The final component is the implementation of technical innovations in the area of transport (steamboats and later the automobile), communication (telegraph, telephone), and the development of infrastructure all over the world (rail networks, tram lines, canal links like the Suez and Panama Canals).

World War I abruptly halted this global expansion. The decades after World War I, with a major crisis in the 1930s and increasing nationalism, fuelled a process of 'de-globalization'. The years after 1945 launched a long phase of unseen economic expansion. It was sustained by a huge growth in world trade, but was mainly the result of the construction and reconstruction of national economies (recovery of Europe, rise of the Eastern bloc, and the independence of former colonies). For a new phase in globalization, we must wait for a new world crisis.

### Globalization is 30 years old

This vision argues that recent global shifts (since the 1970s) are unique and not comparable with earlier processes of increasing interconnection. The major difference is that in the past, contacts took place within a politically fragmented world, between states. States (or other political units such as empires or cultures) remained the basic scale, but sometimes the relations between them intensified. In this vision, the state was increasingly omitted as a basic link in the global system at the end of the twentieth century, resulting in supranational systems. A distinction can be made between the processes of:

- Internationalization: since the creation of national states. This means increasing contact between states without these states losing power and influence, quite the contrary. The growth of international trade as of the sixteenth century fits in this concept.
- Multinationalization: since the end of the nineteenth century with the development of multinational companies. Companies were increasingly organized across national borders. As a result, flows of goods and capital were increasingly controlled by companies rather than by states. These companies still operated within the international state system (with parent companies and branches).
- Globalization: since the end of the twentieth century with increased worldwide flows of capital and information without state intervention. Money and goods become stateless; products become 'made in the world'. Decisions are no longer traceable or coordinated geographically. National politics have lost their grip on the economy.

The new phase of globalization was preceded by an unprecedented increase in world trade, which grew by a factor of 40 between 1970 and 2010. This was twice as fast as total global production. The share of trade in the total GNP was 50 per cent at the beginning of the twentieth century, compared to 25 per cent in the 1960s.

The breakthrough of this globalization is generally linked to a new crisis in historical capitalism. Since the middle of the 1970s, capital flows have been increasingly detached from the 'production sphere' and oriented towards financial investments and speculation (stock markets). The mobility of capital has been increasing quickly, just as in the late nineteenth century.

This financialization of capital is linked to a neoliberal political revolution in the Western world in which deregulation became the new motto. First, there was economic deregulation, which amplified pressure on the twentieth-century social welfare

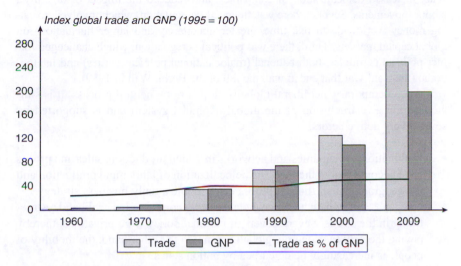

*Figure 8.3* The growth of global trade and global GNP, 1960–2009.

Source: *World Bank World Development Indicators* (http://data.worldbank.org/data-catalog/world-development-indicators).

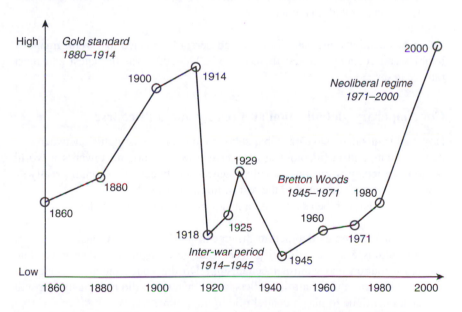

*Figure 8.4* A stylized picture of the mobility of capital between 1860 and 2000.

Source: R. Kaplinsky, *Globalization, poverty and inequality: Between a rock and a hard place*, Polity Press, 2005, p. 24.

state, increased delocalization of companies, and reduced the impact of organized labour movements. Second, there was financial deregulation, which involved investing money worldwide in real time, greater uncertainty and larger fluctuations on global capital markets. Third, there was political deregulation, which challenged former political certitudes, both national (major national political parties) and international (the Cold War that ended with the fall of the Berlin Wall in 1989).

This contemporary, neoliberal globalization is not a neutral process. It is situated within a restructuring of the global capitalist system and is supported by several very active actors.

- Multinational companies and networks in which production, sales and profits have become global themes. The delocalization of labour and production and the geographical shifting of profits has become a daily business strategy.
- National states, which became wholeheartedly committed to neoliberal restructuring in the 1980s. Several levers of national policy were privatized, thereby paving the way to economic globalization. On the other hand, the mobility of people is increasingly being curbed by nation states.
- A new technological, digital revolution has increased the speed of information exchange as well as of capital and digital goods.
- Capital owners have been sending more money than ever around the world, searching for new profit. Most of this capital is detached from the 'real production sphere', in other words detached from investments in production. The concentration of massive amounts of money in insurance and retirement funds accelerated this process.

These accelerations, increases in scale and deregulations led to several financial bubbles and economic crises; the crisis of 2008–2009 was the latest and most intense to date.

## Contemporary globalization as a reality and a discourse

How real is this new wave of globalization? How do we distinguish between real developments and an ideological discourse? Are we moving towards a world without borders, towards one global village? Is the twenty-first century really so new and different compared to the rest of human history?

Questions that can be asked from a historical perspective include:

1   Are national states doomed to disappear, and will international and global institutions assume political power? Can new institutions take over state redistribution and control mechanisms? Do they have enough democratic support? Can they control conflicts better than states did previously? Or will states continue to play a central role in the future?
2   Is there a trend of cultural homogenization? Is globalization equal to the Internet revolution and 'Coca-Colonization'? Or is there a backlash in the form of new cultural identity movements, including nationalism and fundamentalism?

3    Does globalization blur borders? This seems to be true for information, capital and, to a lesser extent, goods and services. Yet new borders are being erected for people and labour, how is this compatible?

4    Does globalization result in more Americanization? Does this confirm the dominance of the United States on a political-military, financial and cultural level? Or is American hegemony waning and the new global world becoming the battleground for new global (economic, political-military) conflicts?

5    Many questions can be reduced to the contrast between convergence and divergence. Does globalization stand for a more unified world, with smaller differences and more equality (convergence)? Or are we growing apart in this 'smaller' world (divergence)? If so, can those differences be reduced to economic inequality, or are new cultures/civilizations developing that will inevitably clash?

It is clear that contemporary globalization stands for a new acceleration in societal processes. It is also clear that this does not automatically lead to a more equal and peaceful world. Since globalization is an active process, choices largely determine what the future world will look like. This controversy is being debated in four major domains, in four contemporary arenas. The question is always: how can new balances be found?

1    A new balance between diverse political blocks. Globalization does not seem to lead to a homogenous global governance. A battle between old and new core powers is not out of the question. Regional blocs, such as the triad North America, Europe, Southeast Asia, are reinforcing their ties. Former third-world countries like China, India and Brazil are working their way up, and others are slipping further away. The gap between poor and rich seems to be getting bigger.

2    A new balance between politics and the economy. Over the past decades, political power has lost much of its hold on the economy and capital. The recent financial crisis made clear that the markets need control, regulation and political stability.

3    A new balance between politics, the economy and the aspirations of social groups. The twentieth-century societal model resulted in a strong increase in prosperity and more political participation in the West (a more inclusive system). The challenge is to develop this on a world level. This assumes income redistribution on a global scale, and a new balance between the growing aspirations of social groups and the boundaries of the ecological system.

4    A new balance between the rich West and the poorer non-West. Ever larger differences in a global society where information and knowledge have no boundaries inevitably lead to an explosive situation.

We can summarize the above as follows. First, globalization is not a neutral concept. It refers to the expansion of a specific economic and social model. Globalization has been an ideological lever for reducing national regulation and control in favour of more international economic mobility. Second, globalization is a historical story. Globalization is not new. It has its roots in the first expansion of the new, capitalist world system. This world has experienced several phases of globalization; the most important being the colonial and commercial expansion during the sixteenth century, the industrial and imperialist expansion in the late nineteenth century, and the global financial expansion in the late twentieth century. Globalization stands for consecutive acceleration phases in the development of the capitalist world system. At the same time, globalization does not work in one direction because it is both a fact and an ideological concept. Processes of scaling down and of compacting coincide with trends of fragmentation and divergence. That paradox of contemporary globalization is one of the greatest challenges of today and tomorrow.

# 9 A polarized world

## Development, poverty and inequality

A remarkable, worldwide campaign against global poverty was launched in 2005 entitled 'Make Poverty History'. The campaign peaked during a massive march at the G8 summit in Edinburgh, Scotland. The main goal of the campaign was to remind world leaders about their promise to take fundamental steps, in the short term, to combat extreme poverty in the world. These global promises are called the Millennium Goals. The international community, unified in the General Assembly of the United Nations, formulated eight development goals in 2000 to cut worldwide poverty in half, compared to 1990 levels, by 2015. Developing countries promised to make an effort in these areas and developed countries promised to make enough money available to realize the goals.

The goals are (http://www.un.org/millenniumgoals):

1 Halve, between 1990 and 2015, the number of people living in extreme poverty.
2 Ensure that, by 2015, all children in the world go to primary school.
3 Eliminate gender disparity in primary and secondary education by 2005, and in all levels of education by 2015.
4 Reduce by two thirds, between 1990 and 2015, the under-five mortality rate.
5 Reduce by three quarters, between 1990 and 2015, the maternal mortality ratio.
6 Halt the spread of HIV/AIDS, malaria and other diseases by 2015.
7 Integrate the principles of sustainable development into country policies and programmes by 2015. Halt the irreversible loss of environmental resources. Halve, by 2015, the proportion of the population without access to safe drinking water, and by 2020 achieve a significant improvement in the lives of at least 140 million slum dwellers.
8 Develop a global partnership for development, with agreements about good governance, about the development of an open and fair trading and financial system, about a solution for solving the debt problems, and about the transfer of new technologies.

The millennium goals prove that there is a worldwide consensus to make the fight against poverty a priority. However, a lot of criticism has been leveled at the Millennium Goals. They are called minimal, selective and too strongly oriented towards quantities. They do not take into account the possible discrimination and exclusion of certain people or groups, which enables inequality to grow. More importantly, the fundamental political and economic causes of the poverty problem are not mentioned. The Millennium Goals do not specify that the world's natural resources must be divided more fairly by 2015.

## Poverty on the international agenda

Poverty is high on the international agenda today. Poverty has become the central concept within development thinking by supranational institutions such as the United Nations and the World Bank. Since the 1990s, they have stressed what they call the worldwide fight against multidimensional poverty.

Closely associated with the United Nations Millennium Project is Jeffrey Sachs, development economist and advisor to the International Monetary Fund, the World Bank, the United Nations and other organizations. His book, *The End of Poverty* (Sachs 2005), is a passionate plea that supports the Millennium Project. The book's central thesis is that the poor living in developing countries are in a vicious circle, a poverty trap. The financial resources necessary to neutralize this are present, but collaboration and political courage are lacking. Developing countries have bad economies, health issues (malaria, AIDS), poor infrastructure, bad educational systems, difficult climates etc. Sachs expressed strong criticism of organizations like the IMF and the World Bank, which concentrated on one-sided market principles and trade impediments for a long time. He argues that extreme poverty can be fought by giving people on the bottom rung of the development ladder a boost. Once there is movement, the economy will do the rest. As long as the poor produce less than they need to stay alive, they will never get out of the downward spiral.

The most important criticism of this international focus on poverty is that poverty is equated with a lack of progress. This 'remaining behind' is primarily the consequence of a development impasse in poorer regions. Critics argue that people are primarily poor because they are deprived of the means to support themselves. They are poor because they live in an unequal world. European and North American prosperity is, in their eyes, largely based on resources that were removed from Asia, Africa and Latin America. Consequently, poverty is not the initial stage of human progress that one needs to escape, but the final stage when lopsided development destroys the ecological and social systems of subsistence. People are only poor when they do not have the money to pay for basic facilities, no matter what their income is. In this vision, poverty can only be ended by deactivating the system that robs the poor of their shared resources, livelihood and incomes. In other words, before we can make poverty history, we must first rectify the history of poverty, and this is only possible with more equitable global relations.

*Poverty* cannot be separated from *inequality*, the unequal distribution of poverty and wealth across the entire population. Processes of growing inequality are called *social polarization*. Which shifts have occurred over time?

We need to define these concepts before they can be debated. We do this by briefly analyzing the modern debate about poverty and inequality. Then one of the most pressing questions in world history can be posed: in its millennia-long history, why was humankind not able to banish poverty and inequality from the world?

## Measuring poverty

Over the past two decades, the discussion about global progress and development has become more focused on the fight against (extreme) poverty. This was an important shift in development thinking. It no longer aimed at national development, but rather at individual development. From the 1950s to the 1970s, development thinking departed from the idea of national progress (modernization). From the 1980s this was replaced with a new, two-fold ambition: an integrated world market on the one hand and a local fight against poverty on the other. The role of the state has been limited to implementing plans devised by supranational organizations. An open economic climate that can attract investments and capital flows must be prevalent in order to boost economic growth. In the first instance, that means macro-economic stability. In development thinking, the sovereignty of the state has given way to sovereignty of the market and of individuals.

This sovereignty entailed greater responsibility for the individual. Social policy should not protect people from market risks but help them participate in the market. Within the model of the welfare state, risks are no longer socialized; they are privatized and individualized. The poverty problem is currently seen as the rich world's greatest burden, a modern *Rich Man's Burden*.

Since the international market is considered a solution for poverty, it cannot be viewed as the cause of poverty. Barriers that obstruct access to international markets, such as a lack of education, the presence of epidemics, wars, unstable regimes, gender inequality, certain cultural norms etc. are the major problems. Poverty is then eliminated indirectly by combating these barriers directly. This vision has far-reaching consequences. Measures that reform the market and redistribute incomes are inconceivable from this point of view.

To be able to work with a quantifiable instrument, poverty is usually converted into an absolute income criterion such as the almost-symbolic threshold of $1 or $2 per day. The success of poverty reduction is then measured by the number of people that cross this threshold. According to World Bank figures, the number of people that must survive on less than $1 per day has fallen from 40 per cent of the world population in 1981 to 16 per cent (less than one billion) in 2005. One in every two world citizens must get by with less than $2.50 per day. Regional differences remain huge. The decline is almost entirely due to the strong performances of China and, to a lesser degree, India.

Academics are diligently looking for a more integrated definition of poverty, one that includes social exclusion, discrimination, health and illiteracy. The *human development index* (HDI) is an attempt to bring clarity to the multidimensional concept of poverty. HDI is an international standard that includes indicators about

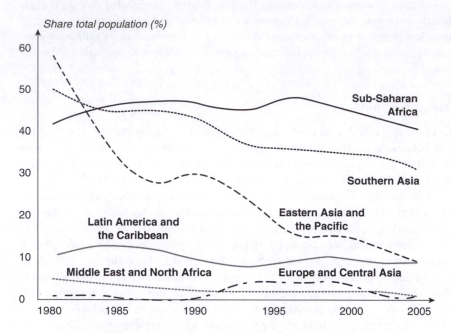

*Figure 9.1* Population with less than 1 dollar per day, 1981–2005.

Source: *World Bank World Development Indicators* (http://data.worldbank.org/data-catalog/world-development-indicators).

health, education and economic welfare (see the annual *Human Development Report*) for almost every member country of the United Nations.

The strategic use of the concept of poverty is not new. Throughout history, poverty has always been an ideological battleground in which the poor were frequently unrecognizable. The way that we 'see' and approach poverty is the result of social preferences and political imagery disseminated by those who are not poor. At the beginning of the twentieth century, sociologist Georg Simmel phrased it very radically: poverty reduction always answers the needs of the non-poor. The poor themselves are not the real goal.

In historical research, processes of impoverishment and enrichment are studied in relative terms, in relation to the social constitution of the population. The income is related to the cost of living; this gives an impression of the purchasing power and standard of living of diverse population groups. It remains a difficult and risky exercise, especially since the income level and composition of individuals and families are hardly known.

There have been big differences between rich and poor in every civilization and culture. At the same time, it is generally assumed that the regional differences between civilizations before 1500 and even 1800 were much smaller than after 1800. Anthropometric indicators such as mortality rate, life expectancy and physical height do not show divergent tendencies. The same is true of real wages and family incomes; those differences became substantially greater only after 1800. The standard of living primarily depended on agricultural output until the nineteenth century. In the 'organic regime', the standard of living could rise via processes of intensification, but only gradually and within margins. Agricultural yields differed strongly within the same civilization areas, but the richest centres were comparable.

## From poverty to inequality

In the contemporary discourse about poverty, social inequality is a largely blind spot. The degree of poverty says nothing about the extent that poverty (or wealth) is spread within a society. The following example illustrates this. Imagine that the richest 5 per cent of people in a society earn $450 on average per capita, and the poorest 5 per cent earn $50. Let us assume that the GNP doubles and, consequently, so does everyone's income. The differences are no longer $450 compared to $50 but $900 to $100. The relative ratio remains nine to one, but the income gap in absolute figures rises from $400 to $800. Therefore, inequality has a relative and an absolute side. If we assume an absolute poverty line of $60 then our example evolves from a society with 5 per cent poverty to a society without poverty even though absolute inequality has increased. This shows that the debate about poverty and inequality cannot be grasped in one or even just a few absolute indicators. The effects of economic growth can even be paradoxical, with less (absolute) poverty but with more (relative) inequality.

Despite an exponential increase in wealth, income inequality on a world scale seems to have grown strongly in the past two centuries. The richest 20 per cent of the population controlled about 60 per cent of the total wealth in 1820, about 70 per cent in 1950 and up to 85 per cent in 2010. The poorest 20 per cent of the population today can only claim less than 1.5 per cent of the total wealth. The growth of income inequality over the past 30 years is striking. Due to a stronger redistribution in rich countries, the share of total wealth of the one per cent highest incomes has fallen from 15 to 20 per cent in the first half of the twentieth century to 5 to 10 per cent in 1950–1980. This share of total wealth increased again after 1980 to more than 15 per cent worldwide and up to 25 per cent in the United States.

Inequality did not disappear with the advent of the modern world, quite the contrary. Social and economic differences that have been present since our earliest agricultural societies are being further deepened. These differences are a consequence of unequal access to wealth, anchored in social and political power relations. That access to social resources is delineated by group limits and demarcated according to gender, age, caste, class, race or ethnicity. One of the most important questions in world history is how and why human groups take on hierarchic forms and reinforce them. Social differences are ascribed to social origin or individual competence. They are expressed via ideas (ideology) and material wealth. Social differences are institutionalized via unequal access to the yields of land and labour; they are anchored in social, economic and political hierarchies.

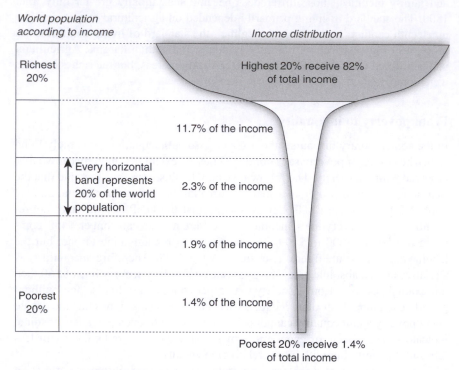

*Figure 9.2* Global income distribution in 1992.

Source: *Human Development Report 1992* (United Nations Development Program).

The expansion of large empires and civilizations resulted in increased economic exploitation by denying large groups free access to land and labour, amongst others via different forms of serfdom. These discrepancies intensified with the spread of large-scale systems of.indentured servitude in the modern world system after 1500. New forms of slavery, colonization and imperialism created new categories of subordinate social groups. Inequality was justified in new, racist-inspired world views. Many forms of formal inequality based on sex and descent were reduced or eliminated in the twentieth century. However, global economic inequality remained high at the beginning of the twenty-first century.

Inequality exists in multiple, often overlapping, forms. Three major areas of tension can be identified: (1) gender – the inequality between men and women; (2) race/ethnicity – the inequality between different complexions or cultural identities; and (3) social class – the inequality between rich and poor. The question is whether a society can be broken down entirely along these patterns of inequality. To what extent are these forms of inequality separate from each other, or do they ratify each other? Is there a certain hierarchy? Is income inequality the prime mover for other forms of inequality? The rich get sick or depressed, but the chance that a poor person gets sick or depressed is even greater. That 'materialistic' vision is not new in sociology or economics. Jean-Jacques Rousseau saw the creation of private property as the cause of inequality in his book *Discours sur l'origine et les fondements de l'inégalité parmi les hommes* (*Discourse on the Origin and Basis of Inequality Among Men*, 1755). According to Rousseau, society is responsible for the maintenance of that inequality. A social contract is needed that gears private and public interests to one another. Karl Marx broadened Rousseau's insights. He defined the phenomena of alienation, impoverishment and income inequality as structural characteristics of a capitalist society. Differentiation becomes discrimination that is no longer situated between individuals but between social groups (classes). The insights of Rousseau and Marx were the start of a fundamental – and still relevant – debate about the causes and consequences of economic inequality. According to 'critical' tradition, inequality is not self-evident; it is a social product, an injustice that must be combated and prevented. Opponents switch this reasoning around. Inequality is unavoidable in a society that is held together by consensus, power, norms and values. Social inequality is also viewed as unconsciously applied by societies to ensure that the most important positions are filled by the most competent people. This emphasis on the inevitable and plural character of inequality does not take into account the contextual and power-based causes of social differences.

Despite the long debate about social inequality, the theories remain incomplete. Inequality is mainly seen as an economic reality between individuals or classes within one country and between countries. Authors like Paul Baran, Paul Sweezy and Raul Prebisch worked out the theory of underdevelopment in the 1950s and 1960s. According to them, there was an unequal distribution of economic surpluses between countries, which leads to a geographic division between peripheral and core countries. This was a reality as of the sixteenth century, and continued through the entire period of colonization and modern imperialism. These insights were a great source of inspiration for dependency theorists like Andre Gunder Frank, historians like Fernand Braudel and historical sociologists like Immanuel Wallerstein. Development and underdevelopment are seen as two sides of the same picture. They reflect a state's power to control its own imports and exports and to dictate those of other countries. The paradigms of *l'économie monde* and *world-system* continue to build on these insights. This historical vision introduced the concept of global polarization to the debate.

## From inequality to polarization

World history implies the study of social inequality in a broad spatial and chronological perspective. Have human societies become more prosperous over time? Does a richer world also imply a less unequal world? Central to this issue is the impact of an increasingly international division of labour on poverty and inequality. In order to understand the effects of social systems, we must do more than simply ascertain the cause of poverty or inequality. We need to show whether processes occur that perpetuate, enlarge or reduce poverty or inequality. Both the processes and the mechanisms behind them must be exposed. This is not easy. We still lack the basic tools to record poverty, inequality and social polarization in the long term and in a global perspective. Not only are the basic data often inadequate or non-existent, one must also study economic inequality within and between different scales (people, households, social groups, states, regions and economic zones). This is probably the most ambitious research agenda in world history. Moving the focus from the global society or world system to states, regions, classes, households and individuals results in the discovery of other forms and proportions of inequality. Then the questions arise as to how these scales relate to each other and to what extent they interact. To what degree is the inequality between regions determined by the inequality between countries or between individuals? The world historian Patrick Manning explains:

> One of the most striking contrasts in all of world history is the development, in the past two centuries, of a widespread ideology of social equality for citizens within nations and equality among nations, at a time when the economic inequality within nations and between nations has grown to unprecedented extremes. Social historians addressed this issue with studies of slavery and emancipation; economic historians have addressed it with studies of wage levels. Meanwhile the categories of class, community, family and ethnicity are each deserving of more thorough analysis at the world-historical level.

In Figure 9.3 we distinguish between inequality in countries and between countries based on the research of Branko Milanovic (2009). The vertical axis shows the Gini coefficient, an indicator of social inequality. A Gini coefficient of zero expresses perfect equality and a Gini coefficient of one expresses maximal inequality. We see a double movement until the 1980s. On the one hand, inequality within countries was pushed back. This was primarily a result of new redistribution systems in welfare societies that alleviated income differences as of the late nineteenth century. However, the inequality between countries increased dramatically. The distance between the regions that did well and those that did less well was still increasing, but at a slower tempo after 1950. As a result, global inequality has been growing due to the impact of growing international inequality. The trends seem to switch as of the 1980s. While the inequality between countries stopped increasing, the inequality within countries started to increase. This is explained by the rise of new emerging economies like China, India and Brazil (international inequality declines) and by the welfare state's decreasing grip (internal inequality grows). Global inequality remains just as high: 0.7 compared to a bit more than 0.4 in 1820. According to prudent estimates, the index of global inequality fluctuated between 0.3 and 0.4 between 1500 and 1800.

The changing composition of global inequality also alters the most important explanation for income differences between world citizens. At the beginning of the nineteenth century, two thirds of global inequality is explained by wealth differences within countries and only one third by inequality between countries. To determine someone's economic position, where they lived was less important

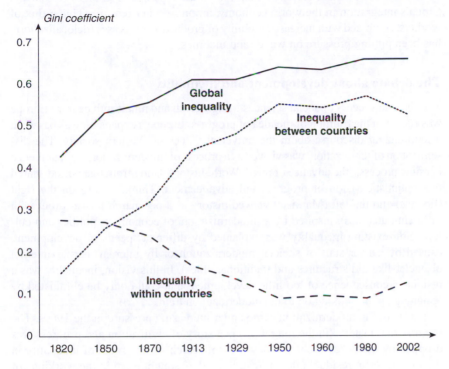

*Figure 9.3* Global inequality, 1820–2002.

Source: B. Milanovic, *Global inequality and global inequality extraction ratio: The story of the last two centuries*, 2009 (http://ideas.repec.org/p/wbk/wbrwps/5044.html).

than the social group they belonged to (free/indentured, man/woman, elite/working class). By the beginning of the twenty-first century, almost 90 per cent of the wealth differences between people are due to international inequality and a maximum of 15 per cent are due to internal social inequality. In other words, today, one's place of birth is by far the most important predictor for one's place on the global income ladder, much more so than one's class in the country of origin. Almost all inhabitants in rich countries are among the 40 per cent most prosperous world citizens, compared to only a small portion of population in poorer countries. More than ever, economic inequality is an international and a global responsibility.

Inequality has not been decreasing on a world scale. At the beginning of the nineteenth century, the most prosperous countries were about three times richer than the poorest countries. This difference increased to one hundred times at the beginning of the twenty-first century. The imbalance of power between capital and labour has been an important driving force. Globalization leads to a global redistribution of income in favour of capital owners at the expense of the working population. That is because the number of available workers worldwide has doubled since 1980 and currently stands at 3 billion people, a result of Russia and China's integration in the world economy, amongst other reasons. This influx of workers, combined with increased mobility of production processes (delocalization), has been putting pressure on wages and incomes.

## The debate about development and inequality

The rise and success of social sciences in eighteenth and nineteenth century Europe was rooted in the triumph of the idea of progress. Europe's expansion was based on a legitimizing discourse about the universal values of Western society. The dissemination of 'civilization' was viewed as a process of 'modernization', as a universal learning process: 'the advance of men'. World history dating from that period shared this optimistic vision of progress and advancement. Thinkers both on the right (liberals) and the left (Marxists) viewed history as a big march forward (but with different outcomes), inspired by a 'modernization' of economics, politics and culture. Still-existing inequality was explained by different speeds of development, caused by a later start of societal modernization or by internal inertia (internal obstacles like old structures and traditional elites). In this vision, inequality was a residue, a consequence of too little development that could only be eliminated by 'catching up' or hooking on to the modernization train.

This belief in modernization came under increasing pressure in the 1960s. The premise that history (in the long term) is a story of civilization and progress was dropped by many researchers. They did not search for the roots of inequality in the far past or in residual internal restraints; they sought them in the workings of new social models. In their view, the modern world system encourages new forms of inequality, primarily via unequal trade relations. More modernization, more integration, means more impoverishment for many parts of the world (outside the core), and therefore greater global inequality. Inequality is not viewed as a consequence of too little development, but of too much.

A third vision of inequality asserts that the causes are to be found in the loss of previous production and community structures. Once again, these researchers point to the current economic order. The thesis is that global capitalism destroys more autonomous and collective survival structures in time. This causes the loss of peasant agriculture (based on family farms), as well as an increasing pressure on the welfare state that was constructed in the twentieth century. The possibilities of (partial) self-sufficiency disappear without the creation of new, stable income perspectives or social security networks. The massive process of urbanization (a *planet of slums*) is the most visible component of this process. Collective facilities are also under growing pressure; this includes social services (education, health care, social security etc.) and ecological facilities (land, water etc.). These three visions still nurture the contemporary debate about globalization.

# 10  A fragmented world
## Unity and fragmentation

In Chapter 1, world history was described as a different way of looking, thinking and doing. World history strives to capture the big picture, but the big picture is not the entire story. So, how big is this picture? How big is this world? We speak about our own world, about the world of children, of music, the business world, lost world(s), the civilized world, or simply 'the world'. Since the concept 'world' can include almost every sphere of human interaction, it sometimes refers to the planet earth, the globe and to 'global'. Global means worldwide as well as complete, total. This semantic discussion points out the need to delineate the concept 'world' in world history. That world is not a constant; it is bound by human activity. The 'world' refers to social change that can only be understood in specific contexts of space and time. For that reason, no single delineation can be absolute. On the contrary, choosing a space and time perspective ('where' and 'when') is linked to an intrinsic, substantive choice (which social change?). Consequently, world history does not apply exclusive frameworks of space and time; it does not draw fixed boundaries. We speak of scales. These scales overlap from small to large so they do not exclude each other. We also speak of zones of contact and interaction. This is where different social systems come together. Scales and contact zones or frontiers are central concepts of analysis in contemporary world history.

There are many scales both in spatial and chronological perspectives. Every research project within world history is confronted with different scales, from small (micro) to large (macro), and these scales interact. Therefore, it is not sufficient to indicate the outer boundaries of the perspective, for example the North Atlantic world or the period 1500 to 2000 CE. In addition to these external boundaries, research projects are also shaped by internal division or scales (smaller spaces or time periods). Contrary to many other historical approaches, world history does not depart from a primary scale, one scale from which all others derive. The primary structure of human society is not the national state, nor the family, the village or the global economy. World history departs from an interaction between the scales on different levels. Every ethnic group is made up of families, and they are usually part of a larger culture or civilization. That is why human actions cannot quasi-automatically be derived from a smaller scale (individual decisions) or a larger scale (economic networks or political organization). Modern migration patterns are the result of countless individual decisions.

They are also shaped by the actions of human traffickers, by national states' attempts to regulate migration, and by unequal relations in the world economy. Global economic shifts over the past 500 years only partly explain nineteenth century industrialization, as do regional processes and individual initiatives. If we want to understand why English agricultural workers moved to industrial towns at the beginning of the nineteenth century, then we must have insight into the actions of households, the social relations in villages, and we must understand why industrial processes were able to develop so successfully in that location as opposed to somewhere else in the world. In other words, every scale measures something else. Human behaviour can never be fully explained by major processes, and these processes are not simply a sum of countless human decisions. Every scale has autonomy, but only partial autonomy due to interaction and interdependence. This requires a diversity of research methods. Evolutionary biologist Richard Dawkins used this metaphor: macrogrowth (of a human) is the sum of lots of little episodes of microgrowth (of cells). The two interlinked forms of growth take place on a very different time and spatial scale and, therefore, require very different research methods and approaches. Microscopes are unsuitable for measuring the height and weight of children, and scales and measuring tapes are unsuitable for studying cell proliferation. However, we need all these instruments to understand the complex phenomenon of body growth.

Global patterns interact with regional and local patterns – that is the core of world history. Those global patterns also have their own, partial autonomy. Research into these broader patterns is not only useful, it is necessary. They are not merely derivatives of processes on a smaller scale (in space and time). Conversely, a world history perspective cannot and must not be detached from more focused research with a more limited spatial and chronological view. Nineteenth- and twentieth-century national historiography was in keeping with contemporary social realities and the need for new knowledge. Likewise, there is currently a clear need to examine and understand economic, social, cultural, ecological and demographic processes on a global level. Studies go wrong when the historical and social analysis is limited to only one level, when the insights are not placed in a context of larger or smaller scales. Each research project in world history must make choices. The project's boundaries and theme must first be determined. The space and time perspective and the applicable scales are chosen depending on the theme and the research questions. Studies related to the impact of climate change on humankind cover a longer period of time and use different scales than research into the globalization of trade or the end of the Cold War.

We distinguish between scales and patterns of space and time. Sections 1 and 2 of this chapter question these scales. Section 3 incorporates the delineation in space and time in a thematic research framework. We learn how world history gains insights by using comparative research strategies (cases), interconnected research strategies (networks) and systemic research strategies (systems). Section 4 shows that a dynamic, multilayered SpaceTime model incorporates shifting contact zones, or *frontiers*. History is the result of constant interaction between and within scales and contact zones or frontiers.

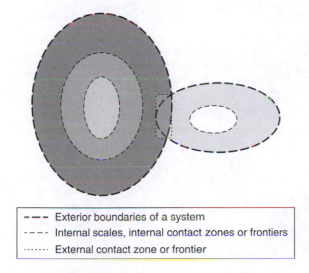

Exterior boundaries of a system
Internal scales, internal contact zones or frontiers
External contact zone or frontier

*Figure 10.1* Scales and contact zones in world history.

## Scales and patterns of space

This scale does not seem problematic initially. After all, world history occurs in a place that we call earth. However, human processes do not cover the entire globe and information does not represent the entire world. We examine the way that we have been making spatial dimensions visible in the past and present, and question the delineation of spaces and boundaries.

Human groups have always had their own world image – knowledge about and an interpretation of their known world, large or small. Humans recorded that global view, primarily to place their own society in the wider world. Most cultures used a spatial representation to make the world tangible, usually in the form of 'world maps'. These maps are never neutral but are always the result of several choices. Those choices reveal their own perspective. Contemporary world maps are still often drawn using the Mercator projection, which was originally intended for navigation. Directions can be accurately determined but the size of countries is not correct. Land masses in the northern and southern parts of the globe are shown much bigger than they really are. The alternative Peters projection indicates the correct surface proportions but distorts the directions.

Earlier world maps departed from the maker's own, known world. That knowledge remained limited geographically until the fifteenth to sixteenth centuries CE. These world maps displayed the cultural view of space and of time. The maps were often completed with scenes from the group's mythical past. This made them a true 'imago mundi' – a representation of the terrestrial and cosmological world. The group's political, cultural and/or religious society was in the centre. The further away from this centre, the more foreign the world became. The oldest

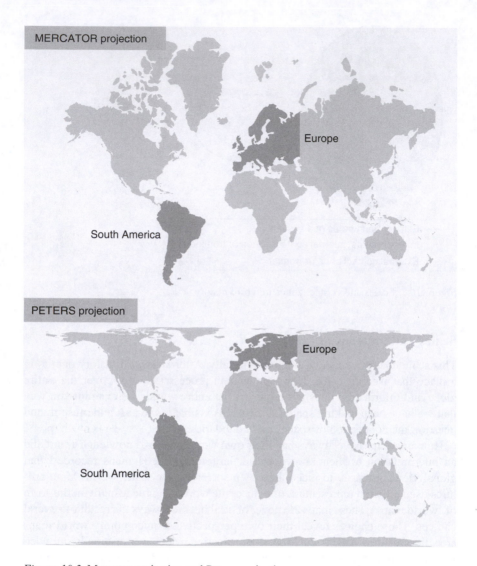

*Figure 10.2* Mercator projection and Peters projection.

'world maps' placed Babylon in the centre (Mesopotamia); Islamic maps placed Baghdad in the centre (for example the Al-Idrisi map, twelfth century CE); Christian maps placed Jerusalem in the centre (for example the Psalter map, thirteenth century CE); and Asian maps placed Mount Meru (India) or The Middle Kingdom (China) in the centre.

World maps have not been sufficient to make the known world comprehensible. People have always used smaller units (scales) to differentiate this world. The first scale was a broad geographic division, usually into continents. The dividing line of seas and major rivers were important beacons. Regions were much more difficult to record geographically since they shifted over time. Few borders were drawn on older maps, but they often divided the human groups/cultures/civilizations into their own civilization and 'the others'. A third scale that was present early on within the spatial interpretation of one's own world was the central locality. Major world cities were regarded as centres of power and reference points in the world, from Babylon, Rome, Baghdad, Beijing and Teotihuacán, to Timbuktu, Constantinople, London and New York.

Spatial approaches took shape by naming zones and drawing borders. These zones and borders usually had a combined character: geographical, political, cultural etc. For that reason, they have not been absolute but shifted depending on the perspective and time period. In the context of world history, geographical borders cannot define a study; rather, they must be part of the analysis. For example, dividing the world into a first, second and third world was a prominent analysis model in the twentieth century. According to a classic modernization perspective, the first world stood for developed, industrial-capitalist countries, the second world for communist countries and the third world for developing countries ('in development' according to the model of the first or second world). When the Cold War ended around 1990, this division lost its meaning. Today global studies speak of 'Global North' and 'Global South' as global-regional concepts. Global South includes all countries that are not part of the Western core and are mostly located in the southern hemisphere.

Zones and borders can never be established on a uniform basis. Europe is a clear example of this. Is an unambiguous division possible, and if so based on what?

The first choice that can be made is a geographic division. As a continent, Europe is surrounded by water in the north, west and south. The eastern border is much more difficult to establish. Over time it was shifted further to the east: from the Black Sea, the Dnieper River, the Volga River, the Ural Mountains and the Caucasus, the Ob River and the Caspian Sea, to the Yenisei River (in central Russia). The line from the Ural Mountains and Ural River to the Caucasus is the most recognized geographic dividing line between Europe and Asia. Between the Ural and the Caucasus there is a 600 km 'gateway' to Europe without natural barriers. Major historical migrations from the east (the steppes) to the west all passed through here. If we respect this border then a quarter of Russia (west of the Ural Mountains, including Moscow) is in Europe and three-quarters is in Asia.

If we place more importance on cultural-historical boundaries then the question becomes even more difficult. Possible criteria include: the Christian tradition (Roman Catholic, Protestant and Orthodox); the values of the Enlightenment (separation of church and state, human rights etc.); political democracy and the state system; and the capitalist market economy. Not only does each interpretation leave room for discussion, they also do not completely overlap. Christian traditions are practiced in Russia and beyond. Enlightenment traditions are not limited to European countries either. This is also true of political democracy and the system of modern nation states. What about the dictatorships that arose in the previous century within Europe? The capitalist economy has become a global economy. For a long time, large areas of Europe were part of non-European empires like the Arabian empire (to Poitiers), the Russian empire (to Berlin) and the Ottoman empire (to Vienna). To which tradition do these areas belong? It is difficult – if not impossible – to define Europe in terms of religion, traditions and values. This also became clear when discussing the European Constitution in 2005. The fiercest debates centred on adding a reference to Europe's Jewish-Christian heritage. In the end, the final version only referred to the ideas of the eighteenth century Enlightenment (such as human rights, freedom and tolerance) and nineteenth century liberalism (such as the democratic constitutional state).

It is clear that Europe's real boundaries will be determined politically. Who will be allowed to join the European Union and who will be rejected? Where are Europe's external borders? The debate concentrates on the position of Russia (and the Ukraine) and Turkey. Referring to history, Russia stands the best chance. Russia has been considered part of Europe by the political elites since the beginning of the eighteenth century. Under the reign of Peter the Great (1689–1725), Russia became a European superpower while concurrently carrying out steps towards 'modernization'. In recent history (the twentieth century), Turkey has become a secularized, stable, more-or-less democratic constitutional state.

Europe's constant discord and great variety of national, religious and cultural identities have been some of its most identifying characteristics. This diversity has prompted the best (openness and tolerance, human rights and democracy) and worst (slavery, militarism and dictatorship) of Europe. In any event, the European space will be demarcated by political choices that will rest much more on contemporary and future concerns than on historical values and traditions.

## Scales and patterns of time

Time measures the speed of change. This is obvious yet subjective. As human beings we are confronted with diverse speeds of change, with diverse forms of time. Along with space, every society attempts to control time. Days and seasons are given a place in calendars. Periods of the day are indicated with time indicators and clocks. This gives the past meaning, the present becomes manageable, and the future is partially cognizable. Every method of time management tells a tale, as a form of perception and world view, and as an attempt to integrate time in social and cultural life. Historians often speak of social time. Different social realities (a personal life versus an economic cycle) have different time regimes. They do not exclude each other but are complementary. Moreover, time and space cannot be disconnected. Spaces change over time, and time is linked to space. Social time and place form one social reality, a so-called SpaceTime.

Every human society constructs a spatial location and its own notion of time. That notion of time had a strong mythical nature for a long time. Rather than recreating the timeline accurately, societies created grand stories in which time was an intangible, abstract concept. The notion of time in older societies was usually cyclical in nature, constructed around day and night, seasons, harvests, generations and dynasties. Time as a straight, mostly ascending line is a relatively recent (mostly Western) perception, based on a new belief in progress. Linear time goes together with the idea of development and modernization. This vision is currently under pressure. Unpredictability was mostly seen as deviant until recently, but in certain visions (such as chaos theory) it seems to have become the rule rather than the exception. From this point of view, history does not develop linearly but by fits and starts, evidenced by consecutive dramatic changes (such as the periods of mass extinction).

History is about changes over time. Time, even more than place, is simply a background factor in many historical works – a given. But this should not be the case. A time perspective is always the result of a choice. This is especially true regarding the way that timelines are parcelled. In world history, periodizations are the subject of much debate; justifiably so, as the choice of a time delineation and a periodization is never neutral. Periodization is a technique that historians use to map and understand processes of change. It departs from the assumption that change is not random or constant; it occurs in phases or waves with much more change in some periods than in others. Distinguishing those periods is a prerequisite for understanding them. Periodization aims to understand which patterns exist and when they change. In a world historical perspective this means that changes occur over geographic and social borders, and include agrarian (agricultural systems), cultural (world religions), commercial (trade systems) and industrial (industrialization) transformations.

General world history overviews use a very similar periodization scheme:

1   Until 8000/5000 BCE. Period of hunter-gatherers, of mini-systems.
2   5000/3500 BCE to 1000/500 BCE. Origin of civilizations ~ agricultural civilizations ~ early complex societies.
3   1000/500 BCE to 500 CE. The flourishing of 'classical' civilizations/societies.
4   500 CE to 1450/1500 CE. Postclassical period ~ decline and recovery ~ divided regions ~ interregional unity.
5   1500 CE to 1750/1800 CE. New modern world ~ rise of the West ~ the world shrinks ~ roots of global dependence.
6   1800 CE to 2000 CE. In one or two periods, nineteenth century: European dominance; twentieth century: a global world.

Three major benchmarks always reappear:

• the rise of agricultural societies, 5000–3500 BCE;
• the split with 'classical' civilizations (and a fragmentation of the world), 500 CE;
• the beginning of the 'Rise of the West' and of globalization, 1500 CE.

The sequence of periods can be interpreted differently, from linear stories (such as the modernization of the world, technological developments and demographic growth) to arguments that refer to cycles in history (such as climate cycles, cycles of civilizations, cycles of economic hegemony and cycles of warfare).

World history explicitly questions the time dimension. As stated above, the time dimension is not separate from the social story, as indicated in these examples.

- Fernand Braudel (1979) is the historian that introduced the concept *longue durée* (the long term). Obviously, he was not the first person to depart from the long term for a historical analysis (in this case the fifteenth to eighteenth centuries CE). He did problematize the relation between diverse timescales: *histoire structurelle* (shifts in the (very) long term); *histoire conjoncturelle* (cyclical movements); and *histoire événementielle* (facts). He also wrote about the seemingly immobile *le temps géographique* (geographic time) and the seemingly fast *le temps individuel* (individual time). When discussing the place of *longue durée* in historiography, Braudel wrote:

  It is not the only approach, but it is the one that can ask big questions about social structures in the past and the present. It is the only language that can link history with the present in order to make one undivided world.

- Jared Diamond (1997) starts his story 10,000 years ago, with the domestication of plants, to analyze the geological and ecological factors in the success or failure of civilizations. Johan Goudsblom (1992) goes back to the domestication of fire by Homo erectus 400,000 years ago.

- The broadest timeframe is in so-called 'Big History' – history from the Big Bang until now. This period of billions of years is the subject of David Christian's *Maps of Time* (Christian 2004). This extreme example of a world history in the long term combines a cosmic scale with human time measured in centuries. He builds further on the discovery of 'deep time' by astrophysicists like Stephen Hawking (*A Brief History of Time*, 1988) and palaeontologists like Stephen Jay Gould (2002). Like other works about the long term, the periodizations become shorter the closer they get to the present day. It is interesting how David Christian brings diverse timescales together:

  - the scale of the universe: 13 billion years;
  - the scale of earth, the biosphere: 4.5 billion years;
  - the scale of multicellular organisms: 600 million years;
  - the scale of mammals: 70 million years;
  - the scale of hominids: 4 million years;
  - the scale of human history: 200,000 years;
  - the scale of agrarian and urban civilizations: 5,000 years;
  - the scale of modernity: 500–1,000 years;
  - the scale of 'national history': maximum of a few centuries;
  - the scale of microhistory: a lifetime.

To reflect those sliding scales he introduced the metaphor 'maps of time': maps condense information about space and time and bring them together in one view.

## The interaction between scales of space and time: which research framework?

World history teaches us that social change is a multilayered process that is anchored in a multilayered time and a multilayered place. The scales of space and place change over time. Relevant chronological scales differ according to place: the larger the space, the 'slower' the time. Time and place are, therefore, dependent variables: SpaceTime. The choice of the scales of space and time is determined by the social reality, the social change that is to be investigated. This is the research theme in world history. This interaction means that many scales of time and place are imaginable in world history. Different scales show different things. Compare this to overview maps and detailed maps. A neighbourhood map shows much more detail than a country map. Country maps offer macro-information that is not available on a neighbourhood map. World history always uses several maps – a map atlas. The ultimate reference map is a world map, both literally and figuratively. How does a certain story fit in the broader view? What does a specific case teach us about human society? The 'big questions' turn social research into world history.

From the above, it becomes clear that for a useful interpretation of history in a global perspective we need a predetermined 'framework', an interpretative construction that is made up of three types of analysis units: time, space and the research theme. This research framework determines the lens that one uses to look at the 'world'. In other words, the framework is the key on the atlas of world history. Maps have no meaning without a key. Only then can one think about strategies for gaining information and about interpretations for answering questions. For example, the concept 'civilization' is a framework that is still important in world history. As seen above, many people question the use of this concept. This dissatisfaction encouraged researchers and writers to seek out and apply new concepts, frameworks and analysis units. The basic question for them all remains the same: what is the best way to understand the world in a broad and cohesive manner? For which concepts do we need to ask 'big' questions about progress/decline in history, about social equality and inequality, about demographic changes, about the rise and fall of economic centres etc.?

The framework for a historical and social analysis is determined by the choice of the analysis units of time, space and theme. This determines, in turn, the research strategy. *Analysis units* can be divided into cases, networks and systems. By *research strategy* we mean the way that we study the cases, networks and systems. Basic strategies in world history include making comparisons, looking for connections, detecting systems, and analyzing scales and contact zones. Cases, networks, systems, scales, frontiers, comparisons and connections are key words in world history research.

The most popular approach in social sciences and in history is still *case studies* (*case analysis*), based on the analysis of a specific 'case' as a more-or-less autonomous unit. The premise is that a case can be/is relevant to the bigger picture, either as a sample study or as an exception to the norm. This case approach is very strong in so-called 'traditional' historiography, but we also find case research in broader contexts (with a focus on individual human communities). Case analysis is important for our knowledge about the world. It contributes to a global perspective when placed in a broader context, either by comparison or by pointing out connections. The designated method or strategy for understanding case studies in a global context is *comparative analysis*, which documents similarities and differences between two or more cases in a systematic manner. This means that the comparison must be reciprocal and integrated. Reciprocal comparison does not depart from a standard model, often based on European history. It acquires information from diverse cases using a similar set of questions that leave room for the individuality of each case, but can still determine similarities and differences in a systematic manner. The comparison is also embedded in broader research perspectives. The integrated comparison avoids static snapshots; instead, emphasis is placed on change and dynamism. Classic research questions such as state-building or economic change gain more significance when analyzed in a bigger picture, without using the particular (European) standard as the norm. Classic examples of reciprocal comparison in modern world history include the studies of Kenneth Pomeranz (*The Great Divergence*) and Bin Wong (*China Transformed*).

The concept *network* is a strong metaphor in contemporary world history. In its most general meaning, it refers to the web that holds the world together. Just like cases, networks constitute spaces but with less visible boundaries (e.g. migration networks or financial networks). Key words include flows, junctions, exchange, connections, influencing, diffusion (e.g. of plants, knowledge or technology), syncretism (e.g. of belief systems) and resistance (to new influences).

In *The Human Web* by father and son William and John McNeill (McNeill and McNeill 2003), the 'human web' is a metaphor for the global human society as shaped from the first major civilizations onwards. Until 1000 CE there were diverse webs with increasingly more contact between them. Between 1000 and 1500 CE these webs 'condensed', and after 1500 CE they were spun into a new worldwide web. The contemporary web is described as an enormous network of collaboration and competition, supported by massive streams of information and energy. New junctions or nodes create increasingly greater complexity. In *Maps of Time*, David Christian (2004) also uses the image of condensing human interaction and of 'collective learning' to summarize world history. Small-scale zones are absorbed by large contact areas (America, Africa-Eurasia, Australia-Polynesia) and later in a global network.

The idea of networks is prominent in the study of economic and trade systems. Contacts between human groups across ecological zones have existed for a very long time. Coastal areas, highlands, steppes, agricultural areas, valleys, mountains, deserts and forests all produced different goods that found a market far beyond the area where they were collected.

Interregional exchange and trade have been important since the beginning of human history due to this unequal distribution of supplies. This interaction accelerated between 500 and 1500 CE, primarily in the Afro-Eurasian zones but also elsewhere. The silk routes through Eurasia were one of the most extensive and long-standing trade networks in world history. They linked China, across central Asia, India and the Middle East with the Mediterranean area. The opening of the silk routes also enabled the passage of knowledge, cultures, religions (Buddhism) and germs (the plague). The trade web of the Indian Ocean Basin was the largest maritime-commercial network until the Europeans opened up the seas in the sixteenth century. It connected the coasts of China with those of India, Arabia and East Africa, and was controlled by an 'archipelago' of trade cities. This space was a strong catalyst for the spreading of Islam from the seventh century CE (for example on the Swahili coasts). The same was true for the trade network through the Sahara, which grew strongly due to the introduction of the camel and the flourishing of commercial centres on the southern border (Ghana, Mali and Songhai) in the first millennium to 1500 CE. During this period, trade networks also flourished in pre-Columbian America: along the Mississippi River, in Mesoamerica and in the Andes. In each case, diverse ecological zones were spanned. Expansion of the Incan empire in the fifteenth century was based on state-controlled interregional trade. Trade towns were established and a network of roads more than 12,000 miles long connected the coasts with plateaus at 16,000 feet and linked valleys with high mountain ranges.

Urban networks are also a good indicator of economic and political growth, since urban centres need considerable surpluses. The paradigm of the global city network (Peter Taylor, *World City Network* and Saskia Sassen (2002)) focuses on a global network with cities as central nodes. The starting point is that modern society is not (or no longer) designed by an interaction of national states but by more-or-less autonomous power bases that have become global cities; in other words, by the network of those global cities. Global cities are central links in a global network of production, trade and services, as well as being central nodes of decision-making and monopolizing of information. Financial centres and so-called 'global firms' are located in every global city. Global cities also attract large flows of labour (including illegal, often foreign labour). They provide the flexible, often informal 24-hour economy. The question is to what extent systems of global cities can be found in the past. Historians often work with the concept of urban networks but on a smaller scale. An example of historicizing the concept of global cities is the work of George Modelski (2000). In a first phase of urbanization (3000 to 1000 BCE, cities with at least 10,000 inhabitants), cities became the basis of an urban knowledge culture that included writing, mathematics and time management. In the 'classical' phase (1000 BCE to 1000 CE, cities of at least 100,000 inhabitants), cities received a growing social role as centres of world religions that dominated social life. The third, modern phase (after 1000 CE, cities of at least 1 million inhabitants) is defined by a growing political power of cities as centres in a globalizing system. Modelski predicts a fourth phase (global cities with tens of millions of inhabitants) in which cities also have economic power and become the most important basis for material wealth in the world.

Another frequently used metaphor in world history is *system*. This includes specific systems (e.g. trade systems, political systems, migration systems) and general systems (a so-called world system). The perspective is that of interactions within a unit. An essential difference with the case study is that the unit – the system – is not studied in parts but as a whole, as a combination of diverse subsystems (the Atlantic system as of 1500 CE is more than the sum of trade activities of various European nations). The difference with a network analysis is that interconnections are part of systemic shifts (human migration and slave trade in the Atlantic system were also a consequence of changing intercontinental power shifts). The current political system is more than a sum of national systems. The central focus in the research shifts from a comparative analysis of national cases to the links between those cases and the overarching inter-state system. This interconnection has its own logic that cannot be understood by merely looking at the subsystems (the states).

In other words, world history is not only about connections, it is also about systems of interconnection such as patterns in trade relations, in migration networks, and in the diffusion of technology, culture and diseases. The direction in those patterns is also determined by interregional power relations. The diffusion is not random; it is promoted and magnified by the major shifts between societies throughout history. As a result, a system theory needs to be holistic. A whole can never be understood only by looking at its parts; there is a meta-level that has its own dynamism. System theory pointedly asks about the 'analysis unit'. If we take national states as the unit then we get a different image than if we expand the analysis to an inter-state system or a world system. The same can be said of national versus global cultures and economies. These metasystems are not closed but open, historical systems with their own time course (origin, growth and decline). A system approach not only clarifies the connections between human groups, it also makes clear which structural processes influence the actions of human groups. A system approach maps horizontal connections (between equivalent subsystems) and vertical connections (between microstructures, macrostructures and ditto processes).

Inspired by Fernand Braudel's *économie-monde*, Immanuel Wallerstein introduced a system approach in world history. The units of analysis are 'world-systems', social systems that have their own coherence and logic and that form a 'world in itself' (that's why world-system is written with a hyphen). Diverse types of world-systems existed alongside each other until a few centuries ago. Wallerstein distinguishes between mini-systems (small-scale social systems such as hunter-gatherers and small agrarian cultures), regional world-systems (world-empires) and world-economies. In a world-economy the economic organization has become the 'prime-mover'. A world-economy comprises several political and cultural systems. The most important world-economy to date is what Wallerstein calls the 'modern world-system' – historical capitalism. He locates the origin of historical capitalism at the intersection of the European Middle Ages and the modern era (long sixteenth century). It integrated the whole world in diverse steps. Diverse world-systems existed next to each other (a capitalist world-economy next to world-empires such as the Ottoman empire and China, and next to the last remaining mini-systems) until the nineteenth century. The 'modern world-system' also literally covered the world from the end of the nineteenth century so it became a real global system. A global (capitalist) economy overarches a fragmented political system (a system of nation states, an inter-state system) and a fragmented cultural system (e.g. world religions). This modern world-economy has several specific characteristics: inequality in development (phases, crises) and inequality in composition (geographic: centre, semi-periphery and periphery; social: social groups). At the same time, that inequality is a necessary condition for the existence of a world-economy. Another characteristic is that successive political conjunctures arose within one economic system. This is contrary to a world-empire where the economic and political cycles coincided. Those political cycles were characterized by an intense struggle in the core regions and by successive hegemonies (Northern Italy, Holland, Great Britain, the United States etc.).

This world-systems analysis is an example of a paradigm, a heuristic model that uses systems as a starting point for a global analysis of the world. These systems are open, historical systems: they crop up, flourish and disappear. The study of world-systems also combines diverse methodological approaches: comparative (comparison of diverse systems such as trade networks), interconnective (flows or chains of commodity production in world-systems) and global (such as climate changes). Systems analysis also pays attention to connections in a horizontal (between systems) and in a vertical (within the system) sense.

## The frontiers of world history

World history incorporates diverse, overlapping scales of place and time in its research strategy. This enables historians to investigate the combined action of small and large, of local and global. Contrary to a structuralistic macro-approach, this research model leaves space for action, interaction and agency. World history shows how social change takes place, how it is incited, and within which limitations. World history connects the time of the 'event' with that of the 'world', thereby showing the complexity of the human journey.

We labelled this multiple stratification in research social SpaceTime. The combined action of place and time creates a constant dynamism, with shifting zones of transition. These border zones or *frontiers* are a central focus of contemporary world history. Frontiers are not defined boundaries or borders. They are constantly shifting zones of contact between different social spaces and social systems. Contact zones originate via the interaction between social systems with their own characteristics. They disappear when the interaction ends or when one system is incorporated by another system. Frontiers can be external and internal, part of a changing system (see Figure 10.1). The delineations between social groups, and the extent to which they are included or excluded, also create transition zones. Synergies develop in such spaces, as do reactions. There is room for collaboration, but also for resistance. Frontier zones are permanently reproduced by converging and dialectical processes of homogenization (the reduction of frontiers) and heterogenization (the creation of new frontiers). History is made by permanent shifts in and between frontier zones. They originate, shift and disappear. The study of these contact areas in world history puts the focus on divergent, interacting scales. It avoids a static micro/

macro-approach and defies essentialist, fixed and pre-defined zones and social systems. Place and time are historical, dynamic and multilayered.

The frontier-focus in world history requires research into similarities and differences, into connections and systemic changes. It primarily concerns the border zones of contact, of cultural, social and economic interaction. Those zones are fluid; they change, grow or disappear, together with the rise and decline of empires, civilizations, states and economies. These zones are the peripheries of larger systems. They often have intense traffic and interaction between merchants, conquerors, pilgrims, missionaries, settlers and tourists. Pilgrimages from peripheral areas (Christian pilgrims in the Roman empire, Islamic pilgrims from the Arabian deserts) spread new religious systems. Believers traversed cultural zones, shifted cultural borders and often created new, hybrid frontiers. The people in frontier zones absorb new cultures, create alliances and collaboration, rebel, and take on other identities. Social mobility is a product of geographic mobility within and between frontiers.

Political units exist by grace of borders. They try to define these zones more strictly with clear dividing lines: the Great Wall of China, Hadrian's Wall, the Berlin Wall, the wall between Israel and the Palestinian territories, the fences between the United States and Mexico. The system of national states and the associated citizenship make political borders more absolute. They often do not coincide with cultural or economic borders, which are best discovered by mapping the zones of contact and conflict. Historical capitalism grew as an economic system due to the constant incorporation of new frontier zones. Social and ecological frontiers shifted due to the further appropriation of new means of production (land, labour, goods and knowledge). At the same time, this process always fed new social spaces of action and resistance.

The multiple projects of migration and colonization of empires and states constituted a permanent process of breaching existing borders and creating new peripheries and new geographic and cultural frontier zones. The expansion of Russia to the east (the frontier reached the Pacific in the seventeenth century), China to the west and south (the frontier reached Mongolia and the Himalayas in the eighteenth century) and the United States to the west (the frontier reached the Pacific in the nineteenth century) created new frontier zones and new forms of assimilation and conflict. Along the borders of the Chinese Manchu empire many hybrid, barely-defined contact zones developed with Indian, Iranian, Islamic, Turkish, Mongolian and Tibetan cultures. Seas also became large, easy-to-penetrate contact zones: the Mediterranean Sea, the Indian Ocean, the South China Sea and Oceania. Borders were always disputed, zones scarcely protectable. They were spaces for new expansion that made trade and migration possible. They also formed active zones of resistance against territorial powers, with many forms of smuggling and piracy.

New forms of colonization and imperialism from the sixteenth century instigated a gigantic expansion and shift of peripheral frontier zones. This expansion connected large population groups to the European world economy, and often gave them means for new forms of identity and resistance. Economic exploitation incorporated new regions in world economy, but it was also the basis of new forms of peasant agriculture and so-called 'informal economies'. Political incorporation processes nurtured the battle for decolonization and national emancipation in the twentieth century. Cultural association created many new hybrids with the 'creolization' of language, identity, religion and food.

Borders and frontiers modulate world historical processes via political expansion, human migration, economic exchange or incorporation, cultural assimilation, and religious dissemination. Along the borders of social and economic systems, hybrid cultures originate and processes that challenge existing systems often grow. Within social systems frontiers also grow or disappear. Social groups, social zones are excluded or incorporated. The battle for boundaries – which is always about inclusion and exclusion – is a battle for power. Those who have the power define the territory, draw the borders, define the identity and make the difference vis-à-vis 'the others'. Borders are about geographic places on the exterior, and about internal social categories and spaces. The exclusion of women from public spaces – such as during the battle against religious heresy in Early Modern Europe, or during the propagation of the breadwinner/housewife model in the twentieth century – has drawn new borders. Urban survival networks in nineteenth century industrial centres or twenty-first century 'cities of slums' define new, partially-autonomous zones. The new frontiers also give space to new forms of organization and reaction.

External and internal frontier zones play a first-rate role in social change. They build walls as well as bridges. They determine exclusion and inclusion. They enforce new rules but also give space for resistance. New forms of political and social emancipation are often formed in border zones, such as with eighteenth-century slave rebellions in the Caribbean, or with peasant movements in the south in the twenty-first century. The new frontiers also expose the big paradox in the current globalized world: borders have not disappeared. They have been redefined with global networks of money and communication, but also with new regional identities, national walls against migration and immense zones of economic underdevelopment. This is what makes world history: connection and interaction, assimilation, conflict and resistance, in a world that is big but not equal.

Through the multitude of scales and patterns, world history searches for larger, more coordinating stories. They give the human journey meaning, in the past and in the present. This modern world history still wrestles with what Fernand Braudel once called the historiographic inequality between the West and the rest of the world: 'Europe invents historians and makes good use of them. Its own history is well known and can be used both advantageously and adversely. The history outside Europe still needs to be written.' We currently have more knowledge about the most diverse parts of the world and periods of history than ever. There is still an unequal global hierarchy in this knowledge formation, which is still centred in the West. That is the most important frontier in contemporary world history. As long as that inequality exists, historians must remain restrained to unravel 'the Gordian knot of world history' – the question of the roots of modern global inequality.

# Literature guide and references

This list is a personal selection of works that offer a global and historical perspective. Of course, it is only a guide.

## Prelude

Burke, E. III, Christian, D. and Dunn, R. E. (2009) *World history – the big eras: A compact history of human mankind for teachers and students*. The Regents, University of California.

Christian, D. (2008) *This fleeting world: A short history of humanity*. Berkshire Publishing Group.

Dawkins, R. (2004) *The ancestor's tale: A pilgrimage to the dawn of life*. Weidenfeld & Nicolson.

Gould, S. J. (1996) *Full house: The spread of excellence from Plato to Darwin*. Three Rivers Press.

Haywood, J. (2011) *The new atlas of world history: Global events at a glance*. Thames & Hudson.

## 1 World history: a history of the world?

### *Literature as an introduction to world history*

Bentley, J. H. (1995) *Shapes of world history in twentieth-century scholarship*. American Historical Association.

Bentley, J. H. (2007) 'Why study world history?', *World History Connected*, 5(1). Available online at http://worldhistoryconnected.press.uiuc.edu/5.1/bentley.html

Bentley, J. H., Bridenthal, R. and Yang, A. A. (eds) (2001) *Interactions: Transregional perspectives on world history*. Routledge.

Conrad, S., Eckert, A. and Freitag, U. (eds) (2007) *Globalgeschichte: Theorien, Ansätze, Themen*. Campus.

Crossley, P. K. (2008) *What is global history?* Polity Press.

Dunn, R. (ed.) (2000) *The new world history: A teacher's companion*. St. Martin's Press.

Hughes-Warrington, M. (ed.) (2005) *Palgrave advances in world histories*. Palgrave Macmillan.

Jalagin, S., Tavera, S., Dilley, A. (eds) (2011) *World and global history: Research and teaching*. CliohWorld.

Komlosy, A. (2011) *Globalgeschichte: Methoden und Theorien*. UTB.

Manning, P. (2003) *Navigating world history: Historians create a global past*. Palgrave Macmillan/St. Martin's Press.

Mazlish, B. and Buultjens, R. (eds) (1993) *Conceptualizing global history*. Westview.

O'Brien, P. (2006) 'Historiographical traditions and modern imperatives for the restoration of global history', *Journal of Global History*, 1, pp. 3–39.

Stearns, P. N. (2003) *Western civilization in world history*. Routledge.

Stearns, P. N. (2011) *World history: The basics*. Routledge.

Stuchtey, B. and Fuchs, E. (eds.) (2003) *Writing world history 1800–2000*. Oxford University Press.

Vries, P. (ed.) (2009) *Global History*, special issue *Österreichische Zeitschrift für Geschichtswissenschaften*, 2. (With contributions from P. Vries, E. Vanhaute, J. Osterhammel, J. Darwin, J. A. Goldstone, D. Christian, H. Floris Cohen.)

## Textbooks

There is an abundant supply of world history textbooks. A selection of textbooks and several reviews can be found in *World History Connected*, 3(2) (February 2006, available online at http://worldhistoryconnected.press.uiuc.edu/3.2). A selection follows.

Bentley, J. H. and Ziegler, H. F. (2011) *Traditions and encounters: A global perspective on the past* (5th ed.). McGraw-Hill.

Fernandez-Armesto, F. (2007) *World: A brief history* (combined volume). Pearson-Prentice Hall. (Published in paperback, 2008)

Goucher, C. and Walton, L. (2008) *World history: Journeys from past to present*. Routledge.

Spodek, H. (2006) *The world's history* (combined volume, 3rd ed.). Pearson-Prentice Hall.

Strayer, R. W. (2009) *Ways of the world: A brief global history* (2 vols). Bedford/St. Martin's.

## Encyclopedia

*Berkshire encyclopedia of world history*. Berkshire Publishing Group, 2010 (2nd ed., 6 vols).

*The Oxford handbook of world history*. Oxford University Press, 2011.

*Routledge handbook of world-systems analysis: Theory and research*. Routledge, 2012.

*World history encyclopedia*. ABC Clio, 2011 (21 vols).

## Associations

### The World History Association (www.thewha.org)

The *World History Association* was established in 1982 to promote the study and teaching of world history. The association is still mostly made up of North American members but is also strongly represented internationally. The association organizes international congresses and publishes *World History Bulletin: Newsletter of the World History Association*, which includes book reviews, short articles and contributions about developments in the discipline.

### European Network in Universal and Global History (www.eniugh.org)

The affiliated European organization of the *World History Association* is the *European Network in Universal and Global History*, which was founded in 2002 and is domiciled in Leipzig. Together with other international associations, WHA and ENIUGH form the coordinating *Network of Global and World History Organizations*

*(NOGWHISTO)*. ENIUGH organizes international conferences and publishes a journal entitled *Comparativ* (see below). Book reviews and miscellaneous announcements are spread by ENIUGH via an online forum *history.transnational* (http://geschichte-transnational.clio-online.net).

**The New Global History** (www.newglobalhistory.com)

*New Global History* emphasizes globalization themes in world history and attempts to build a historical analysis framework for researching processes of growth and worldwide interconnections. *New Global History* is more a research group than a network like WHA or ENIUGH.

## Journals

**Comparativ. Zeitschrift für Globalgeschichte und vergleichende Gesellschaftsforschung**, European Network in Universal and Global History, from 1991 (www.comparativ.net)

ENIUGH patronizes *Comparativ*, a bimonthly journal in English and German that emphasizes the thematic approach of *comparisons*.

**Global History Review**, China Social Science Press, from 2006 (www.global-history.org)

*Global History Review* is a Chinese journal, linked to the history department at the Capital Normal University.

**Global Networks, a journal of transnational affairs**, Blackwell Publishing, from 2001

This journal looks at how transnational networks of individuals or groups steer processes of globalization. The approach is mainly contemporary.

**Globality Studies Journal, Global History, Society, Civilization**, The Stony Brook Institute for Global Studies, from 2006 (globality.cc.stonybrook.edu)

*Globality Studies Journal* is an open-access journal aimed at interdisciplinary analyses of world history, global society and culture, and interaction with local cultures.

**Globalizations**, Routledge, from 2004

Just like *Global Networks*, the journal *Globalizations* studies growing interconnections on a global scale. The contributions in the journal emphasize the various interpretations of and processes behind globalization.

**Itinerario, International Journal on the History of European Expansion and Global Interaction**, Cambridge University Press, from 1977 (published for the Leiden Institute for History)

This journal uses the history of European expansion between 1500 and 1950 as its central focus.

**Journal of Global History**, Cambridge University Press, from 2006

*Journal of Global History* focuses on global change. Special attention is paid to debates about *the great divergence*, globalization, regional scales and transdisciplinarity in world history.

**Journal of World History**, University of Hawaii Press, from 1990

The *Journal of World History* has been the official journal of the *World History Association* since 1990, and is the oldest world history periodical. From the beginning, it emphasized *communities*, *comparisons* and *connections*, with extra attention paid to broad processes (such as religion, trade, knowledge migration, migration or climate) that influence regional definitions like cultures, states and civilizations.

***The New Global Studies***, Berkeley Electronic Press, from 2007 (www.bepress.com/ngs)

The *New Global Studies* approaches globalization as a whole and across disciplinary lines. The journal is the publication channel of New Global History, the research group of Bruce Mazlish, et al.

***World History Connected***, from 2003 (worldhistoryconnected.press.illinois.edu)

*World History Connected* is an open-access journal that offers a platform for studying world history, with an emphasis on North America. Much attention is paid to world history as a pedagogic project.

***World-Systems Archives*** (wsarch.ucr.edu)

The wide spatial perspective of world history is older than the discipline of world history. This electronic archive compiles documents, bibliographic information, newsletters, reference books and series related to the analytic paradigm of world-systems analysis. With links to two essential journals for this discipline:

*Review. A Journal of the Fernand Braudel Center* (Binghamton University, since 1977; established by Immanuel Wallerstein) (www2.binghamton.edu/fbc/review-journal/index.html)

*Journal of World-Systems Research* (open-access journal, since 1995) (jwsr.ucr.edu)

***Zeitschrift für Weltgeschichte***, Wissenschafts-Verlages Martin Meidenbauer, from 2000

This journal, established by Hans-Heinrich Nolte of the *Verein für Geschichte des Weltsystems,* offers a German-language forum for world history.

## Interesting websites

***H-World*** (www.h-net.org/~world)

One of the many electronic mailing lists on [www.h-net.org]. With a very active forum and book reviews. *H-World* is an important communication network, focusing both on research and education in world history.

***World History For Us All*** (www.worldhistoryforusall.sdsu.edu)

A didactic website that offers a package of lessons on world history. The lessons are also aimed at high school students.

***Bridging World History*** (www.learner.org/courses/worldhistory)

Didactic website, thematically constructed around 26 units.

***World History Sources*** (chnm.gmu.edu/worldhistorysources and www.worldhistory matters.org)

Manual of sources for world history.

***The World History Network*** (www.worldhistorynetwork.org)

> This website is designed as an introduction to the study of world history. The search functions give access to a wide range of information and electronic sources.

***Communities/Comparisons/Connections*** (www.ccc.ugent.be)

> Website of the World History Research Group at Ghent University in Belgium.

***World History Matters*** (worldhistorymatters.org)

> A portal to world history websites developed by the Center for History and New Media, Department of History and Art History, George Mason University, Fairfax, Virginia.

> Associated with this is *World History Matters: A Student Guide to World History Online*, by K. Lehner, K. Schrum and T. Mills Kelly (Bedford/St. Martin's, 2008), a paperback book that reviews 150 world history websites.

***Best History Sites*** (www.besthistorysites.net)

> A portal to world history websites developed by EdTechTeach Inc.

Websites with maps and atlases:

> www.timemaps.com
> www.worldhistorymaps.info
> www.lib.utexas.edu/maps/historical
> www.atlas-historique.net
> www.worldmapper.org
> mondediplo.com/maps
> www.indianoceanhistory.org

## 2 A human world

Adams, P. V., Langer, E. D., Hwa, L., Stearns, P. N. and Wiesner-Hanks, M. E. (2000) *Experiencing world history*. New York University Press.

Cipolla, C. M. (1978) *The economic history of world population*. Penguin Books.

Commire, A. and Klezmer, D. (eds) (1999) *Women in world history: A biographical encyclopedia*. Yorkin.

Fagan, B. (1990) *The journey from Eden: The peopling of our world*. Thames & Hudson.

Hoerder, D. (2002) *Cultures in contact: World migrations in the second millennium*. Duke University Press.

Hughes, S. S. and Hughes, B. (1997) *Women in world history*. M.E. Sharpe.

*Journal of Global History* (2011) Five articles by various authors on the subjects of mobility and migration, issue 2, pp. 299–344.

Kiple, K. (ed.) (1993) *The Cambridge world history of human disease*. Cambridge University Press.

Livi-Bacci, M. (2001) *A concise history of world population*. Blackwell.

Lucassen, J., Lucassen, L. and Manning, P. (eds) (2010) *Migration history in world history: Multidisciplinary approaches*. Brill.

McKeown, A. (2008) *Melancholy order: Asian migration and the globalization of borders*. Columbia University Press.

McNeill, W. H. (1976) *Plagues and peoples*. Anchor Books.

Manning, P. (2005) *Migration in world history*. Routledge.

Mithen, S. J. (2004) *After the ice: A global human history, 20,000–5000 BC*. Harvard.

*Women in world history* website (http://chnm.gmu.edu/wwh, George Mason University).

Wrigley, E. A. (1969) *Population and history*. Weidenfeld & Nicolson.

# 3 A natural world

Aberth, J. (2006) *The first horsemen: Disease in human history*. Pearson-Prentice Hall.

Barbier, E. B. (2011) *Scarcity and frontiers: How economies have developed through natural resource exploitation*. Cambridge University Press.

Burke, E. III (2009) 'The big story: Human history, energy regimes and the environment', in: E. Burke and K. Pomeranz, *The environment and world history*. University of California Press, pp. 33–53.

Cavalli-Sforza, L. L. (2001) *Genes, peoples and languages*. University of California Press.

Chew, S. C. (2001) *World ecological degradation: Accumulation, urbanization and deforestation, 3000 BC–AD 2000*. Altamira.

Crawford, D. H. (2007) *Deadly companions: How microbes shaped our history*. Oxford University Press.

Crosby, A. (1986) *Ecological imperialism: The biological expansion of Europe, 900–1900*. Cambridge University Press.

Crosby, A. (2006) *Children of the sun: A history of humanity's unappeasable appetite for energy*. Norton.

Davis, M. (2001) *Late Victorian holocausts: El Niño famines and the making of the Third World*. Verso.

Diamond, J. (1997) *Guns, germs and steel: The fates of human society*. Norton.

Fagan, B. M. (2000) *The little ice age: How climate made history, 1300–1850*. Basic Books.

Goldstone, J. (2008) *Why Europe? The rise of the West in world history 1500–1850*. McGraw-Hill.

Goudsblom, J. (1992) *Fire and civilization*. Penguin.

Headrick, D. R. (2009) *Technology: A world history*. Oxford University Press.

Hughes, J. D. (2009) *An environmental history of the world: Humankind's changing role in the community of life*. Routledge.

McClellan, J. III and Dorn, H. (2006) *Science and technology in world history: An introduction* (2nd ed.). Johns Hopkins University Press.

McNeill, J. (2000) *Something new under the sun: An environmental history of the twentieth-century world*. Norton.

McNeill, W.H. (1976) *Plagues and peoples*. Anchor.

Marks, R. B. (2007) *The origins of the modern world: A global and ecological narrative from the fifteenth to the twenty-first century*. Rowman & Littlefield.

Morris, I. (2010) *Why the West rules – for now: The patterns of history, and what they reveal about the future*. Farrar, Straus and Giroux.

Mosley, S. (2009) *The environment in world history*. Routledge.

Penna, A. N. (2010) *The human footprint: A global environmental history*. Wiley-Blackwell.

Ponting, C. (2007) *A new green history of the world: The environment and the collapse of great civilizations*. Vintage.

Radhau, J. (2008) *Nature and power: A global history of the environment*. Cambridge.

Richards, J. F. (2003) *The unending frontier: An environmental history of the early modern world*. University of California Press.

Ruddiman, W.F. (2005) *Plows, plagues, and petroleum: How humans took control of climate*. Princeton University Press.
Simmons, I. G. (2008) *Global environmental history.* University of Chicago Press.
Smil, V. (1994) *Energy in world history*. Westview Press.
United Nations (n.d.) *Global environment outlook*. Available online at http://www.unep.org/geo
United Nations (2007) *Climate report 2007*. Intergovernmental Panel on Climate Change. Available online at http://www.ipcc.ch

## 4  An agrarian world

Belasco, W. (2006) *Meals to come: A history of the future of food*. University of California Press.
Bellwood, P. (2004) *First farmers: The origins of agricultural societies*. Wiley-Blackwell.
Crosby, A. (1972) *The Columbian exchange: Biological and cultural consequences of 1492*. Greenwood Press.
Diamond, J. (1999) *Guns, germs and steels: The fates of human societies*. Norton.
Donald-Hughes, J. (2001) *An environmental history of the world: Humankind's changing role in the community of life*. Taylor & Francis.
Fagan, B. M. (1999) *Floods, famines and emperors: El Niño and the fate of civilizations*. Basic Books.
Fernandez-Armesto, F. (2002) *Near a thousand tables: A history of food*. Free Press.
Foster, J. B. (1994) *The vulnerable planet: A short economic history of the environment*. Monthly Review Press.
Goodman, D. and Watts, M. (eds) (1997) *Globalising food: Agrarian questions and global restructuring*. Routledge.
Goody, J. (1982) *Cooking, cuisine and class: A study in comparative sociology*. Cambridge University Press.
Grove, R. H. (1997) *Ecology, climate and empire: Colonialism and global environmental history, 1400–1940*. White Horse Press.
Hobhouse, H. (1999) *Seeds of change: Six plants that transformed mankind*. Papermac.
Kiple, K. F. (2007) *Movable feast: Ten millennia of food globalization*. Cambridge University Press.
Manning, R. (2004) *Against the grain: How agriculture has hijacked civilization*. North Point Press.
Mintz, S. (1985) *Sweetness and power: The place of sugar in modern history*. Viking Penguin.
Mintz, S. (1996) *Tasting food, tasting freedom: Excursions into eating, culture, and the past*. Beacon Press.
Pilcher, J. M. (2006) *Food in world history*. Routledge.
Pollan, M. (2006) *The omnivore's dilemma: A natural history of four meals*. Penguin Books.
Pomeranz, K. and Topik, S. (1999) *The world that trade created: Society, culture, and the world economy, 1400 to the present*. M.E. Sharpe.
Sauper, H. (2004) *Darwin's Nightmare* (documentary film). (Website http://www.darwins-nightmare.com/)
Simmons, F. J. (1994) *Eat not this flesh: Food avoidances from prehistory to the present*. University of Wisconsin Press.

Sing Chew (2001) *World ecological degradation: Accumulation, urbanization and deforestation 3000 BC–AD 2000*. Altamira Press.
Tannahill, R. (1988) *Food in history*. Three Rivers Press.
Tauger, M. B. (2011) *Agriculture in world history*. Routledge.
Weis, T. (2007) *The global food economy: The battle for the future of farming*. Zed Books.

## 5 A political world

Black, J. (1998) *War and the world: Military power and the fate of continents 1450–2000*. Yale University Press.
Burbank, J. and Cooper, F. (2010) *Empires in world history: Power and the politics of difference*. Princeton University Press.
Chase-Dunn, C. (ed.) (2004) *Premodern historical systems: The rise and fall of states and empires*. Special issue of *Journal of World-Systems Research*, 3.
Chase-Dunn, C. and Hall, T. D. (1997) *Rise and demise: Comparing world-systems*. Westview Press.
Darwin, J. (2007) *After Tamerlane: The global history of empire*. Allen Lane.
Flint, C. and Taylor, P. J. (2011) *Political geography: World-economy, nation-state and locality* (6th ed.). Pearson-Prentice Hall.
Goldstein, J. S. (1988) *Long cycles, prosperity and war in the modern age*. Yale University Press.
McNeill, W. H. (1984) *The pursuit of power: Technology, armed force and society since AD 1000*. University of Chicago press.
Modelski, G. and Thompson, W. R. (1996) *Leading sectors and world powers: The coevolution of global economics and politics*. University of South Carolina Press.
North, D. C., Wallis, J. J. and Weingast, B. R. (2009) *Violence and social orders: A conceptual framework for interpreting recorded human history*. Cambridge University Press.
Parker, G. (1996) *The military revolution: Military innovation and the rise of the West, 1500–1800*. Cambridge University Press.
Tilly, C. (1990) *Coercion, capital, and European states, AD 990–1990*. Basil Blackwell.
Turchin, P. (2009) 'A theory for formation of large empires', *Journal of Global History*, 2, pp. 191–217.
Wallerstein, I. (1984) *The politics of the world-economy*. Cambridge University Press.

## 6 A divine world

Armstrong, K. (2006) *The great transformation: The beginning of our religious traditions*. Random House.
Braudel, F. (1999 (1963)) *Grammaire des civilizations*. Flammarion.
Denneth, D. C. (2006) *Breaking the spell: Religion as a natural phenomenon*. Penguin Group.
Gress, D. (1998) *From Plato to NATO: The idea of the West and its opponents*. Free Press.
Huntington, S. (1996) *The clash of civilizations and the remaking of world order*. Simon & Schuster.
Johnson, D. and Elliot Johnson, J. E. (2007) *Universal religions in world history: The spread of Buddhism, Christianity, and Islam to 1500*. McGraw-Hill.
Mazlish, B. (2004) *Civilization and its contents*. Stanford University Press.

Noss, D. S. (2003) *A history of the world's religions*. Prentice Hall.

Sen, A. (2007) *Identity and violence, the illusion of destiny*. Norton.

Stark, R. (2001) *One true God: Historical consequences of monotheism*. Princeton University Press.

Tishken, J. (ed.) (2007) 'Religion and world history', *World History Bulletin*, 23(1).

## 7  A divided world

Allen, R. C. (2009) *The British Industrial Revolution in global perspective*. Cambridge University Press.

Allen, R. C. (2011) *Global economic history: A very short introduction*. Oxford University Press.

Amsden, A. (2001) *The rise of 'The Rest': Challenges to the West from late-industrializing economies*. Oxford University Press.

Arrighi, G. (1994) *The long twentieth century: Money, power and the origins of our times*. Verso. (Updated edition published 2010)

Arrighi, G. (2007) *Adam Smith in Beijing: Lineages of the twenty-first century*. Verso.

Austen, R.A. (2010) *Trans-Saharan Africa in world history*. Oxford University Press.

Bayly, C. A. (2004) *The birth of the modern world, 1780–1914*. Basil Blackwell.

Bin Wong, R. (1998) *China transformed: Historical change and the limits of European experience*. Cornell University Press.

Bin Wong, R. and Rosenthal, J.-L. (2011) *Before and beyond divergence: The politics of economic change in China and Europe*. Harvard University Press.

Chaudhuri, K. N. (1990) *Asia before Europe: Economy and civilisation of the Indian Ocean from the Rise of Islam to 1750*. Cambridge University Press.

Curtin, P. D. (2000) *The world and the West: The European challenge and the overseas response in the Age of Empire*. Cambridge University Press.

Frank, A. G. (1998) *ReOrient: Global economy in the Asian age*. University of California Press.

Goldstone, J. (2008) *Why Europe? The rise of the West in world history 1500–1850*. McGraw-Hill.

Goody, J. (2004) *Capitalism and modernity: The great debate*. Cambridge University Press.

Gran, P. (2008) *The rise of the rich: A new view of modern world history*. Syracuse University Press.

Hobson, J. M. (2004) *The Eastern origins of Western civilization*. Cambridge University Press.

Landes, D. (1998) *The wealth and poverty of nations: Why some are so rich and some so poor*. Norton.

Inikori, J. (2002) *Africans and the industrial revolution in England: A study in international trade and economic development*. Cambridge University Press.

Liu, X. and Schaffer, L. (2007) *Connections across Eurasia: Transportation, communication and cultural exchange on the Silk Roads*. McGraw-Hill.

Maddison, A. (2007) *Contours of the world economy, 1–2030: Essays in macro-economic history*. Oxford University Press.

Marks, R. B. (2007) *The origins of the modern world: A global and ecological narrative from the fifteenth to the twenty-first century*. Rowman & Littlefield.

Northrup, D. (2002) *Africa's discovery of Europe, 1450–1850*. Oxford University Press.

Palat, R. (2010) 'Convergence before divergence? Eurocentrism and alternate patterns of historical change', *Summerhill Indian Institute of Advanced Study Review*, 1, pp. 42–58.

Parthasarathi, P. (2011) *Why Europe grew rich and Asia did not: Global economic divergence, 1600–1850*. Cambridge University Press.

Pomeranz, K. (2000) *The great divergence: China, Europe and the making of the modern world economy*. Princeton University Press.

Thornton, J. (1998) *Africa and Africans in the making of the Atlantic world, 1400–1800*. Cambridge University Press.

Vries, P. (2003) *Via Peking back to Manchester: Britain, the industrial revolution, and China*. Leiden Studies in Oversees History.

Vries, P. (2009) 'Global economic history: A survey', in: P. Vries (ed.), *Global History, Österreichische Zeitschrift für Geschichtswissenschaften*, 2, pp. 133–169.

Vries, P. (forthcoming) *A world of surprising differences: State and economy in early-modern Western Europe and China*.

Wallerstein, I. (1974, 1980, 1989, 2011) *The modern world-system* (4 vols). Academic Press and University of California Press.

# 8 A global world

Arrighi, G. (2003) *The social and political economy of global turbulence*. New Left Review.

Arrighi, G. and Silver, B. (eds) (1999) *Chaos and governance in the modern world system*. University of Minnesota Press.

Bagchi, A. K. (2005) *Mankind and the global ascendancy of capital*. Rowman & Littlefield.

Bayly, C. A. (2004) *The birth of the modern world, 1780–1914: Global connections and comparisons*. Wiley-Blackwell.

Bordo, M. D., Taylor, A. M. and Williamson, J. G. (eds) (2003) *Globalization in historical perspective*. University of Chicago Press.

Cooper, F. (2001) *What Is the concept of globalization good for? An African historian's perspective*. African Affairs.

Dicken, P. (2003) *Global shift: Reshaping the global economic map in the 21st century*. Sage.

Friedman, T. (2000) *The lexus and the olive tree: Understanding globalization*. Anchor Books.

Gunn, G. C. (2003) *First globalization: The Eurasian exchange, 1500–1800*. Rowman & Littlefield.

Held, D., McGrew, A., Goldblatt, D. and Perraton, J. (1999) *Global transformations: Politics, economics and culture*. Polity Press.

Hirst, P. and Thompson, G. (1996) *Globalization in question: The international economy and the possibilities of governance*. Polity Press.

Hobsbawm, E. (1996) *The age of extremes: A history of the world, 1914–1991*. Vintage.

Hopkins, A. G. (ed.) (2002) *Globalization in world history*. Norton.

Maddison, A. (1995) *Monitoring the world economy, 1820–1992*. OECD.

Maddison, A. (2007) *Contours of the world economy 1–2030 AD: Essays in macroeconomic history*. Oxford University Press.

O'Rourke, K. and Williamson, J. (2001) *Globalization and history: The evolution of a nineteenth century Atlantic economy*. MIT Press.

Osterhammel, J. and Petersson, N. P. (2009) *Globalization: A short history*. Princeton University Press.
Roberts, J. T. and Hite, A. (eds) (2000) *From modernization to globalization: Perspectives on development en social change*. Blackwell.
Robertson, R. (2003) *The three waves of globalization: A history of a developing global consciousness*. Zed Books.
Rosenberg, J. (2002) *The follies of globalisation theory*. Verso.
Stearns, P. N. (2010) *Globalization in world history*. Routledge.

## 9  A polarized world

Atkinson, A. and Piketty, T. (eds) (2009) *Top incomes: A global perspective*. Oxford University Press.
Davis, M. (2006) *Planet of slums*. Verso.
Frederickson, G. M. (2002) *A short history of race*. Princeton University Press.
Kaplinsky, R. (2005) *Globalization, poverty and inequality: Between a rock and a hard place*. Polity Press.
Kerbo, H. (2006) *Social stratification and inequality: Class conflict in historical, comparative, and global perspective* (6th ed.). McGraw-Hill.
Kohonen, M. and Mestrum, F. (2009) *Tax justice: Putting global inequality on the agenda*. Pluto Press.
Korzeniewicz, R. P. and Moran, T. M. (2009) *Unveiling inequality: A world-historical perspective*. Russel Sage.
Lindert, P. H. and Williamson, J. G. (2003) 'Does globalization make the world more unequal?', in: M. D. Bordo, A. M. Taylor and J. G. Williamson (eds) *Globalization in historical perspective*. University of Chicago Press, pp. 227–270.
Maddison, A. (n.d.) Home page at University of Groningen (http://www.ggdc.net/maddison).
Milanovic, B. (2005) *Worlds apart: Measuring international and global inequality*. Princeton University Press.
Sachs, J. (2005) *The end of poverty: How we can make it happen in our lifetime*. Penguin.
United Nations (2005) *Human Development Report 2005*. Available online at http://hdr.undp.org/reports/global/2005
World Bank (2006) *Equity and development: World Development Report 2006*. Available online at http://web.worldbank.org

## 10  A fragmented world

Aveni, A. F. (2002) *Empires of time: Calendars, clocks, and cultures*. University Press of Colorado.
Barnett, J. E. (1999) *Time's pendulum: From sundials to atomic clocks, the fascinating history of timekeeping and how our discoveries changed the world*. Harcourt Brace.
Bentley, J. H. (1993) *Old World encounters: Cross-cultural contacts and exchanges in pre-modern times*. Oxford University Press.
Bentley, J. H. (2007) *Seascapes: Maritime histories, littoral cultures and transoceanic exchanges*. University of Hawaii Press.
Braudel, F. (1979) *Civilisation materielle, economie et capitalisme, XV–XVIII siècle* (3 parts). A. Colin.
Chase-Dunn, C. and Anderson, E. N. (eds) (2005) *The historical evolution of world-systems*. Palgrave Macmillan.

Christian, D. (2004) *Maps of time: An introduction to big history*. University of California Press.

Diamond, J. (1997) *Guns, germs, and steel: The fates of human societies*. Norton.

Gell, A. (1992) *The anthropology of time: Cultural constructions of temporal maps and images*. Berg.

Goucher, C. and Walton, L. (2008) *World history: Journeys from past to present*. Routledge.

Goudsblom, J. (1992) *Fire and civilization*. Penguin.

Gould, S. J. (2002) *The structure of evolutionary theory*. Harvard University Press.

Kearny, M. (2004) *The Indian Ocean in world history*. Routledge.

McKeown, A. M. (2008) *Melancholy order: Asian migration and the globalization of borders*. Columbia University Press.

McNeill, J. R. and McNeill, W. H. (2003) *The human web: A bird's-eye view of world history*. Norton.

Modelski, G. (2000) *World cities, −3000 to 2000*. Faro.

Nolte, H.-H. (2005) *Weltgeschichte, Imperien, Religionen und Systeme 15.−19. Jahrhundert*. Böhlau.

Sachsenmaier, D. M. (2011) *Global perspectives on global history: Theories and approaches in a connected world*. Cambridge University Press.

Sassen, S. (2002) *Global networks, linked cities*. Routledge.

Sassen, S. (2006) *Territory, authority, rights: From medieval to global assemblages*. Princeton University Press.

Stearns, P. N. (2011) *World history: The basics*. Routledge.

Taylor, P. (n.d.) *Globalization and world cities study group and network*. Available online at http://www.lboro.ac.uk/gawc

Wallerstein, I. (1974, 1980, 1989, 2011) *The modern world-system* (4 vols). Academic Press and University of California Press.

Wallerstein, I. (1995) *Historical capitalism, with capitalist civilization*. Verso.

# Index and key concepts

# Key concepts

## 1/ Hunter-gatherer societies

*Homo sapiens*
Migration (divergence)
Extensive biological energy regime
Mini-systems / clans, families, tribes
Reciprocity
Cultures
Proto-religions / folk religions
Language
Fire

## 2/ Agricultural societies

Agricultural / Neolithic revolutions
Domestication
Demographic transition (Neolithic)
Migration (convergence)
Intensive biological energy regime
Chiefdom
Empires
Tribute / redistribution
Regional world systems
(Early and classic) civilizations
World religions
Regional / long-distance trade networks
Technological toolkits

## 3/ Rise of the Modern World / The Great Divergence (15th–19th centuries)

Global migration
Columbian exchange
Fossil energy regime
States and inter-state system (informal)
Sovereignty / territoriality
Citizenship
Revolutions
Mercantilism
Colonialism / imperialism (formal)
Capitalist world economy / commercial capitalism / industrial capitalism
Hegemony (The Netherlands, United Kingdom), new peripheries
Industrial revolutions / industrialization
Rise of historical capitalism, expanding frontiers
Globalizations / global hegemony (Great Britain)
Atlantic trade system / Rise of Europe – the West / global trade networks
Scientific / technological revolutions
Proletarianization
Regional inequality

## 4/ Triumph and decline of the Modern World
## (20th–21st centuries)

Demographic transition (modern)
Limits of fossil energy regime / climate change
Ecological overkill
Welfare state / social state
Regionalization and inter-state system (formal)
Apogee and decline of historical capitalism, internal frictions/frontiers
Neoliberalism / neoliberal state / neoliberal globalization
Capitalism world system / global capitalism / financial capitalism
Global hegemony (United States) / global crisis (21st century)
Decolonization / imperialism (informal)
Modernization (developmentalism) / underdevelopment
Agro-industry
Depeasantization / global urbanization
Global inequality / global polarization
Global cities / city networks
Global firms / global commodities